M.

Berkeley's Metaphysics

Berkeley's Metaphysics

Structural, Interpretive, and Critical Essays

Edited by
Robert G. Muehlmann

The Pennsylvania State University Press
University Park, Pennsylvania

Library of Congress Cataloging-in-Publication Data

Berkeley's metaphysics : structural, interpretive, and critical essays
/ edited by Robert G. Muehlmann.

    p.   cm.
Includes bibliographical references and index.
ISBN 0-271-01427-X (alk. paper)
  1. Berkeley, George, 1685–1753—Congresses. 2. Metaphysics
—History—18th century—Congresses. I. Muehlmann, R. G.
B1349.M47B47   1995
192—dc20   94-23007
                                           CIP

It is the policy of The Pennsylvania State University Press to use acid-free paper
for the first printing of all clothbound books. Publications on uncoated stock satisfy
the minimum requirements of American National Standard for Information
Sciences—Permanence of Paper for Printed Library Materials, ANSI Z39.48–
1984.

To
Edwin B. Allaire

Contents

Preface   ix
Bibliographical Note   xi
Contributors   xiii

Introduction   1

Part I   Idealism

1   Berkeley's Idealism: Yet Another Visit   *Edwin B. Allaire*   23

2   On Allaire's "Another Visit"
      Alan Hausman and David Hausman   39

3   A New Approach to Berkeley's Ideal Reality
      Alan Hausman and David Hausman   47

4   On the Hausmans' "A New Approach"   *Fred Wilson*   67

5   The Substance of Berkeley's Philosophy
      Robert G. Muehlmann   89

6   Berkeley's Manifest Qualities Thesis
      Phillip D. Cummins   107

7   Berkeleian Idealism and Impossible Performances
      George Pappas   127

Part II   Volition, Action, and Causation

8   Berkeley's Problem of Sighted Agency
      Robert G. Muehlmann   149

9   Berkeley and Action   *Robert Imlay*   171

10   On Imlay's "Berkeley and Action"   *Catherine Wilson*   183

11   Berkeley's Case Against Realism About Dynamics
                                        Lisa Downing   197

Part III   Vision and Perceptual Objects

12   Seeing Distance from a Berkeleian Perspective
                                        Robert Schwartz   217

13   Berkeley Without God   *Margaret Atherton*   231

14   Godless Immaterialism: On Atherton's Berkeley
                                    Charles J. McCracken   249

Index   261

Preface

This volume is the outgrowth of a conference on Berkeley's Metaphysics held at the University of Western Ontario in London, Canada, on March 13–14, 1992. Aside from the success of the conference in bringing together and facilitating critical dialogue between so many important Berkeley scholars, and aside from the general excellence of the papers read at the conference, there are two additional reasons for assembling yet another collection of essays on Berkeley's philosophy. The first is to bring together contributions by every recipient to date of the Colin and Ailsa Turbayne International Berkeley Essay Prize Competition; before publication of this collection only one of the prize-winning essays, in its original form, had appeared in print. This volume provides a convenient vehicle for publishing together—for the first time—most of these essays. The second reason for assembling this collection is the same as that for organizing the original conference: to shed new light on Berkeley's metaphysics, particularly on his idealism but also on his theories of causation and perception. The focus of previous anthologies on Berkeley has been more diffuse than this.

Of the fourteen essays assembled here, eleven were delivered at the conference, including one (Essay 3) of the prize winners. The contents of this volume, however, cannot properly be considered "conference proceedings," even if one ignores the three other recipients of the prize (Essays 5, 6, and 11). Although four of the essays delivered at the conference, as well as the critical commentaries, are reproduced here essentially unaltered, in two instances (Essays 7 and 12) the commentators declined to work up their comments for publication, and in one (Essay 8) the critical commentary has been incorporated into a revised version.

One essay, in its present form (Essay 6), has been published previously, and three (Essays 5, 8, and 12) were extracted from larger works that have seen publication since the time of the conference. I am grateful to the *Journal of the History of Philosophy*, to Hackett Publishing Company, and to Basil Blackwell, Ltd., for permission to reprint these materials.

Special thanks are due to my colleague Thomas Michael Lennon. A distinguished historian of philosophy and notable commentator on Berkeley, Lennon gave spiritual support to the ideas of both conference and anthology. But it was in his capacity then as Dean of Arts at the University of Western Ontario that he provided the material support that made the conference, and thus this volume, a reality.

Berkeley's Metaphysics: Structural, Interpretive, and Critical Essays is dedicated to Edwin B. Allaire, the father—both through the electricity of his teaching and the incisiveness of his writing—to a whole generation of Berkeley scholars.

Bibliographical Note

Cross-references to this anthology are by parenthesized page numbers: (#) or (#–#). Except for those to Berkeley's writings, all other (external) page references are preceded by *p.* or *pp.*

For Berkeley's writings, we have used A. A. Luce and T. E. Jessop, editors, *The Works of George Berkeley, Bishop of Cloyne*, 9 volumes (London: Nelson, 1948–57); hereafter referred to as *Works*. More specifically, references to Berkeley's writings in this volume include the following abbreviations:

A *Alciphron* (*Works* III). References are by dialogue, section, and page number.

D *Three Dialogues Between Hylas and Philonous* (*Works* II); hereafter, *Dialogues*. References are by page number.

DM *De Motu* (*Works* IV). References are by section number.

IN Introduction to the *Principles* (*Works* II). References are by section number.

NTV *An Essay Towards a New Theory of Vision* (*Works* I). References are by section number.

PC *Philosophical Commentaries* (*Works* I). References are by entry number.

PR *A Treatise Concerning the Principles of Human Knowledge* (*Works* II); hereafter, *Principles*. References are by section number.

S *Siris* (*Works* V). References are by section number.

TVV *The Theory of Vision Vindicated and Explained* (*Works* I). References are by section number.

Contributors

Edwin B. Allaire. Ph.D. University of Iowa, 1960. Professor, University of Texas–Austin. Has also taught at Iowa, Michigan, and Swarthmore. Publications: Articles on ontological topics and figures in the modern period.

Margaret Atherton. Ph.D. Brandeis University, 1970. Professor, University of Wisconsin–Milwaukee. Publications: *Berkeley's Revolution in Vision* (Ithaca: Cornell University Press, 1990); *Women Philosophers of the Early Modern Period* (Indianapolis: Hackett Publishing Co., 1994); numerous articles on the history of philosophy, particularly on Locke and Berkeley.

Phillip D. Cummins. Ph.D. University of Iowa, 1962. Professor, University of Iowa. Has published widely in the history of philosophy, particularly on Berkeley, Hume, and Reid.

Lisa Downing. Ph.D. Princeton University, 1992. Assistant Professor, University of Pennsylvania. Publications: papers on Berkeley's philosophy of science and Locke's corpuscularianism. She is currently pursuing research on philosophical debates surrounding early modern dynamics.

Alan Hausman. Ph.D. University of Iowa, 1964. Professor, Southern Methodist University. Has also taught for many years at Ohio State University. Publications: numerous articles on metaphysics, history of philosophy, and contemporary philosophy, particularly on Descartes, Berkeley, Hume, and Goodman.

David Hausman. Ph.D. University of Iowa, 1971. Professor, Southern Methodist University. Publications: with Alan Hausman, *Turing Early Modern Philosophy: Machines, Meaning, and the Theory of Ideas* (University of Toronto Press, forthcoming); with Alan Hausman, "Descartes' Secular Semantics," *Canadian Journal of Philosophy* (18:2) (November 1992). Author of articles on history of philosophy, metaphysics, and the philosophy of science.

Robert Imlay. Ph.D. University of Glasgow, 1967. Professor, University of Toronto. Publications: "Descartes, Montaigne, Beyssade et le Critère de

Vérité," *Studia Leibnitiana* 18 (1986); "Frankfurt, van Inwagen, and the Principle of Alternate Possibilities," *The Modern Schoolman* 66 (1989); "Ckeptizismus und die Ewigen Wahrheiten bei Descartes," *Studia Leibnitiana* 23 (1991); "Berkeley and Scepticism: a Fatal Dalliance," *Hume Studies* 18 (1992); and other articles, principally on Descartes and Hume.

Charles J. McCracken. Ph.D. University of California–Berkeley, 1969. Professor, Michigan State University. Publications: *Malebranche and British Philosophy* (Oxford: Oxford University Press, 1983) and numerous articles on seventeenth- and eighteenth-century philosophy.

Robert G. Muehlmann. Ph.D. University of Iowa, 1968. Associate Professor, The University of Western Ontario. Publications: *Berkeley's Ontology* (Indianapolis: Hackett Publishing Co., 1992); articles on Berkeley, Russell, and Wittgenstein.

George Pappas. Ph.D. University of Pennsylvania, 1968. Professor, Ohio State University. Has published widely in epistemology, metaphysics, and the history of philosophy, particularly on Berkeley, Hume, and Reid.

Robert Schwartz. Ph.D. University of Pennsylvania, 1970. Professor, University of Wisconsin–Milwaukee. Publications: *Vision: Variations on Some Berkeleian Themes* (Oxford: Blackwell Publishers, 1994); papers in philosophy of psychology, philosophy of science, and epistemology.

Catherine Wilson. Ph.D. Princeton, 1972. Professor and chair, University of Alberta. Publications: *The Invisible World: The Microscope in Early Modern Philosophy* (Princeton, Princeton University Press, 1989); *Metaphysics* (Princeton, Princeton University Press, 1989); articles on seventeenth-century metaphysics and early modern science, Kant, and philosophy of literature.

Fred Wilson. Ph.D. University of Iowa, 1965. Professor, University of Toronto. Publications: *Explanation, Causation, and Deduction* (Dordrecht: D. Reidel, 1985); *Laws and Other Worlds* (Dordrecht: Kluwer, 1986); *Psychological Analysis and the Philosophy of John Stuart Mill* (Toronto: Toronto University Press, 1990); *Empiricism and Darwin's Science* (Dordrecht: Kluwer, 1991); numerous articles on metaphysics and history of philosophy, particularly on David Hume.

Introduction

The great figures in the Western philosophical tradition were system builders. Not content with specialized knowledge, they sought a vision of the whole, a principle or set of principles in terms of which the cosmos, in all its myriad detail, could be explained. Too often, their extraordinary systems of thought are conveyed to us in ordinary prose: a literary style pedantic, dull, and sometimes even tortured. Yet these philosophical systems, once understood, have a beauty and transparency that rivals the greatest works of art and architecture. Like a symphony they soar into our consciousness, displaying an integration of evocative themes, a penetrating clarity, a profundity that astonishes and enlightens. Like architectural treasures, the great philosophical systems exhibit breathtaking originality, intricate design, and ingenious substructure. The system constructed by George Berkeley (1685–1753) dazzles us with these qualities, and it is all the more dazzling because conveyed in a style of lucid and captivating prose rare in the philosophical literature. But as is often the case in art, architecture, and philosophy, Berkeley's system presents us with unique puzzles, particularly at its foundation. One aim of this volume is to examine these underlying Berkeleian puzzles.

At the foundation of Berkeley's system is its metaphysics: his account of the nature of, and the relations between, the various items, deemed 'existing things', in his ontological inventory. This inventory, its logical lattice and metaphysical motif, is the focus of the essays assembled in this volume. But while the target is Berkeley's ontological inventory, the authors of the essays contained here do not ignore other aspects of his system. Nor could they, since any philosophical system worthy of serious consideration coherently integrates its various components.

Within Berkeley's system we can distinguish three principal theses. Berkeley is, of course, best known for his metaphysical motif: the notorious thesis that trees, houses, mountains, and rivers cannot exist without being perceived, that the *esse* of sensible things is *percipi*. This is his *idealism*. A second thesis, *immaterialism*, has a positive and a negative component: sensible things are collections of sensible qualities, and their ontological analysis yields no material substance. A third Berkeleian thesis, *realism*, also has two components, the first of them epistemological: bodies are known by, and exist independently of, human (finite) minds. From Berkeley's point of view, a description of his philosophy that omitted its epistemological component would be seriously misleading, for he was convinced that his system contained the only cure for the philosophical skepticism he found in the writings of the major philosophers of his time. As in other great philosophical systems, these ontological and epistemological components are logically latticed, or at least closely related. (Precisely how they are related, and how closely, is the subject of several essays in this volume.) They are integrated, too, with other components of Berkeley's philosophy, including those on language, mathematics, causation, vision, and moral responsibility. Thus, while the attention here is on Berkeley's metaphysics, the fourteen essays of this volume range rather freely, as they must, over other philosophical domains.

All of the essays in Part I ("Idealism") bear, one way or another, on an influential account of the route Berkeley takes in arriving at idealism. According to this account, advanced by Edwin B. Allaire thirty years ago,[1] Berkeley's idealism rests on his acceptance of the Aristotelian-Scholastic principle of inherence. The principle of inherence states that qualities, being dependent existents, must be supported: they must *inhere in* entities that have an independent existence; their existence depends upon, to use the traditional designation, *substances*. Coupled with Berkeley's rejection of material substance (negative immaterialism), the principle of inherence yields the conclusion that sensible qualities are dependent upon, must inhere in, mental substances. In his 1963 paper, "Berkeley's Idealism," Allaire put it this way: "Qualities need a support, a substance in which to exist. But the only substances available are minds. Hence, qualities must be supported by minds, they must be in minds."[2] This argument exhibits what Allaire has called the 'inherence pattern', and if it is joined by two other premises, it yields Berkeley's notorious thesis. The first premise is Berkeley's account of sensible things as mere collections of sensible qualities (positive immaterialism). The second is another feature of Allaire's account, that *inheres in* explicates 'is perceived by'. The conclusion is idealism: the existence of sensible things consists in their being perceived, their *esse est percipi*.

Allaire's account, 'the inherence interpretation', quickly gained a wide

1. "Berkeley's Idealism," *Theoria* 29 (1963), pp. 229–44.
2. Ibid., p. 235.

following.[3] Almost as quickly, however, it became the subject of criticism. Not surprisingly, among the most vigorous critics of the inherence interpretation were some who had formerly been converts to it, including several of the contributors to this volume.[4] The principal complaint about "Berkeley's Idealism" was that Allaire had paid insufficient attention to the Berkeleian texts. A careful analysis of the texts his account draws on, the critics argued, fails to support his interpretation: while the texts provide clear evidence that Berkeley is a substantialist, they provide little support for the definitive claim that Berkeley employs the inherence pattern in his argument for idealism.

A decade ago Allaire responded to the earliest criticisms in the second of his papers on Berkeley's philosophy: "Berkeley's Idealism Revisited" (1982).[5] In this second paper he conceded the principal complaint, going so far as to describe the Berkeley of his earlier paper as "fictitious"[6] But Allaire nevertheless insisted on the usefulness of the fiction, arguing that it serves to reveal important 'structural' connections between substantialism and idealism. His emphasis on the structural basis of an interpretation finds its way into the essay that opens this volume, Allaire's third essay on Berkeley's philosophy: "Berkeley's Idealism: Yet Another Visit."

A structural interpretation begins with the assumption that no philosopher, steeped in the ethos of his time, can make a completely clean break with philosophical tradition. In the early modern period—beginning with Descartes, Hobbes, and Gassendi—every major philosopher struggled to overcome one or the other of two legacies: the Platonic or the Aristotelian-

3. Among the early defenses are Phillip D. Cummins, "Perceptual Relativity and Ideas in the Mind," *Philosophy and Phenomenological Research* 24 (1963), pp. 204–14, and Richard A. Watson, "Berkeley in a Cartesian Context," *Revue Internationale de Philosophie* 65 (1963), pp. 381–94. Alan Hausman's more recent defense of Allaire's original account appears in "Adhering to Inherence: A New Look at the Old Steps in Berkeley's March to Idealism," *Canadian Journal of Philosophy* 14 (1984), pp. 421–43.

4. Among the critiques by former converts are Phillip D. Cummins, "Berkeley's Ideas of Sense," *Nous* 9 (1975), pp. 55–72; Robert Muehlmann, "Berkeley's Ontology and the Epistemology of Idealism," *Canadian Journal of Philosophy* 8 (1978), pp. 89–111; and, more thoroughly (and adequately), idem, *Berkeley's Ontology* (Indianapolis: Hackett Publishing Co., 1992). Other critiques include Harry Bracken, "Some Problems of Substance Among the Cartesians," *American Philosophical Quarterly* 1 (1964), pp. 129–37; Nathan Oaklander, "The Inherence Interpretation of Berkeley: A Critique," *The Modern Schoolman* 54 (1977), pp. 261–69; and George Pappas, "Ideas, Minds, and Berkeley," *American Philosophical Quarterly* 17 (1980), pp. 181–94.

5. Included in *Berkeley: Critical and Interpretative Essays*, ed., Colin M. Turbayne, (Minneapolis: University of Minnesota Press, 1982), pp. 197–206.

6. Ibid., p. 198.

Scholastic. This struggle was most successful in the realm of physics, with the nearly complete rejection of animism, anthropomorphism, and teleology. However, in the realm of metaphysics there remained an ontological inertia more resistant to change. A structural account seeks evidence of this ontological inertia and then advances analyses of a philosopher's system in the light of that evidence.

Allaire's second paper, "Berkeley's Idealism Revisited," left some with the impression that 'structural' is opposed to 'textual', but it should be clear that a structural account, being a species of the interpretive, cannot be divorced from the texts. Nor does Allaire divorce himself from them, for where else could evidence of ontological inertia be found? Indeed, it is in passages such as the following that the inherence interpretation gains its textual toehold and prima facie plausibility. Here, in Berkeley's major work, originally titled *A Treatise Concerning the Principles of Human Knowledge*, allegiance is given to substantialism when Berkeley succinctly expresses his system's ontological inventory: "*Thing* or *Being* . . . comprehends under it two kinds entirely distinct and heterogeneous, and which have nothing common but the name, viz. *spirits* and *ideas*. The former are *active, indivisible, incorruptible*, substances: the latter are *inert, fleeting, perishable passions* or *dependent beings*, which subsist not by themselves, but are supported by, or exist in minds or spiritual substances" (PR 89). Thus Allaire insists again, in his third Berkeley essay, that "if one reads PR 86–95 with no more than a hint of sympathy for the [substantialist] dialectic" (31), one cannot avoid seeing the inherence pattern at work.

Sympathy aside, is there a serious alternative to Allaire's reading? Specifically, is there a structural interpretation that finds Berkeley responding to a different historical tradition, one that discovers its own 'structural pattern' underlying idealism? One approach to this question is provided, indirectly, by the last essay in Part I, George Pappas's "Berkeleian Idealism and Impossible Performances" (Essay 7). The subject of this paper, Berkeley's master argument, confronts any interpretation with a formidable challenge. And the way a structural account meets this challenge serves as an interpretive 'litmus test' of its adequacy. Before I describe the challenge, however, some preliminary comments are necessary.

The master argument is so called because Berkeley evidently rests his entire case of idealism upon it:[7] "I am content to put the whole upon this

7. Nearly every recent commentator on the argument has assumed that the designation

issue" (PR 22). Its gist is that a counterexample to the idealist thesis is inconceivable, since anything we can conceive is, by virtue of being conceived, "in the mind." Berkeley's prefatory comments to the argument suggest that he regarded it a conclusive proof of idealism, but it is held by most commentators to be an embarrassment, since it is usually regarded as committing at least one elementary logical fallacy. (For example, "Whatever is conceived is in the mind" is one of the propositions at issue.) As a result Berkeley scholars have, until recently, passed over it with little more than silence. J. O. Urmson, for example, confines himself to observing only that the master argument is "surely fallacious."[8] I. C. Tipton's response to the argument, to take a more surprising example, is one of complete omission. Commenting on a different Berkeleian argument, he writes that "Berkeley *needs* the argument from the relativity of perception to pull the things we immediately perceive into the mind, and . . . the *only* alternative he has is to appeal to what is 'evident to any one who takes a survey of the objects of human knowledge'."[9]

The citation at the end of Tipton's remark is part of Berkeley's first sentence in the *Principles*—an opening sentence in an opening section that has long puzzled commentators. The puzzle arises from the fact that in the next twenty sections Berkeley alludes to an argument for idealism he has already provided, but a careful examination of these sections fails to discover it. It is not until the master argument appears, twenty-two sections into the *Principles*, that Berkeley directly argues for idealism. Thus Tipton's concern: Does Berkeley, from the outset, take idealism for granted? The assumption that he does is unpalatable, since it threatens to undermine Berkeley's stature in the philosophical pantheon. What, then, is the argument to which he alludes, what is his argument for idealism? Such an interpretive puzzle is the very substance of a structural interpretation.

Tipton's concern is not misplaced; nevertheless, he is mistaken on two other counts. The first is his assumption that Berkeley appeals to the fact of perceptual relativity among his arguments for idealism, arguments designed "to pull the things we immediately perceive into the mind." For

---

of 'master' to the argument is apt (see note 25). The only exception I know of—an exception unjustly ignored—is Peter S. Wenz, "The Books in Berkeley's Closet," *Hermathena* 123 (Summer 1980), pp. 33–40.

8. *Berkeley* (New York: Oxford University Press, 1982), p. 45.

9. I. C. Tipton, *Berkeley: The Philosophy of Immaterialism* (London: Methuen, 1974), p. 238; second emphasis added.

how is the argument from perceptual relativity supposed to do this? The argument takes for granted that sensible qualities vary with the *physical* state of the perceptual environment—the situation of the perceiver's body, the nature of the sensing apparatus, the location of the object, and so on—and at best proves only that naive realism[10] leads to absurdities. I submit that Berkeley fully appreciates this fact[11] and that this submission is startling only if one fails to distinguish between Berkeley's arguments *for* idealism and his arguments *against* materialism.[12]

Tipton's second mistake is more relevant to my present concern, the master argument. With 'the only alternative he has', Tipton ignores it completely. Pappas's essay, in diametric contrast, focuses on it exclusively. Thus, in the sense indicated some paragraphs back, Pappas's analysis is not structural. Moreover, "Berkeleian Idealism and Impossible Performances" is the only essay of the group composing Part I that does not bear directly on the inherence interpretation. It does have an indirect bearing, however. To see this, consider the following suggestion: since Berkeley regarded the master argument conclusive proof of idealism, we ought to take him at his word and confine ourselves to advancing only nonstructural explanations—perhaps merely logical diagnoses—of his arguments for idealism.

This suggestion (call it S) should be greeted with contempt,[13] for it does Berkeley a grievous disservice. If the master argument is the exclusive ground of '*esse est percipi*' and a nonstructural explanation is the best we can do, why should we take idealism seriously enough even to advance such an explanation? To say that Berkeley's idealism can be explained *in toto* by means of a master-argument reconstruction along with a diagnosis of his blunder is to speak as a philistine. For it would make a virtue of

10. The initial stance, in the first of the *Dialogues*, of Berkeley's caricatured materialist Hylas.

11. For details, see my "Role of Perceptual Relativity in Berkeley's Philosophy," *Journal of the History of Philosophy* 29 (1991), pp. 397–425, and also *Berkeley's Ontology*, esp. chaps. 4 and 5.

12. Although Berkeley uses 'materialist' to label his philosophical opponents, 'dualist' or, even more specifically, 'representative realist' would be more accurate. His arguments 'against materialism' include arguments against naive realism and representationalism (see note 20); more generally, they include any arguments not specifically directed at establishing his idealism.

13. Two disclaimers: As becomes clear almost immediately below, I am not implying that only structural explanations have value. Nor, of course, am I implying, despite its proximity, that Pappas would endorse S. It is the subject matter of his essay (the master argument itself), not Pappas's analysis, that brings S to mind. The valuable results of his analysis are described later.

ignoring Berkeley's immersion in the philosophical controversies of his time, of ignoring the conceptual background of his environment.

Our contempt, however, should not blind us to S's merit: in its naked exclusiveness S calls our attention to the fact that nothing prevents us from advancing *both* a nonstructural and a structural explanation, *provided that* they complement each other. Berkeley's master argument begins with a challenge to his readers—to conceive it possible for a sensible thing (a tree, for example) to exist without the mind—and it would be fitting to call this his master challenge. But it is nevertheless appropriate in this interpretive context to call *the master challenge* the challenge of satisfying that proviso: to advance, as integrated complementaries, a structural as well as a nonstructural explanation of Berkeley's master argument.

The inherence interpretation (call it *II*) is one of at least two possible structural accounts of Berkeley's idealism, the other one being the nominalist interpretation (call it *NI*). In *Berkeley's Ontology* I advance a nominalist interpretation that addresses the master challenge.[14] I cannot repeat the details of that engagement here, but by contrasting *NI* with *II*, I can convey its gist; and this may be of some service in meeting the demands placed on an anthology's introduction: both to describe its essays and to partake sympathetically, yet critically, of their argumentive content.

The early modern philosophers struggled with at least two legacies, the Aristotelian-Scholastic and the Platonic. On *II*, as we have seen, the focus is on the former, and the structural pattern—the line of reasoning that leads to idealism—derives from substantialism, an ontological position deeply rooted in the tradition. On *NI* the focus is on Platonism, and the structural pattern derives from nominalism, an ontological stance with equally deep roots. Plato's ontological inventory includes, most prominently, transcendent universal qualities, and this inclusion has been under attack for a long time, beginning in fact with Plato's student, Aristotle. The controversy ebbed and flowed during the medieval period until the fourteenth century, when William of Ockham (c. 1285–1349) applied his "razor," shaving Platonic Universals from the ontological facade. By the early seventeenth century an uncompromising nominalism, energized by the endorsement from Thomas Hobbes (1588–1679), had gained ascendency. Thus Berkeley, on *NI*, is more in debt to Ockham and Hobbes than

14. All the claims of *NI*, including the more startling ones, are dealt with in detail in this book, and henceforth I shall not bother to document them.

he is to Aristotle; indeed, *NI* and *II* could not be much more antithetical, since on *NI* Berkeley takes his structural pattern from Ockham and Hobbes, while taking nothing of significance from Aristotle.[15]

Now, Berkeley is convinced that the only alternative to Platonism is nominalism. But 'nominalism' is ambiguous, referring to either or both of two theses. (1) Qualities are as individual and determinate as the objects that possess them. As Berkeley succinctly puts it, *"every thing which exists, is particular"* (D 192).[16] Thus (1) amounts to the ontological thesis that there exist no universal qualities, either immanent or transcendent. (2) Qualities do not exist in isolation or separation from one another; they are, again as Berkeley puts it, "mixed, as it were, and blended together, several in the same object" (IN 7). These two theses are closely related, of course, but though (1) probably entails (2), (2) does not entail (1). As a proponent of *NI* reads him, Berkeley fails to appreciate the difference between (1) and (2), appealing to (2) in his argument that abstract ideas do not exist, while drawing on (1) for his conviction that they *cannot* exist (IN 21).

Few commentators doubt that Berkeley is both a substantialist and a nominalist. The direct textual evidence for the former can be found in many passages of the published works, but particularly, as we have seen, in the middle sections of the *Principles*. Evidence for the latter is more difficult to find, but is nonetheless impressive. Two brief passages, one from the *Principles* (IN 15) and one from the *Dialogues* (cited above), and several passages in a draft to the introduction of the *Principles* (*Works* II, 125–36), provide unambiguous support. Berkeley did not see fit to publish the draft passages; and though they do provide some direct textual evidence of a nominalist underpinning for his antiabstractionism, the evidence supporting *NI* is largely indirect, not only because Berkeley does not repeat his draft arguments in the published texts but also because he does not explicitly appeal to a 'nominalist pattern' either in his arguments for idealism or his arguments against materialism.

In his 1963 paper, Allaire contended that the inherence pattern *does* find explicit textual support in section 91 of the *Principles*. The principal barrier to accepting his contention, Allaire recognized, was the difficulty of squaring it with Berkeley's remarks at section 49. Heroically storming

---

15. It is worth noting that PR 11 is only one of many places where Berkeley speaks of the ancients and scholastics with contempt, whereas PC 795–99 make it clear that he takes Hobbes seriously.

16. Berkeley's emphasis.

that barrier, Allaire advanced an ingenious supporting interpretation of section 49. However, with the appearance of the 1982 paper, this interpretation, along with the contention it supported, has been abandoned. Thus, proponents of both *II* and *NI* have to build for Berkeley an "implicit" idealist argument, since on neither is the structural pattern to be found in the texts.

Some might consider this a fatal drawback of both interpretations, but if so, they would be mistaken. The 'drawback' is, in fact, an inevitable concomitant of taking seriously Tipton's concern, the central interpretive puzzle of the *Principles*. The aim of structural analysis is to find an underlying onotological doctrine and its associated "structural pattern" that motivate—without their presence being fully understood or appreciated—the puzzling claims of, or defective arguments for, a metaphysical thesis. Explicit textual evidence of a structural pattern at work would be, of course, a decisive boon to the interpretation, but the interpretation cannot be doomed by the absence of an explicit argument.

On *II*, the structural pattern exemplified in Berkeley's argument for idealism is as follows:

(*a*) There exist no material substances and sensible things are merely collections of sensible qualities (immaterialism).
(*b*) Qualities must inhere in substances (the principle of inherence).
(*c*) Only mental substances exist.

Hence: (*d*) Sensible things inhere in minds.
Since, on *II*,
(ι) *inheres in* explicates 'is perceived by'
the conclusion, (*d*), is equivalent to
(*e*) The *esse* of sensible things is *percipi*.
The "nominalist pattern" begins and ends in the same way:
(*a*) There exist no material substances and sensible things are merely collections of sensible qualities.
(*f*) If a sensation and a sensible quality are separable, then we can form abstract ideas of them.
(*g*) Abstract ideas are impossible because they violate the principle of nominalism [the conjunction of (1) and (2)].
Hence: (*h*) Sensible things are inseparable from sensations.
Since, on *NI*,
(v) sensations cannot exist unperceived

the conclusion, (*h*), is equivalent to

(*e*) The *esse* of sensible things is *percipi*.

On each account, Berkeley's justification for the next-to-last step, (ι) or (ν), is perfunctory: if we ask what the ground of (ι) is, *II*'s Berkeley must appeal, narrowly, to his agreement with the substance tradition, while, for (ν), *NI*'s Berkeley can appeal, more broadly, to what "is agreed on all hands."[17] This may be thought a slight advantage for *NI;* however, proponents of *II* can argue that the appeal of *NI*'s Berkeley has no structural basis: if the account seeks to avoid any appeal to the principle of inherence, the mind-dependence of sensations will rest on no identifiable ontological ground.

While this appears to be a serious objection, it serves at best only to focus our attention on the crucial point separating the two accounts. On *NI*, sensible qualities (and thus, given positive immaterialism, sensible things) are mind-dependent, not because they inhere in mental substances, but rather because they are inseparable from sensations. As for the mind-dependence of the latter, this is an entirely distinct question, one that Berkeley does not address. Given that his minds are substances, his answer might well involve an appeal to the principle of inherence; but *this* Berkeleian use of the Aristotelian principle (i.e., its use in grounding the mind-dependence of *sensations*) is not ruled out by *NI*.

The foregoing considerations, then, are not decisive. Is there any compelling evidence that supports *NI*'s contention that (*f*), (*g*) and (*h*), rather than (*b*), (*c*) and (*d*), play the underlying role in Berkeley's argument for idealism? The answer to this question lies in the explicit Berkeleian arguments. In addition to the master argument, Berkeley seems to draw on at least four others in his effort to make idealism plausible. Textual analysis reveals, however, that one of these arguments, from the meaning of 'idea', is not taken very seriously; and another, from perceptual relativity (discussed above), is used by Berkeley only to undermine naive realism.

This leaves us with two arguments, both in the first of Berkeley's *Dialogues:* the "heat-pain argument" (D 176) and the "tulip-smelling argument" (D 194–96). Both arguments are developments of their embryonic forms found (in retrospect) at section 5 of the *Principles* and else-

---

17. Berkeley uses this expression sparingly, for example, in defense of (2) at IN 7. In the present context perhaps the appeal to the generally accepted (epistemic) doctrine of the mind's transparency to itself and its contents would be more specific. For a discussion of this doctrine and the role it plays in the master argument, see the paper by Eric Saidel cited at the end of note 25.

where.[18] The heat-pain argument is designed to establish the conclusion that sensible qualities are essentially (i.e., inseparably) sensational, and the tulip-smelling argument constitutes Berkeley's rejection of the distinction between *perceiving* and *sensible quality* perceived. Both arguments tacitly appeal to the impossibility of abstract ideas; and if *NI* is correct, this appeal founders in the absence of its grounding in nominalism.

Proponents of *II*, not surprisingly, have remained unconvinced. Indeed, one early proponent argued that a fatal solipsism must powerfully drive Berkeley away from nominalism;[19] and while not going to this extreme, Allaire contends that Berkeley "needs [nominalism] neither for his attack on Locke's doctrine of abstraction nor for his attack on representationalism" (27n.2). By 'nominalism' Allaire has (1) in mind, for it is plain that Berkeley needs (2) in the attack on Locke's doctrine.[20] Consequently, if we ignore the need to explain Berkeley's belief that he has "shewn the *impossibility* of Abstract Ideas" (IN 21, emphasis added), Allaire's contention is certainly correct.

However, if I am right either that (1) is required to secure the impossibility of abstract ideas or that Berkeley only dimly discerns the difference between (1) and (2), then Allaire's contention, respectively, either is incorrect or does not rule out nominalism as the ground of Berkeley's idealism. Suppose true the first alternative of the antecedent: then while it is correct to say that (1) is not needed to make plausible the conclusion that Locke's doctrine is (contingently) false, it is incorrect to say that he does not need (1) to show that abstract ideas are impossible. Consider the second alternative: Berkeley's blurring the difference between (1) and (2) is, to be sure, a mistake—made the more colossal by the fact that (1) is, as Allaire says, "foolish" (27). But this cannot help us decide between the two structural interpretations, for a Berkeleian appeal to the principle of inherence would also be a mistake of colossal proportions—as Allaire himself has pointed out repeatedly.

Given that neither interpretation finds an explicit Berkeleian use of its

18. At PC 692 we find an embryonic version of the heat-pain argument, and the tulip-smelling argument is suggested by Berkeley's claim that his reader will find it impossible "to separate in his own thoughts the *being* of a sensible thing from its *being perceived*" (PR 6).

19. Richard J. Van Iten, "Berkeley's Alleged Solipsism," *Revue Internationale de Philosophie* 16 (1962), pp. 447–52.

20. For his attack on representationalism, Berkeley uses the "likeness" principle: "an idea can be like nothing but an idea" (PR 8).

structural pattern, the balance of textual evidence now shifts in *NI*'s favor, since it appears to do a better job of explaining Berkeley's actual arguments, particularly his use of the master argument, but also his use of the subsidiary ones. To see this, consider the following five points. First, on *II* Berkeley is seen as drawing on perceptual relativity in his argument for idealism, when the textual evidence, as indicated above, suggests otherwise. Second, proponents of *II* have displayed little more than passing interest in the heat-pain argument, when, again, the textual evidence suggests Berkeley invests it with great significance. A third point, related to the second, is that proponents of *II* have tended to play down the significance of Berkeley's antiabstractionism, though Berkeley himself seems to regard it as crucial. Fourth, while the importance of the tulip-smelling argument is recognized, it tends to be dismissed as obviously fallacious, its underlying rationale ignored. Finally, a fifth point, related to the fourth, is that the master argument has been totally ignored, or to put it a bit differently, proponents of *II* have not engaged the master challenge. If we are to judge which of the two interpretations does a better job of explaining Berkeley's explicit arguments, then these five points obviously, militate in favor of *NI*.

This victory for *NI*, if it be such, is a shallow one: a victory largely by default. (It will have served its purpose if it stimulates proponents of *II* to address these points more fully.) Regarding the fifth point, moreover, the victory is even more shallow than I have admitted, since I have said next to nothing about *NI*'s response to the master challenge. But having sketched *NI* above, conveying the gist of a structural explanation of the master argument (jointly with a nonstructural one) will not be difficult. Very briefly, then, the following is *NI*'s response to that challenge.

First, the structural account: the heat-pain argument rests on the impossibility of abstracting sensible qualities from sensations, and the tulip-smelling argument rests on a similar impossibility of abstracting an act of perceptual awareness from its target, a sensible quality or collection of such. The master argument, finally, rests on the impossibility of abstracting a conceiving from its target, the object conceived.[21] If this diagnosis is right—that Berkeley takes inspiration for the master argument from his uncompromising antiabstractionism and his success with the heat-pain and tulip-smelling arguments—then his logical lapse be-

---

21. For an analysis of the connection between Berkeley's antiabstractionism and his master argument, see George Pappas, "Abstract Ideas and the '*Esse Is Percipi*' Thesis," *Hermathena* 139 (Winter 1985), pp. 47–62.

comes less puzzling: these two arguments, particularly the heat-pain argument, are, though flawed, less obviously flawed than the master argument. Second, a nonstructural explanation: if I am right that Berkeley recognizes the paucity of the argument from perceptual relativity as well as the argument from the meaning of 'idea', then the fervency with which he embraces the master argument—his willingness to stake his whole case for idealism upon it—also becomes less puzzling. While the master argument may not be circular (see Pappas's Essay 7), it is surely confused. Fervor and confusion, however, are often companions; and the master argument, sweeping as it is, projects such enormous potential— more potential even than the heat-pain or tulip-smelling arguments— that Berkeley is compelled to use it.[22] I shall have occasion to return to the subject of Berkeley's confusion and circularity at the end of this introduction.

The analytical historian who undertakes structural analysis may both advance an interpretation and critically explore its ramifications. In "Berkeley's Idealism: Yet Another Visit" (Essay 1), Allaire concentrates on the latter of these tasks and presents a new angle on his account of Berkeley's ontology, this time focused on Berkeley's realism. Employing a "variant of the ideal-language method" (26)—a symbolism designed to represent perspicuously an ontological inventory—Allaire contends that in a substance ontology the only genuine relation, the only item exhibited by means of the *juxtaposition* of signs, is inherence. But in the Berkeleian symbolism the only items a mind can experience are those designated by *signs* for simple ideas, items that traditional substantialists called 'accidents'. The upshot is that "knowledge of objects must be indirect and representational." Allaire writes that during the reign of substantialism, skepticism "was a crisis waiting to happen"; his insight is that "idealism was its inevitable offspring" (30). But Berkeley's system fails to solve the skeptical problem because, Allaire now argues, since it cannot come to grips with perceptual variation—the fact that the apparent sensible qualities of an object vary with the conditions under which the object is perceived—it cannot account for our knowledge of bodies; and, he also argues, since it has no way to accommodate the mind's ability selectively

22. 'Nonstructural' covers a wide range of interpretive perspectives, including the analytical, critical, historical, and psychological (as this one is). Any nonstructural account approaching adequacy would have to include these other perspectives. Berkeley's master argument is just beginning to get the attention that will generate the rich account it deserves; see Pappas's Essay 7 as well as the papers cited in note 7 above and note 25 below.

to attend to items in the ontological inventory, it cannot account for knowledge of the self. Allaire concludes his essay, hoping to "sharpen and broaden my attack on idealism," with a brief examination of the system of another philosopher who employs the ideal-language method, namely, Gustav Bergmann, "an ontologist as heroic as the tradition has known" (35).

In their reply, "On Allaire's 'Another Visit'" (Essay 2), Alan and David Hausman raise several challenges. They question Allaire's claim—which they find to be largely unsupported—that substance ontologies can accommodate no relation other than inherence; and they advance several interesting explanations, none of which they think justificatory, for Allaire's making this claim. They also surmise that he confuses the problem of perceptual variation with the problem of false belief. And finally, doubling Allaire's lead, the Hausmans briefly explore the ontologies of Bergmann and Goodman, advancing a series of considerations leading them to conclude that "the problem of [perceptual variation] does not obviously force one to idealism" (45).

In "A New Approach to Berkeley's Ideal Reality"[23] (Essay 3), the Hausmans offer their own account of Berkeley's route to idealism. While they stress, with Allaire, Berkeley's struggle against representationalism, they argue that Berkeley attempts to solve what they see (drawing on the work of Daniel Dennett) as the 'semantic' problem at the root of skepticism. They conclude, however, that this solution comes at a high price: "Berkeley . . . fails to see that once sensible qualities . . . are treated as information, they cannot also be treated as the very objects that the information is about"(64–65).

In "On the Hausmans' 'A New Approach'" (Essay 4), Fred Wilson argues that the appeal to Dennett's emphasis on semantics is not only "Whiggish" (69) but also mistaken and that the Hausmans are unable to explain why Berkeley retains the category of mental substance. Exploring and locating Berkeley within a tradition stretching from Plotinus through the Cambridge Platonists to Hume and beyond, Wilson concludes that Berkeley needs a substantial self in order to ground the unity of the world of bodies. Berkeley's problem, he writes, "is the traditional one of order, not that of understanding meaningful speech" (85). Wilson's struc-

---

23. The Hausmans' essay was delivered at the 1992 conference on Berkeley's Metaphysics (London, Canada) and subsequently shared the 1993 Turbayne Prize with George Pappas's "Berkeley and Skepticism." The latter essay has not been included in this volume. Author and editor concurred that it would be misplaced here, given its nearly exclusive focus on epistemology.

tural analysis yields a Platonic, not an Aristotelian, basis for the retention of mental substance; but he nonetheless argues that his explanation supports *II*, since it "does justice to Berkeley's arguments and commitments and makes clear why the inherence account . . . really does make sense of what he has to say" (69).

One, perhaps the principal, assumption underlying the argument of "The Substance of Berkeley's Philosophy" (Essay 5) is expressed by this conditional proposition: if the notebooks' Berkeley manages to arrive at idealism without mental substance, it is unlikely that he needs mental substance to secure idealism. Berkeley's notebooks, written some years before the publication of the *Principles*, reveal a sweeping antisubstantialism united with an uncompromising idealism. Thus the question addressed in "The Substance of Berkeley's Philosophy": Why does Berkeley, in the published works, introduce the category of mental substance? (This question is similar to, though not identical with, Fred Wilson's in Essay 4.) In this essay, I argue that Berkeley has no need for mental substance either as individuator, support, or agent and—drawing heavily on his notebook entries—that Berkeley's principal reason for introducing mental substance is theological. Moreover, if there is a compelling ontological reason for Berkeley's introduction of mental substance, it has to do, I conclude, with securing the distinctness of bodies from (finite) minds. This conclusion shares a certain affinity with Wilson's in that both of us explain the introduction of mental substance as part of Berkeley's attempt to ground his realism. But it is also at odds with Wilson's, since I argue that Berkeley does not introduce (Wilson says 'retain') mental substance for the purpose of shoring up idealism.

At the outset of this introduction, I described three principal theses of Berkeley's philosophical system: idealism, immaterialism, and realism. If I were to add a fourth, no better choice could be made than his thesis on causation. Berkeley holds that the only causally efficacious items, the only items capable of *production*, are the volitions of minds. Call this causal thesis *volitionism*. Volitionism is the subject of the four essays composing Part II of this anthology, and Phillip D. Cummins's "Berkeley's Manifest Qualities Thesis" (Essay 6) provides a bridge both backward and forward.

Recall that 'immaterialism' labels Berkeley's analysis of "unthinking things" (apples, mountains, rivers, and so on). That analysis has positive and negative components, and in this context, there is an addendum to the latter: Berkeley insists that the analysis of unthinking things, or bodies, yields the conclusion that they are causally inert, that "there is nothing of power or agency included in them" (PR 25). Now, Cummins's target in

Essay 6 is the relation between immaterialism and idealism. He argues that a significant part of Berkeley's immaterialism is "inherently idealistic" (125): it depends on, and cannot be established apart from, his idealism. The part that so depends is Berkeley's addendum to immaterialism, the denial that sensible things are causally active. The reason is that the crucial premise behind his denial—that sensible things, Berkeley's "ideas," have all and only those qualities they are perceived to have (the manifest qualities thesis)—can be established only by an idealist reading of 'idea'.

Essay 6 takes us forward toward Part II because Berkeley's immaterialism underlies his volitionism, and thus, if Cummins's analysis is right, it follows that Berkeley's volitionism is also "inherently idealistic." Essay 6 takes us backward because, though an early convert to *II*, Cummins was one of the first to reject it. While he does not belabor the point in this essay (it appears, subtly, only in his last footnote), his conclusion is also at odds with *II*, since on that interpretation Berkeley arrives at idealism only after having *first* established immaterialism.[24]

George Pappas's "Berkeleian Idealism and Impossible Performances" (Essay 7) is a welcome contribution to the more recent trend of taking the master argument seriously.[25] Careful analysis reveals, he argues, that while the argument is indeed unsound and implausible, Berkeley's misstep is not the sophomoric blunder it is usually thought to be. But Pappas's primary aim in this essay is to determine what the master argument reveals of the logical character of '*esse est percipi*'. He concludes that it is "not understood by Berkeley to be a logically or conceptually necessary truth" (145), but rather is understood to be necessary only in the sense that any attempt to refute it is self-defeating. If Pappas is right, another

---

24. Although it is "at odds" with *II*—and therefore also with *NI*, since their different structural patterns share the same immaterialist premise—Cummins's conclusion does not rule out either account (nor does he make this claim for it). Proponents of both can insist that Cummins's analysis serves only to expose the circularity of Berkeley's system, and it would hardly be surprising for the circle to show up in his underlying argument; indeed, it would be surprising if it did not.

25. We owe the naming of the master argument to André Gallois, "Berkeley's Master Argument," *Philosophical Review* 83 (1974), pp. 55–69. But more recently and perhaps of more value are I. C. Tipton, "Berkeley's Imagination," in *Essays on the Philosophy of George Berkeley*, ed. Ernest Sosa (Boston: Reidel, 1987), pp. 85–102—this article more than makes up for the omission in Tipton's book (see note 9)—and Thomas Lennon, "Berkeley and the Ineffable," *Synthese* 75 (1988), pp. 231–50. Noteworthy, too, is the just-published essay by Eric Saidel, "Making Sense of Berkeley's Challenge," *History of Philosophy Quarterly* 10 (1993), pp. 325–39. All of these commentators assume, as I have above (and continue to do so below), that the master argument is aptly named. But see note 7 above.

piece of the master argument puzzle may fall into place: we can trace this pattern of thought back at least to Descartes's *'cogito ergo sum'*.

"Berkeley's Problem of Sighted Agency" (Essay 8) begins Part II: "Volition, Action, and Causation." In this essay I offer an explanation for Berkeley's failure, in his mature works, to explicate the concept of volition. The explanation, I argue, resides in Berkeley's difficulties, revealed by his notebook entries, in accounting for the relation between volitions and what I call their 'guiding ideas'. Robert Imlay's "Berkeley and Action" (Essay 9) raises additional problems for Berkeley's theory of action, particularly the difficulty of explaining how we can be held responsible for our intentional bodily behavior when, in Berkeley's system, only God qualifies as the cause of such behavior. On a more positive note, Imlay defends Berkeley against the charge that the appeal to volitions is "explanatorily otiose" (176) and—drawing on William James's example of a woman whose will only seemed, 'from the inside', to be causally efficacious—concludes his essay with the suggestion that Berkeleian volitions be understood as 'rehearsals' for action. This last suggestion, in particular, is ably criticized in Catherine Wilson's "On Imlay's 'Berkeley and Action' " (Essay 10). Wilson points out that "such rehearsals may occur without the will being engaged at all," and taking up the examination of James's example, she concludes that exercising one's will "is either having the experience of doing something voluntarily or having the illusion that you are doing so" (195).

Lisa Downing's "Berkeley's Case Against Realism About Dynamics" (Essay 11) concludes Part II. Carefully examining the relevant texts, with a special emphasis on *De Motu* and *Siris*, Downing demonstrates that Berkeley's case against 'forces' is based neither on his immaterialism nor on his idealism—as is usually thought—but rather on what she calls his "rigidly empiricist view" (199) of the criteria for reference. If, once again, we distinguish between Berkeley's arguments for his theses and his arguments against the materialists', perhaps we can forestall the suspicion that her conclusion is at odds with Cummins's in "Berkeley's Manifest Qualities Thesis" (Essay 6).

Part III, "Vision and Perceptual Objects," completes the volume with three essays on the theory of perception and its relations to Berkeley's metaphysics. Robert Schwartz's "Seeing Distance from a Berkeleian Perspective" (Essay 12) sets the theory of vision in the context of a long tradition of vision research. This rich essay advances, among other things, a very helpful account of Berkeley's distinction between "immediate" and "mediate" perception.

This distinction serves as another bridge between the essays of this anthology, directing us (as does Cummins's Essay 6) both backward and forward. It takes us back to several of the essays in Part I, for the distinction between immediate and mediate perception may underlie Berkeley's realism: he seems to hold that since bodies are mediately perceived, they can both be known by and exist independently of human perceivers. And it takes us forward to the last two essays, for Berkeley's realism is also premised on his thesis about the existence and causally efficacious nature of God.

In "Berkeley Without God" (Essay 13), Margaret Atherton argues that Berkeley's theory of vision supplies him with a theory of sensory representation that does not presuppose the existence of God. She concludes that Berkeley can thus, without begging the question, make use of the theory in his argument for God's existence. In his lively reply, "Godless Immaterialism: On Atherton's Berkeley" (Essay 14), Charles J. Mc-Cracken argues that a godless Berkeleianism either is equivalent to J. S. Mill's phenomenalism—in which case it is misleadingly described as 'Berkeleian'—or is more distant from common sense than Atherton believes. The argument between the authors of these last two essays hinges on the nature of Berkeley's objects of perception, and this, finally, returns us to the beginning of the volume and Allaire's critique of Berkeley's realism.

The essays assembled in this volume are contributions to a continuing dialogue on Berkeley's philosophy, a dialogue that will not soon end. Despite the extraordinary elegance and clarity of Berkeley's philosophical prose, his system is so subtle and complicated that the opportunities for scholarly analysis and debate are nearly inexhaustible. His system is also highly integrated and often leaves us with the impression that circles abound, that one part of the system is based on another, which depends on a third, which in turn is grounded in the first. But even if the essays in Parts II and III provide materials to support this impression, and even if the essays in Part I lead us eventually to the conclusion that no structural explanation of Berkeley's idealism is adequate—that we have to fall back upon a logician's impoverished dissection of master-argument form and fallacy—this should not be cause for great scholarly alarm: a philosopher's stature in the philosophical pantheon should not be measured in terms of blunders committed, however enormous they may be. Berkeley is not the first confused, circular, and great philosopher, nor will he be the last. A philosopher's stature should rather be measured in terms of originality and profundity. And these are certainly qualities that Berkeley possesses in abundance. Indeed, we might with justice conclude by echoing a comment Allaire once made about Descartes, that a profound, confused, and circular Berkeley is more compelling than a shallow, clear, and consistent one.[26]

26. In "The Circle of Ideas and the Circularity of the *Meditations*," *Dialogue* 5 (1966), pp. 131–53, esp. p. 151.

PART I

Idealism

1

Berkeley's Idealism:
Yet Another Visit

Edwin B. Allaire

I n these remarks, I try to show that Berkeley's idealism was inevitable and that its failings continue to be instructive. Being too long indifferent to epistemological matters, I have only recently come to believe the former. All *ontological* solutions to the problems of knowledge issue in idealism or a variant of it, I think.

Berkeley's ontology contains two basic kinds: minds and ideas, as he

This is a revised version of a paper I gave at the March 1992 conference on Berkeley's Metaphysics in London, Ontario. By way of explaining the odd title, let me say that in 1963 I published "Berkeley's Idealism" (*Theoria* 29, pp. 229–44) and in 1982 "Berkeley's Idealism Revisited" (*Berkeley: Critical and Interpretative Essays,* ed. Colin M. Turbayne [Minneapolis: University of Minnesota Press, 1982], pp. 197–206). In the former, I advanced what has come to be called the inherence interpretation; in the latter, I discussed some criticisms of it. Some took me to retreat from the inherence interpretation. If I did, I did so only to stress that the interpretation was more structural than textual. In the present essay, I offer further reasons for the inherence interpretation. Whether they are merely more of the structural, I leave to those who *know* the texts.

calls them. The former—also called spirits, souls, and selves—are acknowledged to be (mental) substances (PR 7); the latter, except for some simple ideas that are deemed qualities, though not relative to substances, are not otherwise categorized by Berkeley. Why that is so is of concern later.

I want now to develop a simple representational device in order neatly to exhibit some features of Berkeley's ontology. Let lowercase *exes* with subscripts stand for minds; lowercase *efs* with subscripts, for simple ideas. That "vocabulary" suggests that the schema has only one combination rule, 'fx'. That cannot be. Berkeley distinguishes between simple ideas and collections of them, the collections serving primarily to assay trees, mountains, chairs, and so on ontologically. Berkeley also distinguishes between sense, imagination, memory, and emotion ideas.

Let 's', 'i', 'm', and 'e' be used as superscripts of *ef* signs, thereby enabling the schema to reflect the different kinds of simple ideas. Also, let a pair of brackets, between which are *ef* signs, stand for a collection of simple ideas. Now for several comments: (1) Some *ef* signs agree in subscript, differ in superscript. Speaking loosely, a simple idea—a shade of red, say—may be a sense as well as an imagination idea. (2) Every bracket expression contains more than one *ef* sign, and all the *ef* signs in a bracket expression have the same superscript. Again speaking loosely, an idea composed of the idea red and the idea square is not half imaginary, half real. (3) Different bracket expressions may contain the same *ef* signs. That is, different collections may contain one and the same simple idea. (4) I ignore the rules for specifying which combinations of *ef* signs are permissible within a pair of brackets. I ignore a great deal. For example, one would have further to distinguish between *ef* signs by using, for example, more superscripts in order to reflect the differences between a color, a shape, an odor, a texture, and so on, differences that would enable the schema to ground, for example, that everything colored must have a shape. Much that I ignore is interesting, but what is of concern on this occasion is dialectically independent of what I ignore.

I turn now to combination rules. Bracket expressions are signs, notwithstanding that they contain simple signs. In other words, a bracket expression cannot stand alone to represent a thing or complex or whatever. Accordingly, one formation rule is 'x[   ]'. Another is 'xf^e'. Neither a solitary 'f^m' nor a solitary 'f^i' may combine with an *ex* sign. I shall also assume that 'xf^s' is not a combination rule, an assumption to be remarked on later.

The schema used to exhibit Berkeley's ontology is plainly odd, not at all of the customary sort. First, it contains two levels of vocabulary, the bracket expressions being made from simple *ef* signs, using rules, even though the use of them yields signs, not sentences. Second, there are two formation rules but only one "tie," if I may so speak. That is, the connection between a mind and an emotion idea is the same as the connection between a mind and a collection idea, be the collection a sense, an imagination, or a memory collection. Somewhat differently, 'f^{e}' and '[   ]' expressions stand for items of the same ontological kind.

Since Berkeley categorizes minds as substances, one is likely to insist that 'f^{e}' signs and bracket-expression signs stand for *accidents* or *qualities* or *properties* and that the connection between a mind and an emotion or a mind and a collection is that of *inherence*. That, to be sure, would nicely explicate Berkeley's claim that sensible objects cannot exist without the mind or unperceived by the mind. There is, of course, something right about using 'inherence' as the word for the connection, but there is something wrong about it as well. For now, Berkeley's dependence claim is best left as merely reflected by the schema. Nothing is gained at this stage by insisting on introducing a word for the connection. Indeed, no word is wholly suitable, just as no traditional category term is wholly suitable for ideas. Berkeley himself prefers 'experience' for the connection, though that word is particularly unsuitable for ontological purposes.

The foregoing schema neatly allows for depicting the truth makers of such ("true") sentences as 'Michelle imagines a red square', 'Michelle remembers a red square, "Michelle sees a red square', and 'Michelle feels pleasure'. (The examples are, of course, rough and ready. I take 'Michelle' to stand for a mental substance and let a red square serve for a tree or table or whatever. The liberties are harmless, I believe.) The differences between seeing, remembering, imagining, and feeling are all on "the side of the object" and reflected by the differences in superscripts that encode the differences in kind of the simple ideas, thus serving to capture Berkeley's talk of liveliness (PR 30), or vivacity, to use Hume's term. That is as it should be: Berkeley does not have mental acts, either as relations or as qualities.

The reason for *not* using 'accident' or 'quality' as the category word for emotions or sensible objects is that Berkeley would construe the above examples to express that Michelle experiences this or that and not to attribute a quality to Michelle. Statements about minds are not like statements that express, for example, what color an object is. Somewhat differently, 'Michelle is in (or has a) pain' is best understood as 'Michelle feels, experiences, pain'. Berkeley thus prefers to use 'perceive' or 'experience' as the word for the relation between a mind and "its object." He nonetheless wishes to insist that sensible objects cannot exist without or independently of a mind; and that insistence is rooted in his being driven to categorize sensible objects as accidents of the mind even though they are not, in everyday talk, attributed to the mind. In a substance ontology, there is room for only one genuine relation: namely, inherence. (By a "genuine relation" I mean one that is not represented by means of a sign that is classified as a sign for an accident. That the only genuine relation in a substance ontology is a "tie" is pleasantly ironic.) What, however, is the basis for the dependence claim? Why is Berkeley an idealist?

On the variant of the ideal-language method I am presently using, one designs a schema in order to represent the truth makers of the sentences that are assumed to describe the world, and to represent the truth makers such that the ontology of the world is shown by features of the representation. The schema is for ontological, not logical, purposes. The nature of validity is, so to speak, of no concern whatsoever. Relatedly, the aim is not to "translate" ordinary talk into the schema or symbolism.

A far as concerns the description of the world, that is a datum; and an ontology is given for a world; but what the world is, for which the ontology is given, is not an ontological issue. (Whether there are lions or tigers is not an ontological issue, though whether they are substances or congeries is.) I thus do not challenge Berkeley's description of the world, except to remark on how impoverished the world of the *Principles* is.

The world for which Berkeley provides an ontology is one whose description is exhausted by statements about what minds experience. (Statements, suitably recast, about trees, tables, and so on are construed to "refer to" that which is experienced!) One class of statement conspicuously absent is that to the effect that someone knows he or she is in pain or knows he or she is seeing a white wall or the like. (Also absent are statements to the effect that a person is thinking or believing or judging such and such.) The absence is striking; after all, Berkeley is intent on providing an account of knowledge. He is aware of the absence, though. He waves at but does not wrestle with it (PR 30, 89; and part II of the *Principles* is absent). That is understandable: 'xx[   ]' is not a combination rule. To put the point simply, a mind cannot experience itself as experiencing an emotion or sensible object. I could, of course, have simply noted that Berkeley cannot account for a mind's knowing that it exists ('xx' is not a combination rule); but that failure is not the interesting one. Berkeley cannot accommodate one of the necessary conditions for a mind's knowing that *it* sees a tree or a chair or a stream.

Let me now explain why I exclude 'xf^s' as a formation rule. Sentences such as 'Michelle senses red' and 'Michelle senses the odor of a banana' do not occur in the description of the world for which Berkeley gives an ontology. That may strike one as mad, since it plainly conflicts with what Berkeley says in the very first section of the *Principles*. Let me explain my willingness to be mad. (1) If such sentences do occur in the description of the world, Berkeley's discussion of abstraction runs aground. (2) PR 1 is used in Berkeley's argument for idealism, and that argument is not the heart of the matter. About that, more later. (3) PR 1 is a clear invitation to Kant; it tempts one to dream up a causal or quasi-causal explanation for how a mind constructs or makes sensible objects. Berkeley is best spared that kind of nonsense. Besides, such "explanations" have nothing at all to do with ontology. (4) Berkeley's use of 'idea' in PR 1 is wholly unanchored.

I need now to make several more framework comments. (1) One can do without superscripts on the *ef* signs, except for 'e', by using 's', 'm', and 'i' as superscripts on bracket expressions. (2) I ignore how God is to be differentiated from "finite" minds; indeed, I construe Berkeley's world and its ontology as if there were no God.[1] (3) I ignore Berkeley's causality and activity talk; it is vacuous as far as concerns ontology. (4) I ignore for now how Berkeley might individuate sensible objects and how he might solve the problem of identity through change of sensible objects. (5) I have given Berkeley a solution to the one-many problem by allowing the same *ef* sign to occur in different bracket expressions. (6) I have also allowed for different minds to experience the same emotion or the same sensible object. Have I in (5) and (6) been too generous? I think not, though I confess that my largess flows from my having no sympathy at all for the view that Berkeley is a nominalist. Apart from nominalism's being foolish—fashionable though it is these days, all decked out in tropes—there is no point in burdening Berkeley with the bewildering complications that are unleashed by committing him to nominalism.[2]

Berkeley's thought is driven by his preoccupation with skepticism: more specifically, by his attempt to defend what he takes to be a truism, namely, that people—gardeners and carpenters—sometimes *know* that an object is a rose or a lily, a chair or a table. His defense of that truism is guided by what I call the comparison model of knowledge (CMK), the first appearance of which is in *Theaetetus* (191c–195b). The model dominates

---

1. If God is included in the ontology, he can at best serve to experience sensible objects.
2. What reasons could Berkeley have for nominalism? He needs it neither for his attack on Locke's doctrine of abstraction nor for his attack on representationalism.

the tradition and underlies much of what goes on in Descartes and Locke. The structure of the model is as follows: A person applies a word to an object. The word is true of the object provided that the object and the standard for (or the meaning of) the word match, or agree, in the appropriate way; and a person *knows* the word is true of the object— knows that the object is W—provided that he or she discerns the match.

Here is an illustration of CMK. A "yardstick" is a standard for 'one yard (long)', as well as for a family of measurement words. Suppose a person applies 'one yard' to an iron rod, says of the rod that it is one yard. The word/phrase is true of the rod provided that the end points of the stick and those of the rod coincide; and the person *knows* that the stick is one yard (in length) provided that he or she discerns the coincidences of the end points.

On the CMK, a necessary condition for knowing is that the knower *experience* the object about which he or she has knowledge. Doubt is present or can, at any rate, be engendered whenever the object about which a claim is made is not experienced, not in plain view.

In the tradition, the model was so construed that the standard for a word was "in the mind" and was called a concept or an abstract idea or an idea or a notion. Though few philosophers paid much attention to the word, their thought was nonetheless guided by the model.[3] The model, I should say, has a deep hold on us quite apart from its presence in the tradition. For example, alleged cases of ESP are puzzling because they are exceptions to the CMK.

Berkeley interprets Locke and Descartes to hold that everyday physical-object words ('chair', 'apple') are applied to objects that *cannot* be experienced. For them, judgments to the effect that something is a tree or table express that that which is experienced or sensed has a correlate, the latter matching or failing to match the former (if indeed there is a correlate). That which is experienced (sensed, perceived) is taken to be both a sensed object and in effect a standard. Berkeley's strategy is simple: a physical-object word is applied to that which is experienced (PR 1), and that which is experienced is not a representative entity, for it cannot be like anything different in kind from what is experienced (PR 8).

Skepticism is rooted, supposedly, in representationalism; and to preclude the former, one must reject the latter by collapsing the idea-thing

---

3. Descartes's search for a "new" criterion of truth is inspired by his belief that the CMK does not accommodate the sort of knowledge he demands. His clarity-distinctness criterion, even if accepted, will not provide for the kind of knowledge Berkeley wishes to account for.

dichotomy. Berkeley collapses it to the side of ideas. Why? The simple answer is that he merely follows his predecessors in using 'idea' as the category word for sensed objects and thus drifts or stumbles into idealism. That answer, though somewhat suggested by the early sections of the *Principles*, is not very illuminating, if only because Berkeley himself is of at least two minds concerning his use of 'idea'. His idealism stems instead from his categorizing minds as substances.

Recall that 'x[   ]' is a combination rule. In order to avoid idealism, that is, to collapse the idea-thing distinction to the side of things, one would, first, have to allow that instances of '[   ]^s' may stand alone in representing part of the world and, second, have to introduce a relation such that 'xR[   ]^s' is a rule ('R' being interpreted as, say, seeing). A substance ontology, however, has no room or place for a relation other than inherence, as noted above, and as Berkeley himself knew (PR 89). If one insists on having the object of knowledge *related* to the knower and the knower categorized as a substance, then idealism is inevitable.

One might imagine that Berkeley could have allowed instances of '[   ]^s' to stand alone and could also have allowed 'x[   ]^s' to be a rule. But that would make no sense. If a sensible object is to be related to a substance, the sensible object has to be thought of as an accident of, and thus as dependent on, the substance. One cannot allow for an entity's being both dependent and independent in an ontology that countenances substances. That is a moral of Spinoza's *Ethics*, one that he neatly expresses as Axiom 1: "All things that are, are either in themselves [substances] or in something else [modes, affections]."[4]

Representationalism and thus skepticism were latent throughout the tradition, becoming manifest only after Galileo and Descartes managed to give plausibility to the claim that the cause of that which is sensed need not be like that which is sensed in order "causally to explain" why one senses what one does. On a substance ontology, the only items that can be experienced are accidents; therefore, knowledge of objects must be indi-

---

4. *The Ethics and Selected Letters*, trans. Samuel Shirley and Seymor Feldman (Indianapolis: Hackett Publishing Co., 1982), p. 32. Wittgenstein makes a similar-sounding claim in the *Tractatus* (2.0122), but its meaning is altogether different. Spinoza's claim expresses merely that if one uses 'substance' in the traditional way, then that which is not a substance but combines with a substance must be an affection or mode—it must be what the Aristotelian-Scholastics labeled an "accident," that is, an inessential feature possessed by, and depending for its existence upon, a substance.

rect and representational. Skepticism was a crisis waiting to happen; idealism was its inevitable offspring.[5]

Berkeley's idealism is a consequence of his attempt to defeat skepticism while clinging to a substance ontology. In order to depict the truth maker of a physical-object judgment as something the mind experiences or with which the mind is "directly acquainted," Berkeley has no choice but to insist that the truth maker is mind-dependent and thus *in effect* an accident of the mind. However, he cannot explicitly categorize the truth maker an *accident:* chairs and trees are not ascribed to the mind.

The rudimentary structure of a substance ontology is as follows: Given a subject-predicate sentence, the subject of which is used to refer to an individual, the subject is said to refer to a substance, the predicate to an accident, and the sentence expresses that the instances of the kinds are related by *inherence.* (I ignore the complications deriving from distinguishing between accidents and forms.) Berkeley knows that that which is expressed by 'Michelle sees a white horse' cannot be analyzed in the way that that which is expressed by 'Michelle is walking' may be analyzed. And that is so even when 'seeing a white horse' is construed to stand for a complex having a suitable mark of vivacity. The fact is, Berkeley does not quite know what to do with that which is expressed by 'Michelle sees a white horse'. He knows only that he cannot analyze a white horse as a substance having accidents, since that leads to representationalism and thus to skepticism.

Berkeley does not, I believe, break with the substance ontology. True, he gives a nonsubstantialist, immaterialist, analysis of a tree or a chair; but he does so only in order to make the object mind-dependent and thus in effect an accident. Whether or not he did so wittingly, Berkeley, I submit, embraced Spinoza's first axiom.

A more generous, perhaps more illuminating way of stating the point just made is to say that Berkeley tries to use a substance ontology for a purpose that cannot be served by such an ontology. The ontological depiction given by Berkeley for the truth maker of, say, 'Michelle sees a green leaf' does not mirror the grammatical structure of the sentence. The sentence is relational, and thus no substance ontology can handle it.

5. The peculiar status of sensed items and the latent skepticism in the Aristotelian tradition were ignored because before Galileo there was no appreciation of the difference between direct realism and the view that the cause of what is sensed "completely" resembles what is sensed. Curiously, in the *Third Meditation* Descartes remarks that he once held the latter, representationalist view; but he seems not to have realized that it alone suffices to bring on a skeptical crisis.

Berkeley's predecessors managed, however, by construing the sentence as 'Michelle *is* seeing a green leaf' and then analyzing the truth maker as a substance having an accident of the "idea of" sort; but that leads to skepticism. Berkeley must thus analyze the truth maker of the sentence as a substance having an accident, which accident cannot, however, be ascribed to the mind.[6] For Berkeley, then, the ontological representation in no way mirrors the grammar of the sentence. Berkeley deserves celebration, not scorn: he begins the assault on the conviction that grammar is a reliable (the only?) guide to ontology. That Berkeley fails to appreciate the consequences of that assault should not distress us: seminal philosophers rarely know their offspring.

Berkeley is no happier with his use of 'idea' as the category term for sensible objects (PR 38). He sometimes remarks that his unhappiness is owing to the fact that his use of 'idea' yields nonsense: for instance, 'A chair is an idea'. That is not much of a reason; mixing ontological talk with everyday talk always begets nonsense. He has a much deeper reason for his unhappiness, though. One premise of the argument that opens the *Principles* is that an idea cannot exist unperceived or without the mind. He is entitled to it only if he is using 'idea' in the "idea of" sense; but he is well aware that is not how he uses 'idea'.[7] For him, an idea is not *of* anything. He thus uses 'idea' in a new, philosophical sense, shorn of 'of', and thus must acknowledge that on that use he has no ground for the above premise. In the third dialogue (D 235) Berkeley remarks that he used 'idea' because a necessary relation to the mind is understood to be implied by that term. In so remarking, he suggests that he has available an argument for idealism that does not make use of 'idea'. The argument is hard to find; however, if one reads PR 86–95 with no more than a hint of sympathy for the dialectic, one sees there the only argument that Berkeley could give; and it is the nakedly transcendental one I have given above: idealism is the only way out of skepticism.

Berkeley's organization of the *Principles* is puzzling in the light of the dialectical flow of his thought. Surely he would have been better off to begin with a discussion of skepticism and representationalism. Had he done so, he could have explained his odd use of 'idea' and spared himself the bad arguments that depend on that use. (PR 1–7 is a torturous stretch

---

6. PR 49 encapsulates Berkeley's agonies.

7. That an idea cannot exist without the mind is at best a grammatical truth and, as such, supports no ontological claim. However, when 'idea' is shorn of 'of', there is not even a grammatical truth that Berkeley can think is of use to him. PR 49 is also to the point here; in fact, it bears on many points central to Berkeley's position.

of writing. It needs an exhaustive commentary.) Of course, had Berkeley so organized the *Principles* that it began with a discussion of his central problem, thus making the dialectic transparent, he would have been an exception to what seems to have long been the rule: first things last.

Why did Berkeley categorize minds as substances? Why did he not stick with the congeries analysis he entertained in the notebooks? And could he have avoided idealism had he insisted on a nonsubstantialist account of mind? These are rather daunting questions, and on this occasion I shall do no more than broadly sketch some guesses. (1) Berkeley is not a Humean when it comes to cause. He needs an agent, something that can be said to be *active*. Only substance will do.[8] (2) A congeries account of mind allows one to avoid idealism only if one can analyze experience as a relation that is external to the relata and such that the relata can exist independently of the relation. Berkeley is not able to master such a view of relations; indeed, no one even thought that they could do so until this century. (3) Had Berkeley allowed a sensible object to be a part of a "mind congeries" and also held that the part could exist independently of such a congeries, he would not have avoided idealism, at least not in any more than a verbal sense: that which can be a part of mind has to be categorized as mental. More accurately, Berkeley would not have been made any happier by the claim that chairs are mental than he was by the claim that chairs are ideas (and thus cannot exist unperceived or without the mind).

I return to Berkeley's idealism. There is nothing wrong with it as far as it goes, which is not, as I have indicated, very far; and, as I show shortly, it goes even less far than initially said. Nonetheless, Berkeley's ontology is able to exhibit truth makers for such sentences as 'Spina sees a red ball', 'Tietjens imagines Sylvia's face', and 'Valentine remembers Mark's face'. The superscripts are powerful devices indeed. Furthermore, the schema can be supplemented such that the individuation problem is solved—the problem, that is, of depicting the truth maker of, say, 'Spina sees two red squares' (same size, etc.). Bare particulars will do nicely! (It is sheer prejudice to insist that the members of a collection must be of the same kind, a prejudice that stems from the thought that the ontological depiction of an object must mimic the grammatical form of the sentence used to describe the object, such that 'This is red', about a square, must be so analyzed that the demonstrative refers to the particular, 'red' to a qual-

---

8. Though "causal" explanations have no place in ontology, Berkeley believes they do. Indeed, his primary reason for categorizing mind as substance seems to be that he needs a cause for imaging, sensing, and so on.

ity.)[9] Berkeley's ontology can be made to accommodate a good deal, but it cannot accommodate an account of knowledge. Berkeley's idealism simply cannot do what it was designed to do.

Berkeley's idealism secures only what *appears* to be a necessary condition for one's knowing that a sensed object is a chair or table or horse. In the *Principles*, Berkeley seems to believe that error is possible only if representationalism is the case; or perhaps he thinks that the only kind of error that needs to be handled is error of the mislabeling sort, calling something a horse when it is a donkey, an error that could be explained as due to carelessness in comparing the standard for a word and the object to which the word is applied. Some errors result, however, from a thing's appearing other than it is, as Berkeley himself comes to realize in the *Three Dialogues*. It is errors of this sort that undermine his account of the truism that "we" sometimes *know* that an object is a tree or table.

Suppose that Spina asserts that the wall is red and later claims that he was wrong, explaining his mistake by claiming that the wall appeared red at the time he asserted that it was red. If Berkeley allows that Spina senses a collection that contains "red" (at the time he asserts it is red), and allows, as surely he must, that there is no *mark* that differentiates veridical from nonveridical sensings, then that which is experienced cannot ground the true application of a physical-object judgment. (I ignore the difference between applying 'wall' and 'red wall' and assume that one can be mistaken about an object as well as an object's color. A mirror image of a red wall should do.) The truth maker for a physical-object judgment is not experienced. Accordingly, 'x[ ]^s' does not actually represent the truth maker for someone's seeing an object that grounds the application of a physical-object word; it grounds at best the fact that someone experiences a sensible "something."[10]

Berkeley is not helped, I should add, by being read as a phenomenalist

9. The prejudice gains a foothold early. It is present in Aristotle's *Categories* and dominates the thinking of all the analytical ontologists who take this inspiration from Russell and the early Wittgenstein. It is rather amusing that the analytical ontologists, having liberated themselves from grammatical form, submit to domination by logical form, especially so since the difference between the two does not come to that much.

10. Berkeley's failure on this score is elegantly laid out by Richard H. Popkin in "The New Realism of Bishop Berkeley," in *George Berkeley: Lectures Delivered Before the Philosophical Union of the University of California in Honor of the Two Hundredth Anniversary of the Death of George Berkeley, Bishop of Cloyne (1685–1753)*, University of California Publications in Philosophy, no. 29 (Berkeley and Los Angeles: University of California Press, 1957), pp. 1–19; reprinted in Popkin, *The High Road to Pyrrhonism* (San Diego: Austin Hill Press, 1980), pp. 319–38.

or, more generously, as an incipient phenomenalist. First, phenomenalism does not permit *experiencing* the ground for a physical-object judgment. Second, that which is experienced is the ground for a judgment that has no ordinary use; it is a judgment contrived as part of a philosophical explanation of a kind of error. That is, the claim that Spina experiences a collection containing red is a philosophical claim, as is the claim that Spina could have made or did make an everyday assertion that was about it and made true by it. If Spina speaks everyday language, none of his judgments are about the sorts of items posited by the phenomenalist.

Let us assume for the sake of the argument, however, that Berkeley is headed toward phenomenalism in the *Dialogues* and that phenomenalism is able to provide an account of "our" knowledge of trees, walls, chairs, and so on. Berkeley would still be an idealist, for phenomenal collections would have to be accidents of the mind, at least insofar as his account of knowledge—however Pickwickian the knowledge claims—rests on the comparison model; and if it does not rest on that model, what does it rest on?

Berkeley's ontology fails, first, because it cannot accommodate "our" purported knowledge of chairs, tables, streams, and so on and, second, because it cannot accommodate knowledge at all—at least not if the account of knowledge is shaped by the CMK. The former, resulting from the fact that "things sometimes appear other than they are," is daunting; the latter is disastrous and results from the fact that 'x[ ]' is not a combination rule. That means that the ontology cannot represent a truth maker for, say, 'Michelle knows that she senses a red something' or, more generally, for 'I know this is red' asserted by anyone.

One could try to skirt the disaster by claiming that the ontology can at least accommodate the truth maker for, say, 'Michelle knows the ball is red'. After all, the ontology allows for, say, '$x_m[X]^m$ & $x_m[Y]^s$'. (I use 'x_m' to stand for the referent of 'Michelle', 'X' for the content of what serves as the standard, and 'Y' as the content of the sensed collection.) Quite apart from the question of what role is to be assigned to the mind and quite apart from how one is to exhibit the matching relation such that one is not simply knowing the same object over and over again, the salvage operation saves little, if anything. What can be done with a situation in which Michelle senses two objects of different colors and is said to have knowledge of the color of but one? In this situation, one must account for the discerning of the match between the standard and the appropriate sensed object; but the ontology lacks the resources for that. That is, the ontology lacks the resources to represent a mind's *attending* *to* one of several sensed objects—not to mention that there is no way to represent the discerning of a relation between a standard (assuming it can be marked as such) and a sensed object. Accordingly, Berkeley's ontology cannot accommodate more than the necessary conditions for knowing a something, however one categorizes it over and above its being an "accident" of the mind. True, one could retreat to the only dry ground possible: namely, that a mind senses only one collection at a time and that when the mind does, the appropriate standard is always also an accident of the mind. Actually, one could push the poverty one step farther, claiming that knowing *is* experiencing.

The foregoing attack on the failure to accommodate ontologically the CMK has something in common with the later Wittgenstein's skeptical attack on the model, an attack that assumes that the object of purported knowledge has favored status as "in the mind." Wittgenstein, insisting that knowledge involves putting the right word to the object, presses the problem of how the ostensible knower *knows* that he or she has got the right standard for the word and how she or he can be certain that the matching has been properly carried out. The aim of Wittgenstein's attack is to produce a *reductio* of the comparison model itself, not merely of phenomenalism or, if one will, mentalism.[11] My attack is meant to show that even if one thinks one can surmount the skeptical attack, one cannot devise an ontology within which to locate or ground the CMK.

I want now both to sharpen and to broaden my attack on idealism by reflecting briefly and structurally on Gustav Bergmann, an ontologist as heroic as the tradition has known. Bergmann's ontology has, among other kinds of entities, particulars, universals, and relations. Further, he has two basic kinds of "atomic facts," mental ones and nonmental ones, the difference resulting from his having two kinds of radically different universals, propositions and nonpropositions. The former are used to accommodate "thinking something is green," "believing something is square," and so on; the latter are used to accommodate shapes, colors, tones, and so on.

Bergmann's ontology leads to an utter catastrophe: it is unable to get mind and nonmind together, unable to get a mental act related to a

11. My critique of Berkeley does not require that the word be a feature of his account. I presuppose merely that experience is only a necessary condition of knowing and that a standard, however characterized, must be brought into play.

nonmental state of affairs, notwithstanding that he, unlike Berkeley, has relations other than inherence or exemplification at his disposal. (1) It will not do, even though the syntactical rules allow for it, for Bergmann to make experience a relation between a mental particular and a nonmental particular. Not only would that violate his Principle of Acquaintance, the basis for his insistence that particulars always exemplify at least one universal, it would also provide no ground for knowing that something is, say, red: that which is the object of acquaintance must contain the ground for the truth of the sentence, not merely for the application of the subject of the sentence. (2) Bergmann cannot allow the mental particular to be related to a state of affairs, for in order to do that, one would have to introduce a so-called pseudorelation. Such a relation is objectionable not because of its odd syntactical nature ('xRfy') but rather because a relation cannot be exemplified without there being the relata, and the relatum associated with 'this is red' may not exist, since the sentence can be false. On Bergmann's conception of the ideal-language method, sentences of the natural language are mapped onto strings of the formalism, but none of the strings need be true. That means that for Bergmann the mere possibility that something is not the case puts the nonmental world beyond the reach of mind. Somewhat differently, Bergmann is forced to analyze an act of sensing on analogy with an act of thinking. Notwithstanding his insistence on the principle of acquaintance, Bergmann's ontology has no room for acquaintance, at least not as a genuine relation. All that mind (mental acts) *experiences* are, so to speak, its own propositional characters. The nonmind world is lost, utterly lost, to mind.[12]

Bergmann's fate is not, upon reflection, particularly surprising. His mental acts are particulars and as such not that different from Berkeleian minds. After all, a Berkeleian mind is in effect an enduring particular; the Bergmannian mental act, a momentary Berkeleian mind. Further, though Bergmann has relations, the relata of all of them are particulars; and no particular provides a ground for a knowledge claim. Finally, Bergmann's method dictates that sensing is as problematic as believing. Just as false belief is possible, so too false sensing is possible.

My ontological representation of Berkeley was not designed to make translation possible. My representation was designed to depict only the

---

12. Bergmann's difficulties come to the surface in "Realistic Postscript," in *Logic and Reality* (Madison: University of Wisconsin Press, 1964), pp. 304–40, and stalk him for the rest of his career.

truth makers of true sentences. I was thus able to represent a mind as acquainted with, experiencing, a complex entity, a "something" having properties. Berkeley is spared the problem of false sensing, but that does not save his account of knowing.[13]

13. If there is anything of worth in this essay, it is due, I should think, to others. Virtually all of my thoughts on Berkeley have grown out of conversations—many of them from long ago, though some of them quite recent—with members of the "Iowa School": Bracken, Popkin, Bergmann, Watson, Cummins, Van Iten, Muehlmann, Flage, Alan Hausman, and David Hausman. I have also benefited over the years from conversations with, among others, Pappas and Winkler. If only I could remember the things I have read!

2

On Allaire's "Another Visit"

Alan Hausman and David Hausman

I n his seminal 1963 paper "Berkeley's Idealism," Allaire wrote: "That chairs, tables, mountains and so on must be perceived seems beyond understanding, let alone conviction."[1] Thirty years later, in "Berkeley's Idealism: Yet Another Visit," Allaire makes the rather startling claim that all "*ontological* solutions to the problems of knowledge issue in idealism or a variant of it, I think" (23). Given that his current essay is a defense of the basic ideas of the 1963 paper, it appears that we must conclude that ontology is also beyond understanding or, at best, in strong danger of being so. We hope to show the danger illusory.

In his current paper, Allaire lays out what he believes to be Berkeley's ontology. Indeed, Allaire's concerns are almost exclusively ontological; his arguments attempt to show not only the ontological underpinnings of Berkeley's epistemology but also how ontological positions—Berkeley's

---

1. Edwin B. Allaire, "Berkeley's Idealism," *Theoria* 29 (1963), p. 229.

and seemingly everyone else's—drive one to epistemological consequences; for example, Berkeley cannot distinguish ontologically between veridical and nonveridical ideas, so we cannot have knowledge about physical objects. The startling claim quoted above is the end result of this ontological preoccupation. This claim is made all the more puzzling by Allaire's argument, at least in the case of Berkeley, that he fails to solve the problems of knowledge. If that is true, and if Berkeley's idealism is typical, then why would idealism be the end of the epistemological-ontological progression rather than just another dead end? One might as well say that the ontological problems with idealism lead back to direct realism.

Allaire claims that Berkeley is forced to idealism for two reasons: (1) There can be no genuine relations between substances; the only genuine relation in a substance ontology is inherence, in the sense that an accident (quality, property) inheres in a substance. Hence a substance ontology cannot accommodate an analysis of, say, 'Jones perceives that P' in terms of a relation between the mental substance Jones and the physical substance P. (2) Given (1), there are only two alternatives: either one allows a quality of a mental substance to represent a physical substance, a move that allegedly ends in skepticism, or one claims that the object of perception is a quality of the knowing mind. In effect this is, as mentioned previously, a somewhat revised version of the so-called inherence account Allaire first championed years ago.[2]

For reasons that are not clearly spelled out, Allaire claims that no substance metaphysics can accommodate a commitment to a relation other than inherence. Perhaps this contention is based on familiar accounts of Aristotelian substances by Spinoza and Leibniz, accounts that require all relations to be internal and hence "unreal"; or perhaps it is just that neither the substance tradition nor any other had any real grasp of external relations until Russell. Allaire's conclusion is that an analysis of direct realism as a perceiving relation between a perceiver and a material substance is not, logically speaking, even a possible position in the substance-metaphysical tradition.

There are certainly many substance philosophers who would be surprised by Allaire's claim: Aquinas, who believed there could be relations between substances, and, to the extent they are substance ontologists— momentary-substance ontologists as Allaire himself characterizes those who believe there are momentary particulars—the early Russell, Price,

2. In ibid.

and the Moore of "The Refutation of Idealism." Allaire owes us an explanation here.

For certainly, if he is right, the traditional objections to direct realism that revolve around the facts of perceptual variation and that historically appear to be a major motivation in the move to either representationalism or phenomenalism would be muddled, in fact wrongheaded. Had these philosophers realized that no genuine relations could exist in their substance metaphysics, direct realism would have succumbed without epistemological angst. However, if there were in fact the relations he claims cannot exist, the fact of perceptual variation would in any case force one to abandon the use of such relations to analyze the perception of material objects when analyzed as substances. The reason, of course, is that cases of, say, hallucination face one with the perception of properties that do not obviously belong to a material substance. The ensuing dialectic, at least in the seventeenth century, can be seen to lead to representationalism or perhaps even phenomenalism, and this dialectic is often repeated in the twentieth century. Allaire himself, speaking of Gustav Bergmann's view of perception, says that for Bergmann, "the mere possibility that something is not the case puts the nonmental world beyond the reach of mind" (36). We suspect that it is the problem of false belief, which we presently shall distinguish from that of error, that leads Allaire to say that any ontological attempt to solve the problems of knowledge ends in idealism.

Let us, however, grant Allaire (1) above. Then, one is driven either to representationalism or to a collections analysis of material objects, the latter being some variant of phenomenalism. The move to representationalism posits properties that inhere in mental substance. These properties represent the material object of which we have no direct experience. Such representationalism allegedly leads to skepticism. But, as Allaire sees it, a collections analysis of material objects will not do either; on Allaire's account Berkeley is a substance ontologist. What he takes this commitment to amount to, among other things, is that properties must inhere in substances. On a collections analysis a collection of properties needs a substantial ground; if it did not, we would no longer have a substance ontology. The only substance remaining is mental substance. The result is an idealist metaphysics. Hence, beginning with a substance metaphysics and the commitment to inherence and with the impossibility of relations, the inevitable result is idealism.

So far, then, it appears that whether one takes Allaire's ontological road or the road of error, one ends, if one is a substance ontologist, with the idealism of Berkeley—if (2) presents the only alternatives. We argue that there is another.

We have argued elsewhere that Descartes's representationalism is a response to a scientific problem:[3] given that the new science seems to call for intermediaries of a certain kind, the only way to avoid an infinite regress of such intermediaries is the positing of an entity that has none of the characteristics that cause the regress. Descartes's ideas, we argue, are meant to be genuinely intentional entities; this is the argument, found in the *Third Meditation*, that revolves around his distinction between objective and formal reality. Descartes's theory is a kind of representationalism, and he arrives at this view—contrary to what Allaire believes—neither via the problem of error nor via the limitations of a relationless substance ontology. Furthermore, this sort of representationalism is crafted to avoid the skeptical objections that could be raised against a view that takes representing entities to have the same structure as the entities represented.

As we argue in the next essay of this volume, Berkeley's likeness argument is intended to show that representationalism is not a viable solution to problems about perceiving the physical world. If a sensible quality is unlike a physical entity, it cannot represent it (whether this does real justice to Descartes's intentional entities is a matter we shall discuss presently); if it is like it, then the physical entity would have to be, contrary to fact, directly perceived. This argument, however, cuts against entities allegedly represented by sensible qualities no matter what those entities' ontological analysis. Thus, neither Descartes's argument for representationalism nor Berkeley's argument against it makes use of the substance-property categories per se.

That Berkeley does not seem to do justice to Descartes's intentional view seems surprising, given that–as we argue in the next essay in this volume—he is quite aware of the problems that lead Descartes to those entities. A case in point is Berkeley's move to idealism. After the attack on representationalism Berkeley is left with sensible qualities. Why not be a direct realist? The issue is not necessarily error. In fact Hylas entertains a quite different possibility when he challenges Philonous to explain why, if we distinguish the act of awareness from the object of awareness, sensible qualities need to be mind-dependent. Philonous's answer is not Allaire's; he does not say that such sensible qualities can only inhere in

3. Alan Hausman and David Hausman, "Descartes's Secular Semantics," *Canadian Journal of Philosophy* 22 (1992), pp. 81–104.

minds. Rather, we argue, the answer is in terms of consequences Berkeley fears if the sensible quality is independent. Briefly to rehearse our argument: Berkeley fears that if the act of awareness is 'external' to its object, as would be the case if the object is mind-independent, an intermediary would be necessary for the mind to grasp the object. Such intermediaries, given Berkeley's likeness argument, do lead to skepticism.

Thus, Allaire leaves out a crucial step in Berkeley's move to idealism. It is not merely that all that is available to Berkeley are substances and accidents. Berkeley is more innovative than even Allaire, who gives him some innovative credit, sees. He flirts with making a new tie between an idea and a substance because he sees that his sort of idea cannot be treated quite like an accident, and he flirts also with making things into independent collections of sensible qualities. The reason for the failure of the latter, then, is not a blind adherence to substantialism but a belief that the mind-independent existence of physical objects, no matter what their ontological analysis, can lead to nothing but representationalism.

To put our point differently, if Allaire were correct, Berkeley's idealism would be totally unmotivated, a purely logical deduction from the basic principles of a substantialist ontology. Allaire, who in the past was critical of Berkeley's failure to produce arguments for idealism, has now turned Berkeley's vice into virtue: to argue for idealism is to argue for the whole edifice of substantialist metaphysics. Berkeley becomes a mere keeper of the Aristotelian flame.

Allaire believes that all attempts to do justice to the problems of knowledge reach an ontological end in idealism. We already have indicated our puzzlement with this view. Let us now diagnose why Allaire might think this. First, we wish briefly to distinguish the problem of perceptual 'error' from that of false belief. If one has jaundice or takes LSD, one might see colors that are not actual features of any physical object that one can be truly said to be seeing. One may then wonder, as at least some philosophers do, whether these colors are features of anything and, if so, of what. People of course sometimes make false judgments on the basis of such perceptual states. But this is not a logical necessity. Even if no one ever made a single judgmental error on the basis of such cases, the problem of assigning these colors to something would remain. On the other hand, false belief and the question it engenders—what is there that I am believing if it is not an actual fact?—is a problem that enters with judgments. Although the philosophical atmosphere has decidedly changed, there is a long tradition in which perceptual states, sometimes spoken of in terms of sensations or sensings, are not considered to be properly describable in terms of judgments.

We have some reason to think that Allaire confuses this distinction and that this confusion may lead to the rather radical view in question. In speaking of the ontology of Gustav Bergmann, he claims Bergmann cannot allow a "pseudorelation" (i.e., a relation between a particular and an alleged fact) in his analysis of, say, the fact that Jones sees a red something: "[A] relation cannot be exemplified without there being the relata, and the relatum associated with 'this is red' may not exist, since the sentence can be false." He says soon after that for Bergmann "false sensing is possible" (36). But in what sense can 'This is red' be false for Bergmann?[4] We of course do not want to enter into a long discussion of Bergmann's ontology of mind, so we merely suggest the following: If "this" is taken to refer to a physical object, then of course the sentence might be false. But Bergmann's ideal representation, which reflects his ontology, contains no names for physical objects. So, if one sees something red, something red exists, even if there is no physical object to exemplify the color. The sense in which 'This is red,' if true, might have been false is spelled out in terms of the possibility that this, the particular, might have exemplified some other color.[5] But it does not follow from the possibility of falsehood that an act of sensation or acquaintance can intend a falsehood. To make the point somewhat differently, Bergmann believes that no color quality can be sensed unless it is exemplified by a particular, even if the statement that describes this state of affairs is not a necessary truth.[6] Therefore, Bergmann, or any ontologist worried about 'error,' need not worry about a relational analysis of sensing. It is only judgment that causes a problem.

4. Bergmann discusses atomic statements in so many essays that it is difficult to know what works to cite. But see esp. "The Revolt Against Logical Atomism," in *Meaning and Existence* (Madison: University of Wisconsin Press, 1960), pp. 39–72, and "Particularity and the New Nominalism," 91–105, in the same volume.

5. However, it is not clear that this explication will do. For a discussion of Bergmann's views on the possible falsity of true atomic statements, see Alan Hausman, "Bergmann on the Analytic-Synthetic Distinction," in *The Ontological Turn*, ed. M. S. Gram and E. D. Klemke (Iowa City: University of Iowa Press, 1974), pp. 230–44.

6. Could one make a mistake about which particular one was sensing? I might believe, speaking from within common sense, that the entity I saw a moment ago, which was green, is now red, and I might be mistaken in that belief. This would be an error about a physical object, not about a particular. On Bergmann's ontological view, what I saw a moment ago was a different particular than the one I see now, whether I know that or not. Within the philosophical framework, what is depicted in a Bergmannian schema is what I actually experienced.

If we are right about Bergmann, then he is not forced, as Allaire believes he is, "to analyze an act of sensing on analogy with an act of thinking," with the ontological result that "the nonmind world is lost" (36). If this is an example of how non-Berkeleian views lead to idealism, we reject it.

If we are correct, Bergmann's view can be consistently recast as a version of phenomenalism. Let us take as an example a variant on Goodman's scheme in *The Structure of Appearance*.[7] Goodman is a phenomenalist whose view is consistent with direct realism. Although he himself constructs the mental and physical from 'neutral' sense data, a view Allaire might reject, Goodman need not do this. There is no logical reason he could not have the Bergmannian type of mental acts, as described by Allaire, and give an analysis of physical objects in terms of collections of sensed qualities. Indeed, Goodman distinguishes the sense in which a color may be a mere part of a larger complex (a sum, or, if you wish, a class, whose parts [members] are together the physical object) from that in which, if the color shows a certain pattern throughout the stages of the complex, it is a quality of that complex.[8] This pattern need not be construed as causal or contextual: although he would not do so because of considerations of systematic simplicity, Goodman could introduce a primitive relation of quality-of that happens to hold if, and only if, the pattern is exhibited. This ontology would have two kinds of ties; the color one sees in case one has jaundice or is in bad light is part of the object but not a quality of it (qualities are also parts, of course, but not conversely). A sum, or class, that contains only color parts would be a mere appearance; and parts of a sum, or class, that constitutes the analysis of a physical object, which parts are not also qualities, would be mere appearances of the object.

The point, then, is that the problem of 'error' does not obviously force one to idealism, and we conclude that the argument from error and illusion produces no more than the illusion that ontology is a dead end.

---

7. Nelson Goodman, *The Structure of Appearance*, 3d ed. (Dordrecht: Reidel, 1977).
8. Ibid., pp. 166 ff.

3

A New Approach to Berkeley's Ideal Reality

Alan Hausman and David Hausman

A set of old moves against representational realism has recently been brought into clearer focus by functionalist and artificial-intelligence (AI) theorists. The theory of ideas, advocated by both rationalists and empiricists in the seventeenth and early eighteenth centuries, is seen as an attempt to solve an *information problem:* how does the mind get perceptual information about, say, a tree from the physical environment? Descartes believed that in order to perceive the tree, one had to be directly aware of an idea, a mental item, that represents it.[1] This move puzzled many philosophers in the seventeenth

This essay was cowinner (with George Pappas's "Berkeley and Skepticism" [not included in this volume]) of the fourth annual Colin and Ailsa Turbayne International Berkeley Essay Prize (1993).

1. However, we by no means mean to imply that Descartes has a theory of "extrinsic" representation, that is, that he believes one must assign a semantics to ideas as one does to a language. Rather, Descartes's ideas are *intentional,* by their very nature, about their

century (and continues to do so in the twentieth, and it so exercised Berkeley that he tried to overthrow representationalism in terms of a theory that only added fever to already knitted brows. We want to show that Berkeley's moves can be made more intelligible and interesting in the light of the functionalist critique.

If we are correct, we believe that new light is cast on Berkeley's idealism and on the logic of the steps that lead him there. These steps have been the subject of much controversy.[2] We do not intend, in this essay, to present detailed criticisms of any recent interpretation. However, our argument does show the exact relation of three of Berkeley's most important arguments supporting idealism in the *Principles* and *Dialogues:* the likeness argument, the collapse of the act/object distinction, and the rejection of matter. It is the likeness argument that is the main focus of our attention. Despite some interesting clarifications of it in the literature,[3] we feel its real structure is best revealed using a functionalist critique. Once that is accomplished, the collapse of act and object, which in much of the literature is either ignored or only peripherally worked into the structure of idealism, is seen to be an almost inevitable consequence of the same problems that produce the likeness argument.[4]

What we wish to do, then, is rehearse some of the intellectual motives we feel may have moved Berkeley in his attempt to establish idealism. By "intellectual motives" we do not mean "intellectual biography," and we do not mean to be philosophically psychoanalyzing Berkeley. What we are trying to do is suggest a logical pattern of thought that fits with a certain way of construing problems about ideas and their relation to the mind, namely, information-theoretically. We think that there is enough argumentation in the Berkeley texts to lend support to such speculation. That

---

objects. See Alan Hausman and David Hausman, "Descartes's Secular Semantics," *Canadian Journal of Philosophy* 22 (1992).

2. For a review of some recent argumentation, see George Pappas, "Ideas, Minds, and Berkeley," *American Philosophical Quarterly* 17 (1980), pp. 181–94.

3. See Phillip D. Cummins, "Berkeley's Likeness Principle," in *Locke and Berkeley*, ed. D. M. Armstrong and C. B. Martin (Notre Dame, Ind.: University of Notre Dame Press, 1968), pp. 353–63, and Kenneth P. Winkler, *Berkeley: An Interpretation* (New York: Oxford University Press, 1989), esp. 141–48.

4. Only Chisholm followers, for example, Pitcher, have offered any plausible explanation of Berkeley's move here. G. E. Moore, of course, made much of the collapse in "The Refutation of Idealism," in *Philosophical Studies* (London: Routledge & Kegan Paul, 1960), pp. 1–30, but did not adequately explain Berkeley's motivation for it. Perhaps the general decline in the importance of the act that has marked so much of contemporary philosophy has been reflected in historical scholarship as well.

speculation is fueled, as we have previously indicated, by what we believe is the lack of any totally satisfactory account of his idealism in the literature, as well as by the related difficulties of trying to decide which of Berkeley's arguments depend on what others. We also realize that the plausibility of our reconstruction of Berkeley could be thrown in doubt by the fact that any such reconstruction could not be totally coherent. After all, since idealism is incoherent, there must be missteps in the argument for it. What we hope, then, is that the ambiguities we ourselves call attention to in his theory of ideas are Berkeley's, and not ours in reconstructing him.

Dennett's view of the theory of ideas[5] revolves around regresses and circularities:

I think that AI has broken the back of an argument that has bedeviled philosophers and psychologists for over two hundred years. Here is a skeletal version of it: *First,* the only psychology that could possibly succeed in explaining the complexities of human activity must posit internal representations. This premise has been deemed obvious by just about everyone except the radical behaviorists (both in psychology and philosophy—both Watson and Skinner, and Ryle and Malcolm). Descartes doubted almost everything *but* this. For the British Empiricists, the internal representations were called ideas, sensations, impressions; more recently psychologists have talked of hypotheses, maps, schemas, images, propositions, engrams, neural signals, even holograms and whole innate theories. So the first premise is quite invulnerable, or at any rate it has as impressive mandate. But, *second,* nothing is intrinsically a representation of anything; something is a representation only *for* or *to* someone; any representation or system of representations thus requires at least one *user* or *interpreter* of the representation who is external to it. Any such interpreter must have a variety of psychological or intentional traits: it must be capable of a variety of *comprehension,* and must have beliefs and goals (so it can *use* the representation to *inform* itself and thus assist it in achieving its goals). Such an interpreter is then a sort of homuncu-

5. As we use this phrase, it implies that ideas are mental items and that they are what one directly perceives in what we ordinarily think of as sense perception. That, at least was the seventeenth and early eighteenth-century view. We try, in this essay, to clarify this sense of 'mental'. Dennett's discussion of internal representations, of which ideas are a species, does not imply that representations are mental in any dualistic sense.

lus. Therefore, psychology *without* homunculi is impossible. But psychology *with* homunculi is doomed to circularity or infinite regress, so psychology is impossible.

The argument given is a relatively abstract version of a familiar group of problems. For instance, it seems (to many) that we cannot account for perception unless we suppose it provides us with an internal image (or model or map) of the external world, and yet what good would that image do us if we had no inner eye to perceive it, and how are we to explain *its* capacity for perception? It also seems (to many) that understanding a heard sentence must be somehow *translating* it into some internal message, but how will this message in turn be understood: by translating it into something else?[6]

Exactly what are the alleged circularities and regresses? Dennett gives some examples in the quoted passage, claiming they "are a relatively abstract version of a familiar group of problems." Here, we offer what we take to be the keys to these abstract formulations. They fall into two groups. Each group, we show, can be construed to play a role in Berkeley's understanding of representationalism.[7]

(1) Semantic problems: ideas need a semantics—we need to know what they stand for, and their truth conditions. But to assign their semantics, we need to know the characteristics of the domain of objects, the very thing the representation is supposed to provide. Berkeley's way of putting this problem comes, as we show, with the use of his likeness principle.[8]

(2) Syntactic problems: ideas, representations, have a "syntax," a set of characteristics, analogous to a language, that themselves must be grasped, or

6. D. C. Dennett, *Brainstorms* (Boston: Bradford Books, MIT Press, 1978), pp. 119 ff.

7. Of course, we do not pretend here to give anything more than a quick sketch of Dennett. We merely use his critique to formulate and understand Berkeley. We assume for purposes of this essay that the reader is familiar with Dennett-like problems (he calls them Hume's Problem at one point, p. 122) from the functionalist literature.

8. The quotation from Dennett does not support this interpretation in any obvious way, but we think it is strongly suggested, if not actually implied. A brief argument for our interpretation: Since internal representations are not intrinsically representational, a homunculus must assign an interpretation to them. This Dennett says clearly. But to do this, the homunculus must know the domain of objects, the very thing the representation is invoked to provide. When Dennett says that to some it seems as if a heard sentence must be translated into some internal message, and then asks how this message can be understood, we take the alternatives to be either (a) by means of another message, which generates a regress—as Dennett points out—or (b) by means of assigning the internal message a semantics, which involves us in circularity, since it assumes we know the domain of objects.

else no semantics can be assigned them. Interpreting ideas means coordinating their characteristics with what they are about. Thus we *seem* to have a repeat of the original information problem. Indeed, there were those in the seventeenth century—Foucher, for one—who saw it that way.[9]

We believe that the Cartesian view of the mental, as well as Berkeley's, is meant to *avoid* the semantic and syntactic problems. That is, there are metaphysical reasons Descartes and Berkeley do not give up the theory of ideas in light of the obviousness of (1) and (2). Neither theological concerns nor philosophical blindness plays a role here.

Dennett casts the semantic and syntactic problems in terms of a homunculus, an intelligence, that reads representations. Metaphysically, the homunculus, which has haunted AI theory, took two forms in the seventeenth and early eighteenth centuries: the distinction between a mental substance and its modes (ideas), and the distinction between a mental act, the grasping of the information, and its object, the information itself.[10] In both cases, there are entities that are thought to be mental by their very nature: substances, acts, and, in Descartes's case, ideas. Although we do not give the argument here, we think that this list is exhaustive. Berkeley rids himself of one homunculus, the act, only to reencounter it at a deeper level, mental substance. To analyze these steps is to shed light on why he is an idealist, for, as it turns out, sensible qualities—those entities with which we are directly acquainted in sense perception—are also alleged by Berkeley to be mental.

Seeing Berkeley's collapse of the act/object distinction in the *Dialogues* as a response to the information problem not only makes sense of what is otherwise a very puzzling set of moves but also enables us to focus more precisely on the nature of a problem that has pervaded discussion of the theory of ideas: in what sense are objects about which we get information external (to use Dennett's term) to, outside of, the homunculus? This sense, if there is but one, is crucial, since it is this externality that generates the need for a representative to give information. Now, this cannot be just an action-at-a-physical-distance problem, or it would be

9. Watson suggests that some of Foucher's arguments against Descartes's theory of ideas involve the possibility of an infinite regress of representations. See Richard A. Watson, *The Breakdown of Cartesian Metaphysics* (Atlantic Highlands, N.J.: Humanities Press, 1987), pp. 73 ff.

10. Think of an act of awareness of a representation, if Dennett is right, calling forth another act of awareness of the representation of the representation. One could think of this—we think Dennett does—as a series of homunculi reading a series of representations.

solved by taking brain states as intermediaries. What Descartes sees is that the question of the relation between the brain state and the perceptual experience of the tree presents a problem different from that of the *spatially* external tree. The physical process must come to an end, and then either the last physical step is the perception, and we have materialism, or we again are faced with the problem of how one gets information from the physical world—in this case, from the brain state. Descartes, we think, grasps this clearly; for him, it is a semantic problem. While it is not the object of a perceptual act involving the organs of sensation, the brain state cannot itself represent the physical object that gave rise to it without providing it a specific representative function. Could the brain state be assigned such a function? Descartes, we think, sees that to do so would involve one in the semantic problems described in (1) above. Therefore, some entity must be invested with an inherent representational power; that entity is the idea of the tree. Descartes sees that, given (1), the only way to solve the problem is to build a semantics into the idea, make it intentional.[11] Of course, this means that, within seventeenth-century metaphysical constraints, ideas are now radically different sorts of things from any physical state or process. To solve (2), Descartes invokes direct acquaintance, where, by its very nature, one grasps the object without intermediaries because it is *of the same kind* as the act, a mode of mind.[12] *But Berkeley's ideas are not intentional*, they neither are about nor represent anything.[13] What about them, then, is peculiarly mental? Why classify sensible qualities, in other words, as ideas? We hope to give a new answer to this question.

11. As we use 'intentional', a thought is intentional in that it is by its very nature *about* something other than itself. Its aboutness is not derived, in other words, from the *assignment* of an interpretation to it, as one does with a language. Our view of intentionality thus derives from the Meinongian tradition.

12. Whether or not this is itself an error—since they are very different sorts of modes of mind—is an interesting issue in itself. That is, it is not clear what their characterization has in common, which is a problem: how can a substance have more than one essential mode for a Cartesian, or for anybody? Dennett dismisses the point about direct acquaintance; he does not allow that the homunculus scanning a representation can be so important that (2) is blocked. But the Cartesian argument, after all, is (in effect) that we do manage to perceive; and how could we do that if (1) and (2) were true and at the same time representations were unavoidable, unless there was an act that did not engender more representations? We discuss some of these points further on in the essay.

13. We speak here, of course, only about ideas of sense. For Berkeley the representational capacity of ideas of imagination is a matter of their resemblance to ideas of sense.

The Logical Order of Berkeley's Argument

Berkeley writes the *Principles* and then the *Dialogues* in order to reject the skeptical consequences of philosophers' claims to representationalism and material substance (D 167). His goal is to provide a metaphysics for a philosophy of perception that will be free of skepticism and consistent with common sense. In this revealing passage from the *Principles* Berkeley makes the progression of his thinking explicit:

> First . . . it was thought that colour, figure, motion, and the rest of the sensible qualities or accidents, did really exist without the mind; and for this reason, it seemed needful to suppose some unthinking *substratum* or *substance* wherein they did exist, since they could not be conceived to exist by themselves. Afterwards . . . men being convinced that colours, sounds, and the rest of the sensible secondary qualities had no existence without the mind, they stripped this *substratum* or material substance of those qualities, leaving only the primary ones, figure, motion, and such like, which they still conceived to exist without the mind, and consequently to stand in need of a material support. But it having been shewn, that none, even of these, can possibly exist otherwise than in a spirit or mind which perceives them, it follows that we have no longer any reason to suppose the being of *matter*. Nay, that is utterly impossible there should be any such thing . . . (PR 73)

We believe that Berkeley's intellectual motives for idealism conform to the pattern summarized in these passages. Thus, we believe Berkeley's idealism to be a consequence of a series of steps, each with independent purpose, that begins with an attack on the doctrine of representationalism. We will show that while Berkeley is not himself in the grip of representationalism, he is convinced that sensible qualities are mental by arguments closely related to ones his enemies use to escape problems (1) and (2) above. Berkeley is aware that in presenting such ideas to be characteristically nonintentional—since they do not in any classical way represent—he has placed his theory of ideas outside the range of traditional accounts of the mental. Thus, we show that it is for the purpose of establishing the specific relation ideas bear to the mind, inherence in a mental substance, that Berkeley argues for the collapse of the distinction between act and object.[14] The final step in Berkeley's procedure, as stated above, is to use the rejection of representationalism and the newly established ontological status of sensations to repudiate the doctrine of material substance.

Our view avoids the main problems of the "inherence account" and its difficulties with PR 49.[15] It does not accord with the order in which Berkeley presents his arguments in the *Dialogues*. There it may appear that the argument is as follows: he argues first that sensible qualities are mental, using perceptual relativity arguments, then attacks direct realism by arguing against the act/object distinction, then finally attacks representationalism using the likeness argument. On this view, Berkeley arrives at idealism by eliminating all other possibilities for the existence of independent entities once perceptual relativity establishes the mind-dependence of sensible qualities. But on this interpretation, the place of the collapse of act and object is decidedly weak. Why, if one has already established the mind-dependence of sensible qualities, need one then attack direct realism? Our interpretation of Berkeley, we think, gives him a much stronger and more interesting argument for idealism than the bad arguments—which he himself eschews in PR 15—using perceptual relativity. In fact we think that strong case can be made that the perceptual-relativity arguments are used principally to undermine the distinction between primary and secondary qualities, that is, they are *not* used to establish the mind-dependence of sensible qualities.[16] Furthermore, even granting that perceptual relativity establishes the mind-dependence of sensible qualities, what role does this play in Berkeley's attack on representationalism? All Berkeley needs to do, as we argue, is grant, for the sake of the argument, his opponents' belief in the mind-dependence of

14. Our argument combines arguments from the *Principles* and the *Dialogues* in what we think is the logical order of Berkeley's progression to idealism. The merger is a necessary consequence of the fact, which many commentators have noted, that arguments for the crucial claim that sensible qualities are mental are almost entirely lacking in the *Principles*.

15. See Edwin B. Allaire, "Berkeley's Idealism," *Theoria* 29 (1963), pp. 229–44, and Richard A. Watson, "Berkeley in a Cartesian Context," *Revue Internationale de Philosophie* 65 (1963), pp. 381–94. In "Ideas, Minds, and Berkeley" Pappas reviews the difficulties with this account. We also provide a more consistent interpretation overall than the highly interesting analysis presented by Pappas in "Abstract Ideas and the '*Esse Is Percipi*' Thesis," *Hermathena* 139 (Winter 1985), pp. 47–62, which attributes Berkeley's idealism to a denial of abstract ideas.

16. See Robert Muehlmann, "The Role of Perceptual Relativity in Berkeley's Philosophy," *Journal of the History of Philosophy* 29 (1991), pp. 397–425, and idem, *Berkeley's Ontology* (Indianapolis: Hackett Publishing Co., 1992), pp. 111–69.

sensible qualities, no matter how established, to show what is wrong with *their* arguments. Our view presents a marriage of the *Principles* and *Dialogues* that fits pieces from both works into their logical place.

The Attack on Representationalism

Much of Berkeley's program centers on his concept of a *sensible quality*. Sensible qualities are presented to the mind during a sensation or a perception: we experience red, round, C-sharp, and the like. Here, as Philonous, Berkeley attempts to tell Hylas about sensible qualities:

HYLAS. To prevent any more questions of this kind, I tell you once for all, that by *sensible things* I mean those only which are perceived by sense, and that in truth the senses perceive nothing which they do not perceive immediately: for they make no inferences. The deducing therefore of causes or occasions from effects and appearances, which alone are perceived by sense, entirely relates to reason.
PHILONOUS. This point then is agreed between us, that *sensible things are those only which are immediately perceived by sense*. You will farther inform me, whether we immediately perceive by sight any thing besides light, and colours, and figures: or by hearing, any thing but sounds: by the palate, any thing beside tastes: by the smell, beside odours: or by the touch, more than tangible qualities.
HYLAS. We do not.
PHILONOUS. It seems, therefore, that if you take away all sensible qualities, there remains nothing sensible.
HYLAS. I grant it. (D 174–75)

In its next to last step, Berkeley's argument against the existence of material substance requires that we accept two propositions: (i) all sensible qualities are mind-dependent in the specific sense that they inhere in minds, and (ii) there are no qualities of ordinary objects or events in addition to sensible qualities. This section is concerned primarily with the attack on representationalism, from which (ii) follows. Berkeley defends this proposition in the following passage from the *Dialogues*, where Hylas lays out the representationalist model:

HYLAS. To speak the truth, Philonous, I think there are two kinds of objects, the one perceived immediately, which are likewise called *ideas;*

the other are real things or external objects perceived by mediation of ideas, which are their images and representations. (D 203)

Berkeley attacks this model directly.

PHILONOUS. But how can that which is sensible be like that which is insensible? Can a real thing in itself *invisible* be like a *colour;* or a real thing which is not *audible,* be like a *sound?* In a word, can any thing be like a sensation or idea, but another sensation or idea? . . .
HYLAS. Upon inquiry I find it is impossible for me to conceive or understand how any thing but an idea can be like an idea. (D 206; cf. PR 8)

Representationalists believe that in addition to sensible qualities there exist qualities that are neither perceived nor perceivable. They believe also that these qualities, at least in part, are causally responsible for the perception of sensible qualities and are represented by them. It is the sensible quality pressed into the role of intermediary that becomes the focus of Berkeley's attack.

The argument is in the form of a *reductio:* Suppose that sensible qualities are *not like* the material qualities they are said to represent. In this case, Berkeley tells us, in addition to being unperceivable, the material world would be unknowable. Since we would have no means by which to discover what these entities are in themselves, any claim to their existence would be empty of content.

Berkeley's argument here is clearly a version of the semantic problem discussed above. Sensible qualities are the alleged representatives of the qualities of physical objects. If they are unlike what they allegedly represent, then given that we cannot know physical objects without representatives, there is no hope for constructing a reasonable semantics.

Berkeley's rather succinct argument is part of a long dialectical tradition; there is much more packed into it than it appears. When Philonous says that real things, on the representationalist view, are invisible, he means that they can be known *only* via intermediaries. In effect, he takes for the sake of the argument the representationalist view, based on the new science, that there must be a complex causal chain that links sensible qualities with the spatially external object.[17] It is indeed the Cartesians who claim that sensible qualities, even sensed shapes, are not like what

17. Berkeley is very much aware of the arguments of the new science in this regard. For just one example, see D 186.

they supposedly represent. In addition they believe that the new science shows that the older view of something shared between the object and the perceptual state is naive. But there is more to the Cartesian argument than a conclusion of mere *physical* unlikeness; if there were not, one might think that brain states, whose qualities are of the same kind as, but not literally the same as, the entities that cause them, would serve as the requisite information carriers. But they cannot so serve, simply because no physical entity has the requisite semantic properties to overcome the semantic problem discussed above. Only if the representing entities are different in kind from the physical, that is, only if they are *intentional* and represent by their very nature, can the semantic problem be overcome.[18] It is not that sensible qualities cannot be like physical qualities because they are assumed for some reason to be ideas. They are taken to be ideas because they cannot serve their function of representation if they are merely physical qualities.[19] Berkeley, in other words, need not be construed as begging the question by assuming *himself* that sensible qualities are ideas, even though he seems to talk this way. The difference in kind between sensible qualities and what they allegedly represent is a fundamental tenet of Berkeley's *opponents*. It is this very premise that he exploits in the likeness argument.

However, it is also clear that Berkeley does not allow the Cartesian notion of intentionality; unlikeness of idea to thing represented means automatic semantic failure. In this, Berkeley places himself in a long line of seventeenth-century criticism of the doctrine of the unlikeness of sensible qualities and physical qualities. That criticism insists that representation only makes sense if there *is* likeness between the representing entity and what it represents.[20]

18. It is for this reason that one should not construe Cartesian representatives as sense-data. Even if one took such sense-data as somehow mental, the semantic problem would remain, in that such entities would need to be assigned a semantics; as Dennett puts it, they would be extrinsic representations. Intentional representation gives us a sense, whatever its problems, of a real mental-physical difference. In other words, claiming that the representations are mental, without giving them a logical structure different from the structure of the physical, does nothing to overcome the semantic problem; thus the Cartesian distinction between objective and formal reality. See Hausman and Hausman, "Descartes's Secular Semantics," pp. 81–104.

19. The possibility, exploited by some today, of intentional properties that are in some sense physical would not have occurred to philosophers of the seventeenth or early eighteenth century, who take the qualities of bodies to be mathematizable. Intentional properties would clearly not fit this mold.

20. In *The Breakdown of Cartesian Metaphysics*, Watson argues this at length.

But neither can such intermediaries be *like* the qualities they are presumed to represent. Berkeley is totally unrelenting on this point, as is clear from PR 8: "I appeal to anyone whether it be sense, to assert a colour is like something which is invisible; hard or soft, like something which is intangible." According to representationalists any effort to perceive material qualities results in the intervention of that perception by a mediating object of perception, namely, sensible qualities. Material qualities are in that respect inherently unperceivable. If sensible qualities were like them, they too would need intermediaries to be perceived; but they are, everyone agrees, perceived directly. Sensible qualities are inherently perceivable the same way in which material qualities are not. The whole point of the Cartesian move is to claim that representatives are unlike what they represent. But then it is for Berkeley an absurdity to think a visual quality to be like one not visual or a tangible quality like one intangible.

Thus, when Berkeley says that an idea can only be like another idea, he is claiming that representation only makes sense if there is likeness, but that likeness cannot be what the representationalists have or want.

Berkeley would see his argument as having direct application to the model of representationalism held by an idea theorist such as Descartes or Locke. When Descartes puts sensed material qualities in the mind, the qualities cease to have formal reality as material qualities. But then, Berkeley reminds us, sensible qualities, which on Descartes's account now have formal reality only as ideas, are no longer like the material qualities they are purported to represent: *the idea of square, as a mental something, is not just another instance of square; it is not an instance of square at all.*

Descartes himself would not feel damaged by this account of his theory. In both his "Comments on a Certain Broadsheet" and his *Optics* he explicitly acknowledges the failure of intermediaries to be like the qualities of the micro-object they represent.[21] For Descartes, it is innate ideas that take up the gap and provide our judgments with the information that allows us to do science.[22] Berkeley, of course, as an empiricist armed with

21. See John Cottingham, Robert Stoothoff, and Dugald Murdoch, eds., *The Philosophical Writings of Descartes* (Cambridge: Cambridge United Press, 1985), vol. 1, pp. 152–54 and p. 304.

22. Two papers with insights on this issue are C. Normore, "Meaning and Objective Being: Descartes and His Sources," in *Essay on Descartes' Meditations*, ed. Amelie Rorty, (Berkeley and Los Angeles: University of California Press, 1986), pp. 223–41, and John Cottingham, "Descartes on Colour," *Proceedings of the Aristotelian Society* 90, pp. 231–46.

an empiricist meaning criterion, rejects the appeal to innate ideas and takes his argument against sensible qualities as intermediaries to stand.

To put the point in a different way, the results of the likeness argument are as follows: Either sensible qualities are mental—as the Cartesians think—or they are not. If they are mental, they cannot represent unlike physical things, nor can physical things be like them, or else physical things too would be perceivable, which by hypothesis they are not. If sensible qualities are not mental and are like the qualities of physical things, then perceiving them calls for intermediaries as well, and so a regress looms. Hence representationalism cannot work, whether we assume sensible qualities are mental or assume they are not. Thus, the likeness argument shows that any qualities of ordinary objects or events must be like sensible qualities [(ii) above]. But what is the ontological status of these qualities?

The Mind-Dependence of Sensible Qualities

There is no sustained argument in the *Principles* that sensible qualities are mind-dependent, for Berkeley never seriously doubts that they must in some way be mental. In this section we do two things: first, we present the logic by which Berkeley takes this position, and second, we show that his collapse of the distinction between act and object in the *Dialogues* is an effort to establish the specific ontological status of sensible qualities as ideas *inhering* in the mind. In the next section we follow Berkeley's use of this conclusion to repudiate the doctrine of material substance.

Berkeley is aware that in accepting the conclusion that sensible qualities are mind-dependent, he must take care to distinguish the nature of his commitment to ideas from that of the representationalists. For while Descartes's perceptual ideas are about something else, Berkeley's sensible qualities are not *about* at all.[23] Descartes solves the semantic problem with intermediaries, whose special character as intentional ideas warrants placing them in a different ontological category from material things. Berkeley solves the semantic problem by dissolving it. He also

---

23. Berkeley does entertain the view that the awareness of some sensible qualities may remind us of others that are associated with them; thus the visual presentation of the color and shape of a rose may remind us of its smell and feel. But this is not the sense of representation that is crucial to our—or his—argument.

commits to ideas; but with his rejection of representationalism as well, these ideas have no information to carry. Thus, Berkeley must face some crucial questions. In what way are sensible qualities truly ideas? What is the relation of such an idea to the mind on which it depends?

First, it should be clear that Berkeley's likeness argument generates initial support for the claim that sensible qualities must be mental. If they were material qualities of physical things, the necessity for intermediaries would rise. But intermediaries, we have seen, on Berkeley's view lead to insuperable problems. Hence sensible qualities cannot be the qualities of physical bodies (D 194). Perhaps sensible qualities do not belong to the physical world that necessitates intermediaries. Nevertheless, are they not, in a perfectly good sense, external to the perceiver even if they are, as suggested by the argument from perceptual relativity, immediately perceived? There is, says Hylas, the awareness, which is one thing, and the object, which is another. So why claim that sensible qualities are mental?[24] Indeed, Hylas's question is reinforced by the fact that Berkeley does not think that sensible qualities function in the way that was so much a part of the Cartesian tradition.

Berkeley's sudden and unexpected discussion of the act/object distinction in the *Dialogues* calls for some explanation (this discussion is absent from the *Principles*). Traditionally, acts of *perception* are seen as extracting information from objects; the representationalist view says this is done via intermediaries. But the likeness argument eliminates intermediaries. Sensible qualities represent nothing. Does this fact eliminate the need for reading *them* for information, where "reading" implies conveying of information from one entity to another? How, if at all, do we get information from the direct perception of sensible qualities? It is this issue, we believe, that motivates Berkeley's rejection of the distinction between act and object.

Berkeley claims that one is directly aware of sensible qualities. We thus have three elements in this situation: the homunculus—that is, Berkeley's mental substance—the sensible qualities, and the act by means of which the homunculus is aware of those qualities. Now, it may appear initially that Berkeley, given this model, is not in a position for Dennett-like criticisms. Dennett claims (in the passage quoted above) that if *represen-*

24. G. E. Moore makes a similar point in "The Refutation of Idealism" when assessing Berkeley's argument. One could also argue, we think, that Malebranche exploits the same set of distinctions when he claims that primary qualities are outside the mind of the perceiver but not physical. If these entities are mental, that sense of 'mental' is not at all clear.

tations are extrinsic, that is, must be assigned a semantics, then the homunculus is somehow 'external' to the representation—the syntactic problem mentioned earlier. That is, in order to assign something a semantics, its properties have to be grasped, thus reintroducing the original problem all over again. But Berkeley's sensible qualities, because they are not representations of anything, appear not to be subject to Dennett's problems. The appearance is deceptive. What creates Dennett's problems is not that there is a representation but merely that there is an entity that has to be read for information. Dennett's regress depends on the claim that the homunculus is *always* distinct from what it is reading, and on the refusal (or failure) to recognize any sense of direct awareness that does not necessitate an interaction between awareness and its object, even if that object is in some sense mental. It is this interaction that presumably creates intermediaries. Thus it seems Berkeley *should* have the Dennett problems. Let us see if he does.

After a sustained argument in the *Dialogues* in which Berkeley attempts to establish that "light and colours, tastes, sounds, etc. are . . . all equally passions or sensations in the soul" (D 197)—equally, that is, with pain—Hylas introduces the distinction between the act of perceiving and what is perceived. He insists that one is directly aware of sensible qualities, but still entertains the possibility that they may be of a ontological kind different from awareness. Philonous forces Hylas now to present and repudiate the traditional view that sees *perceiving* as some sort of activity that must extract or at least receive and interpret information from a physical object.

Suppose, then, that Berkeley saw the traditional view as tying the existence of the perceiving act to the existence of entities that need intermediaries. Since sensible qualities are experienced without intermediaries, the act that is aware of them cannot be that of perceiving as traditionally conceived.[25] Sensible qualities are directly known. Direct awareness is not an *act* that *interprets* information for the homunculus. Since such acts *do* nothing, they essentially disappear.[26] There is no information gap between such an act and a sensible quality. Once the distinction between act and object disappears, Dennett's syntactic problem also seems to disappear. For if there is no distinction, there is no gap

---

25. It is interesting to speculate that Berkeley's argument here may even cut against traditional direct realist views such as held by Aquinas. For Aquinas, too, needs intermediaries in the sense of sensible species.

26. Gilbert Ryle made similar points about acts many years later in *The Concept of Mind* (New York: Barnes & Noble, 1949).

between homunculus (the act) and its object, and thus no regress. Berkeley, in other words, believes he solves the syntactic problem by collapsing act and object. This is the real meaning of Berkeley's remarks about the passivity of perception, and of his assimilation of the object sensed to the sensing of it.[27]

But why claim, given the collapse, that it is acts that disappear rather than the object of those acts? Berkeley really wants it both ways here. When he wants to reconstitute ordinary objects, the collapse is toward sensible qualities, since, after all, that is what such objects are constructed from. But this would seem to start the Dennett problems all over again, since we now have the mental substance, the homunculus, in some unspecified relation to sensible qualities. Thus, we think, Berkeley's move to collapse the act/object distinction in the direction of the act recognizes that, to get around Dennett-like problems, one must not have an object that needs to be read by the homunculus. The object, *as act*, becomes "part" of the nature of the homunculus; it inheres in mental substance. It then becomes difficult, to say the least, to understand what an apple is. The fudge is best seen in PR 49, where Berkeley truly tries to have it both ways: sensible qualities are in the mind by way of being perceived by it! So, he retains sensible qualities as distinct from acts of awareness, yet tries to classify them as mental because they are tied to the mind by such awareness, that is, assimilated to acts that are in minds (we return to this point in our concluding remarks). As Freud would have it, competing intentions produce a slip.[28]

Moore, in "The Refutation of Idealism," condemns Berkeley precisely on the grounds that he fails to preserve the proper separation between act and object. Moore is correct in his appraisal of the centrality of this claim to Berkeley's program. For having secured the status of sensible qualities as ideas, and ideas as properties to the mind that holds them, Berkeley is ready to take on the existence of matter itself.

27. There is a problem here, of course, since Berkeley collapses the distinction between the sensation and its object in the *Dialogues* yet insists both there and in the *Principles* (e.g., PR 49) that ideas are in the mind as they are perceived by it, as if perception or direct awareness were a *relation* between the substance and its idea. We discuss this point later in the essay.

28. For a discussion of Berkeley's wearing of two different hats here, see Alan Hausman, "Adhering to Inherence: A New Look at the Old Steps in Berkeley's March of Idealism." *Canadian Journal of Philosophy* 14 (1984), pp. 421–43. Clearly, Chisholm-like interpretations are those which favor the collapse toward the act.

The Attack on Matter

Berkeley presents the basic structure of his attack against matter in essentially the same form in both the *Principles* and the *Dialogues*. We see from PR 9, for example, that his procedure follows precisely the outline appearing in PR 73, which we noted earlier.

> By matter therefore we are to understand an inert, senseless substance, in which extension, figure, and motion, do actually subsist. But it is evident from what we have already shewn, that extension, figure and motion are only ideas existing in the mind, and that an idea can be like nothing but another idea, and that consequently neither they nor their archetypes can exist in an unperceiving substance. Hence it is plain, that the very notion of what is called *matter* or *corporeal substance*, involves a contradiction in it. (PR 9)[29]

It is apparent that Berkeley thinks of the situation as follows: A principle of exemplification precludes the existence not only of unexemplified properties but also of unpropertied substance: "[It] seems no less absurd to suppose a substance without accidents, than it is to suppose accidents without a substance" (PR 67). It is enough then to show that there cannot be properties for material substance to exemplify in order for the conclusion to follow that there cannot be material substance. So, we must be convinced that sensible qualities could not exist in matter. To that end Berkeley in effect proposes the following *reductio*. Assume that sensible properties could inhere in material substance. By the nature of material substance, as claimed by those who accept its existence, it is supposed to be possible for material things, that is, material substance and its properties, to exist independently of minds. It is, therefore, one conclusion of the adopted assumption that sensible properties could exist independently of minds. By an earlier argument it has been shown that sensible properties are in Berkeley's special sense mind-dependent. Hence, the original assumption that sensible properties could inhere in material substance is violated. There are no material substances, since there are no properties for them to exemplify.

29. See also PR 7 and PR 73.

Concluding Remarks

Berkeley's arguments reveal the high price he is willing to pay to refute skepticism. Sensible qualities inhere in and depend for their existence upon minds, and there are no qualities beside sensible ones. All that exists is either mind or is dependent on mind. Berkeley's arguments against representationalism and matter have ended in idealism. Yet, Berkeley does not see this as discouraging. Indeed, it provides him with his final challenge: to make idealism commensurate with common sense. While this is not our issue directly, there is a point to be made that is revealing of a confusion that has been on the edge of Berkeley's work from the beginning.

With all perceptions in the mind, Berkeley has totally removed objects from an external world. As we have shown, it makes sense to call such perceptions mental only if sensible qualities are, in effect, acts of a mental substance, something like Chisholm's seeing redly. In that sense, sensible qualities have lost their powers *as* qualities. On the other hand, unlike Descartes's ideas, they are not about anything either; lacking intentionality, Berkeley's ideas do not bring us information—they are what we normally take the information to be *about*. When Berkeley moves to reconstruct ordinary physical-object judgments to be about bundles of sensible qualities, his confusion becomes apparent. For now sensible qualities have somehow regained their original capabilities to qualify. But then in what sense are they in the mind? As perceived by it? If so, and if sensible qualities are assimilated to acts, how can acts have the powers of qualities? Berkeley's ambiguous use of 'idea' thus makes ideas at once bits of information and bits of what the information is about.

In a way, Hume sees what Berkeley apparently does not. By collapsing the distinction between the act of sensory awareness and its object, Berkeley acknowledges that the act no longer has any work to do. Yet, he remains steadfastly committed to the mind. Hume applies to the homunculus itself the same logic that eliminates the act: If the mind does not gather and process information, what *does* it do? In effect, of course, when Berkeley reconstructs ordinary objects by positing causal connections between sensible qualities, he is already doing what the functionalists do later with information bits. Hume simply makes the logic explicit by recognizing that with the elimination of mental substance a new psychology is called for whereby information is manipulated by laws of nature.

Like Berkeley, however, Hume fails to see that once sensible qualities (impressions of sensation) are treated as information, they cannot also be treated as the very objects that the information is about. In trying to make impressions do both jobs—in his terms, constructing minds out of the same entities from which he constructs objects—Hume also fails to solve the information problem, but not for the reasons Dennett believes.[30] Hume's problem, according to Dennett, still involves representational regress. Hume's *real* problem, since his view implicitly shares Berkeley's idealism, is that there is nothing for information *to represent*.

30. See note 6.

4

On the Hausmans' "A New Approach"

Fred Wilson

No doubt most now agree with the Hausmans that Berkeley must be mistaken because idealism is false. The problem then becomes that of finding out wherein lies the error: where does the argument of the mitered empiricist go wrong? There is, alas, no agreement upon precisely where that error is. Why does Berkeley hold, mistakenly, that a sensible quality (and thus a collection of such, i.e., a sensible object) is mind-dependent? One answer to this question has been that Berkeley's error consists in confusing the claim that qualities cannot exist apart from objects (the entities of which they are predicated) with the claim that properties cannot exist apart from substances. In other words, on this account Berkeley's claim that ideas must be in minds derives from his construing ideas as (collections of) qualities and then reasoning in conformity with the traditional dictum that qualities cannot exist apart from substances.

This account of the error of Berkeley's idealism, the inherence account, was first propounded by Edwin Allaire, was amplified by Phillip Cummins and Richard Watson, and was subsequently defended by Alan Hausman.[1] George Pappas, among others, has offered an opposing second account.[2] And now, in "A New Approach to Berkeley's Ideal Reality," Alan and David Hausman offer a third. But if we cannot agree on precisely where Berkeley goes wrong, then that calls into question our right to claim that he does indeed go wrong. Perhaps, after all, his arguments are correct, and the reason we cannot locate the error is that there is no error. We tend to forget that not so long ago the assumption was that Berkeley was correct, that idealism of some form was true, and that materialism and empiricism were vulgar views easily disposed of in the first few lectures of a philosophy course. If this earlier evaluation is correct, then it is no wonder that we cannot find where Berkeley goes wrong.

Now, I do happen to agree that Berkeley goes wrong. But I also think that, to get a focus on his argument, it may well help to return to the earlier view. Looking at Berkeley from that perspective may throw into relief various features that we neglect if we continue to look at him as an empiricist that somehow goes wrong, perhaps by not going far enough, as far as Hume went.

We all know the standard history: Philosophers before Locke had two kinds of substance. The empiricists abolished substance. Locke started this empiricist critique of substance. Berkeley carried it a step further by getting rid of material substance, though he retained mental or spiritual substance. Hume completed the inevitable process by getting rid of mental substance too. The result was the empiricist world consisting of a bunch of sensory atoms, which when grouped together in one way constitute bodies and when grouped in another way constitute minds.

In my view this traditional history is as mistaken as it is common. In particular, it is mistaken with regard to Berkeley. The discussion since the reconstruction of his *Commonplace Book* sees Berkeley as struggling ambiguously to make the move from Locke to Hume. He did succeed in getting rid of material substance. Mental substance did remain, but though he relied upon this to do a lot of work for him at various points, he nonetheless felt the empiricist drive to eliminate it.[3] For, after all, at one point in the *Commonplace Book* Berkeley did state the Humean view of

1. For references, see note 3 to the Introduction.
2. For references, see note 4 to the Introduction.
3. This tension is explored by Robert Muehlmann in "The Substance of Berkeley's Philosophy," Essay 5 in this volume.

mind as a bundle of perceptions. It is just that the traditional view of substance had such a hold upon him that in the end he could not give it up. In particular, he could not give up the view that properties must be in substances—or so at least the inherence account. As a consequence he landed in the idealism that we all agree is false.

The problem is that this account makes Berkeleian substances ontologically unmotivated: they are there, and lead to idealism, simply because Berkeley cannot find it within himself to abandon the substance tradition. It would be better if we could find a motive for substances. I propose that there is indeed such a motive. Moreover, I suggest, once that motive is clear we also see why Berkeley is committed to the position that properties must be in mental substances, that is, why Berkeley is committed to the central thesis upon which the inherence account of his idealism depends. Thus, the account that I suggest does justice to Berkeley's arguments and commitments and makes clear why the inherence account of Berkeley's idealism really does make sense of what he has to say.

These points begin to become clear once we reflect upon the inadequacies of the empiricist account of Berkeley as adumbrated by the Hausmans.

1. The Empiricist Berkeley

The Hausmans begin, not with the philosophers that lay behind Berkeley and whom he had read, but Whiggishly at the other end of the history of philosophy, with Dennett.[4] On Dennett's view, the early modern philosophers were trying to do what he, Dennett, is trying to do, and they should be read, he thinks, in that light; it is just that he is doing it a bit better. What he, and they, are/were trying to do is explain what it is to understand. People, of course, are understanders; so might be other entities. An entity is an understander insofar as it grasps the *meanings* of things.[5] The things that are meaningful include behavior, specifically rational behavior,

4. D. C. Dennett, *Brainstorms* (Boston: Bradford Books, MIT Press, 1978).

5. "[N]othing is intrinsically a representation of anything; something is a representation only *for* or *to* someone; any representation or system of representations thus requires at least one *user* or *interpreter* of the representation who is external to it. Any such interpreter must have a variety of psychological or intentional traits . . . : it must be capable of a variety of *comprehension*, and must have beliefs and goals (so it can *use* the representation to *inform* itself and thus assist it in achieving its goals)" (ibid., p. 122).

and still more specifically verbal behavior, but also ordinary objects. Thus, for example, a tree is, or becomes, meaningful to one when one perceives it. The meaning to one of an object or behavior is the way in which one *responds* to the object or behavior. The sounds I hear, or the marks I see, are meaningful when I respond to them as carriers of linguistic meaning. The object before one is meaningful to one as a tree when one responds to it in ways that are appropriate to trees, that is, discriminates it from the background, identifies it as a tree, and further treats it as a tree. The meaning may vary significantly given only slight variations in the behavior. Consider the different responses to 'Your son was killed' and 'Our son was killed'. Further, an object or behavior may have effects that are not part of its meaning.

To grasp the meaning of an object or behavior is to select those effects that constitute the meaning and to respond appropriately. But no piece of behavior is intrinsically meaningful; its meaning is a matter of certain, but not all, its effects. How do we select those effects that constitute meaning? Here is a first stab: *Meaning is that which understanders select as meaningful*. But this is clearly circular unless we can explain what it is to select. This is what the philosophers of the early modern period were trying to do, according to Dennett.

These philosophers, quite correctly, took ideas to be representations that are internal in the sense of being immediately present to consciousness.[6] One understands an object when one has ideas that represent that object. One understands a piece of behavior, say an uttered sentence, if one has the ideas that give meaning to that sentence. These ideas represent what the sentence means; specifically, the sentence means what is represented by those ideas with which, by established linguistic convention, the sentence is associated.

The object or behavior evokes the response. The response is the presence in a conscious state of the idea. The object or behavior evokes the response because that idea represents or *refers to* that object or behavior. We have here an *empirical pattern* or *regularity* linking the object or behavior on the one side and the idea on the other. This regularity is an instance of the sort of *pattern-governed* responses to objects and behavior that one finds in systems, such as persons, that understand. These patterns are not simply patterns, however; they are also *rule governed.*[7]

6. "[T]he only psychology that could possibly succeed in explaining the complexities of human activity must posit internal representations" (ibid., p. 119).

7. This way of speaking derives from Wilfrid Sellars. For a brief account, see Fred

This is a point that I take up directly. For the present, what is important is the pattern. The patterns I have just noted can be called system-entry transitions. There are also intrasystem transitions, inferences, deductions, and so forth, and system-exit transitions, actions, rational actions, speech acts, and so forth. The system-entry transitions are part of the broader pattern of system transitions that constitute the fact that the ideas *refer to* or *designate* certain things or behavior; they are part of the broader pattern of system transitions that constitute the *semantics of ideas*.

There is no problem here if ideas wear their semantics on their faces, that is, if it is intrinsic. In that case, the meanings of the ideas that are present to consciousness are transparent to consciousness when it perceives objects or understands behavior. Ideas, however, according to the early modern philosophy, and quite correctly, are sensations; and like ordinary objects and items of behavior taken as such or sentences taken as a set of marks or noises, they have no intrinsic meaning. Indeed, nothing has intrinsic meaning.[8] So within the person we need another understander who will select those effects of the ideas that constitute *their* meaning. The consciousness to which the ideas are present must therefore not be mere consciousness but must be, beyond that, an understander. The consciousness to which ideas are present thus becomes the inner homunculus,[9] or substantial self, that we find in Descartes and Berkeley. Every real person thus comes to have, according to the early modern philosophy, a wee inner person. Beyond the real person who is conscious of inner ideas or representations, there must be a further inner person to whom ideas are present as external objects are present to the real person and whose role is to understand the ideas, grasp their meanings, as the real person understands the meanings of perceived objects and behavior.

Dennett suggests, naturally enough, that this does not solve the problem.[10] In the first place, it either is circular or leads to a vicious infinite regress. If one attempts to explain the understanding that a person

---

Wilson, "Marras on Sellars on Thought and Language," *Philosophical Studies* 28 (1975), pp. 91–102.

8. Thus, recall Dennett: "[N]othing is intrinsically a representation of anything; something is a representation only *for* or *to* someone" (see note 5).

9. "[A]ny representation of system of representations . . . requires at least one *user* or *interpreter* of the representation who is external to it. . . . Such an interpreter is . . . a sort of homunculus" (Dennett, *Brainstorms*, p. 122).

10. "[P]sychology *without* homunculi is impossible. But psychology *with* homunculi is doomed to circularity or infinite regress, so psychology is impossible" (ibid., p. 122).

exemplifies by the understanding exemplified by the homunculus, then it is circular, explaining understanding in terms of understanding. And if one insists that understanding at each level is so to be explained, then the little homunculus requires a still smaller homunculus inside it, which requires a further, even smaller homunculus, and so on to infinity, and viciously so because one never reaches a point where understanding has been explained. Moreover, in the second place, from the viewpoint of empiricism the wee inner self remains forever elusive: we seem never to be acquainted with it in our ordinary experience.[11]

On Dennett's view the early modern philosophers attempted to solve the problem of understanding by means of a metaphysics of a substantial mind, a wee inner homunculus. In the end the problems became evident, and philosophers had to reject the homunculus. It was Hume who saw the problems[12] and argued consistently on empiricist grounds that we should eliminate the substantial mind.[13] The result was an inner self that was no more than a bundle of impressions and ideas. Unfortunately this new inner self lacked the resources to account for understanding: impressions and ideas were without any intrinsic meaning, and there was nothing else in the Humean apparatus to explain understanding.[14] So, although Hume saw the problems of the metaphysics adopted by the early modern philosophers, he had nothing adequate with which to replace that metaphysics, and the problem of understanding remained unresolved.

11. "One is conscious only of the *products* of the producer, which one then consciously tests and chooses" (ibid., p. 88).

12. "Hume's internal representations were impressions and ideas, and he wisely shunned the notion of an inner *self* that would intelligently manipulate them" (ibid., p. 122; see also p. 101).

13. David Hume, *A Treatise of Human Nature*, ed. L. A. Selby-Bigge and Peter H. Nidditch (Oxford: Oxford University Press, 1978), p. 252; hereafter, T, followed by page number.

14. "Hume wisely shunned the notion of an inner self that would intelligently manipulate the ideas and impressions, but this left him with the necessity of getting the ideas to 'think for themselves.' His associationistic couplings of ideas and impressions, his pseudo-chemical bonding of each idea to its predecessor and successor, is a notorious non-solution to the problem" (Dennett, *Brainstorms*, p. 101). Abolishing the self that could intelligently manipulate ideas "left [Hume] with the necessity of the ideas and impressions to 'think for themselves'. The result was his theory of the self as a 'bundle' of (nothing but) impressions and ideas. He attempted to set these impressions and ideas into dynamic interaction by positing various associationist links, so that each succeeding idea in the stream of consciousness dragged its successor onto the stage according to one or another principle, all without the benefit of intelligent *supervision*. It didn't work, of course. It couldn't conceivably work, and Hume's failure is plausibly viewed as the harbinger of doom for any remotely analogous enterprise" (ibid., 122).

The Hausmans argue that Dennett's model can provide us with insight into Berkeley's idealism. They take for granted that Dennett's picture is a fair one. The ideas or inner representations that explain perception and other forms of understanding have two (relevant) sorts of meaning: there is their syntax and their semantics. The syntax has to do with their complexity; the syntactical structure of a complex idea, say a proposition, is given by the relations that structure the simple components into that complex. The semantics has to do with the reference of ideas to the objects external to themselves that they represent. For Descartes, Malebranche, and Locke, each in his own way, this external reference is to something other than an idea. This creates a problem for the semantics of ideas: how does the homunculus interpret ideas, that is, understand their meanings, if that which they mean is neither an idea nor like an idea? One perceives an object. This perceiving consists in selecting the object by means of an idea. This idea means the object. But the idea is simply a sensation, without intrinsic meaning. Thus, first, the homunculus must grasp this meaning. Second, given the principles of this metaphysics of understanding, only ideas are present to the homunculus. And third, the meaning of an idea consists of a semantic relation between the idea and the object that is external to and unlike it. These three propositions together entail that the homunculus cannot grasp the meanings, the semantics, of ideas. Hence the skepticism that the earliest critics had already seen to be implicit in Descartes, Malebranche, and Locke.

The Hausmans' suggestion is that Berkeley, along with other early modern philosophers, accepts the first two propositions but, in order to avoid skepticism, rejects the third. When he does this, he eliminates the entities that constitute the external referents of ideas. Since now there are no external objects, only ideas, it follows that there are only two categories of entities that exist, to wit, the ideas and the homunculus that grasps their meaning. But ideas, on the metaphysics of understanding developed by early modern philosophers, are precisely those entities that are present to the wee inner homunculus. For the latter is introduced precisely in order to account for the understanding, not of external objects, but of ideas. Hence, the existence of all entities besides the homunculus consists of their being present to the homunculus: their *esse* is *percipi*. In other words, on the Hausmans' proposed reading of Berkeley, his idealism follows immediately from his attack upon skepticism, given, that is, Berkeley's commitment to the metaphysics of understanding that Dennett ascribes to the early modern philosophers.

Other aspects of Berkeley's thought also fall into place. Thus, according to the Hausmans' proposal, Berkeley rejects the claim of Descartes, Malebranche, and Locke that ideas represent, or mean, objects that are unlike themselves. This rejection is embodied in the Berkeleian formula that only an idea can be like an idea. By making the idea itself the object that is to be known, Berkeley eliminates the semantic problem that is the root of the skepticism: there is no semantic problem because there is no external reference. The meaning of the idea is, as it were, the idea itself. We now understand the weight that Berkeley, when he argues for his idealism, gives to the principle that only an idea can be like an idea. Moreover, the metaphysics of understanding developed by the early modern philosophers requires the homunculus to grasp the meaning of the ideas with which it is presented. It must select that meaning. This it does by means of yet another idea, an *act of awareness* through which the mind, that is, the wee homunculus, grasps the meaning or comes to understand the idea that is before it. When Berkeley eliminates the external reference of ideas and makes the idea mean nothing beyond itself, he also eliminates the need for such an act to be present to the homunculus when it grasps the meaning of the idea. This accounts for Berkeley's collapse of the act/object distinction when he presents his argument against the philosophies of Descartes, Malebranche, and Locke.

This account of Berkeley's thought has the virtue of avoiding the problem of the inherence reading of Berkeley's idealism. The latter argues that Berkeley's idealism arises from his falling into the thesis that ideas inhere in mental substances. This runs into the objection that if ideas inhere in mental substances, then the ideas are predicable of the mind, something that Berkeley explicitly denies: sensations are in the mind by way of idea and not by way of mode (PR 49). The Hausmans' suggestion does not require the relation between the idea and the homunculus to be that of inherence. The problems of the inherence thesis are thus avoided.

Moreover, we discover the way in which to avoid Berkeley's idealism. His is not so much a problem specific to his own metaphysics as it is one that lies more deeply within the general metaphysics of understanding of the early modern philosophy that Berkeley himself accepts. The problem is the homunculus. This wee inner person has only ideas present to it. This creates the problem of how it can grasp the semantic meaning of the ideas that are present to it, that, is, recognize the external referents of the ideas. Once the homunculus is eliminated, we can have both ideas as internal representations and external objects that are meant by these ideas. Thus, when one eliminates the homunculus, one eliminates the problems that are created by the metaphysics of understanding when it introduces an understander whose awareness is restricted to ideas alone: get rid of the homunculus, and both the idealism and the skepticism that motivates that idealism disappear. But the homunculus should on empiricist grounds be eliminated, as Hume saw. The problem is not so much the homunculus as what we should replace it with if we are to account for how persons understand meanings not only of external objects but of inner representations.

2. Problems with Berkeley as Empiricist

Ingenious as this reading that the Hausmans give to Berkeley may be, it does not, it seems to me, do justice to what Berkeley was trying to do or, indeed, to what early modern philosophy was trying to do. In the first place, Berkeley's argument against material objects does, contrary to what the Hausmans assert, *not* solve what they call the semantic problem. In the second place, Dennett's reading of early modern philosophy is far too narrow to do justice either to the problems that early modern philosophy was addressing or to the solutions that they offered.

For the moment take for granted that Berkeley eliminates material substances. That transforms ordinary objects, as he well understands, into collections of sensible events. (These events are, of course, ideas, given the argument for idealism.) These collections are not merely momentary but are spread out through time: an ordinary thing is a lawfully, temporally, and spatially ordered sequence of sensible events. Where previously things were substances, they are now analyzed as processes consisting of many parts, all sensible, and therefore all separable. To perceive an object is to be aware of a momentary sensible event—an idea if you wish—that is part of the larger sequence that *is* the object. We perceive a tree that is a whole, but are aware through our senses of only the part of the tree that is presented to us, and not, for example, the far side. The momentary sense impression, or, in the early modern terminology that Berkeley adopts, the idea of which we are directly aware, it must be insisted, *represents* the object that we are said to perceive but that is not, as such, presented to us.[15] We are in fact aware of only part of the whole that we perceive, and that part is the representative in conscious-

15. Cf. D. Lewis, "Moore's Realism," in L. Addis and D. Lewis, *Moore and Ryle: Two Ontologists* (The Hague: Martinus Nijhoff, 1965), chaps. 3 and 4, and Fred Wilson, *Psychological*

ness of the whole. There is, therefore, a semantic relation between the idea of which we are directly aware and the object that we perceive. Berkeley does eliminate any semantic relation between the idea and an object no part of which we ever do, or even can, be aware, but he does not eliminate the semantic relation between the presented idea and something that is not presented but that the idea represents, namely, the unperceived parts of the object perceived.[16] The Hausmans' notion that Berkeley solves a semantic problem by eliminating the external reference of ideas is, therefore, mistaken: for whatever Berkeley does, he does not eliminate the need for ideas to stand in semantic relations to things other than themselves, things of which, by virtue of those semantic relations, they are the representations in consciousness.

The problem for early modern philosophers is with the notion, not that ideas represent, but that they represent objects that these philosophers argued had to be of a sort that, as it turns out, creates particular difficulties. According to the traditional view deriving from Aristotle and still defended by such Berkeleian contemporaries as John Sergeant,[17] "like knows like": the object known comes to be such by virtue of a causal process through which its properties come to be present in the mind. But the substance philosophy of the early moderns creates problems about knowing that go beyond the traditional Aristotelian account of knowledge. Whatever the specific account one gives for the ontology of the knowing situation, one cannot avoid the fact that knowledge does involve a semantic relation between what is present to consciousness and the object known. Whatever else this means, it means that there is a semantic pattern connecting the object known to the conscious state that is the knowing of it. By virtue of this pattern, the object known is able in a system-entry transition to evoke the conscious state that constitutes the knowing of it. The obtaining of the semantic relation thus requires a causal interaction between the known and the knower. The crucial point is that the metaphysics of substance adopted by the early modern philosophers renders any such causal interaction impossible. Here two points are

---

Analysis and the Philosophy of John Stuart Mill (Toronto: University of Toronto Press, 1990), chap. 5.

16. This point is made by Harry Bracken, *Berkeley* (London: Macmillan, 1974), chap. 9, esp. pp. 95–96, where he emphasizes that the perceptual object, being extended in time, is not wholly presented to one and that if Berkeley did succeed in eliminating the skepticism implicit in the representationalist's veil of ideas, he did not succeed in eliminating the possibility of error that arises from the veil of time.

17. *Solid Philosophy Asserted Against the Fancies of the Ideists* (London, 1698).

relevant.[18] In the *first* place, the early modern philosophers argued that there were two sorts of objects, namely, minds and body or bodies. The essential property of mental substance was thought; the essential properties of body were either extension alone or extension and solidity. According to Descartes and Malebranche—Locke wavered on this in the correspondence with Stillingfleet—extension and thought are contraries: if characteristics of one sort are present, then characteristics of the other sort are excluded. It therefore follows that properties of body cannot be in the mind, and the former can, therefore, not be known by the latter. In the *second* place, mind and body are separate substances, independent of each other. To say this is to say that the one could exist and remain identical with itself even if the other ceased to exist. It follows that the substances can exemplify only nonrelational properties.[19] That being so, it follows in particular that there can be no causal transaction between them.[20] Transeunt causation, though not immanent causation, is impossible on the account of substances adopted by the early modern philosophers. There is, in short, no possibility that a causal process could make present in the mind properties of body and, more generally, no possibility of any causal process of the sort requisite to a semantic relation between the object known and the state of consciousness that is the knowing of it. The skeptical conclusions are inevitable, as Berkeley clearly saw.

Berkeley removes this looming skepticism by giving up the ontology that is its source: he rejects the substance analysis of things. This in turn requires him to rethink the relation between the representative in consciousness of the thing and the thing it represents. In place of the ontology of substances Berkeley offers his analysis of things as wholes consisting of sensible parts. Some of these parts we actually sense; these sensible parts that are present in consciousness are what Berkeley, following the tradition, calls *ideas*. The relation between the thing represented and the sensed sensible part representing is not that of an external substance causing the part to come to be in a second substance. Rather, the relation between the sensed part and the whole that is the thing it represents is that of part to whole and, more specifically, the pattern or regularity among the parts of the whole that defines the sort of whole that it is, for example, a tree in a quad. This avoids the problem of substantial interac-

18. See Richard A. Watson, *The Downfall of Cartesianism* (The Hague: Martinus Nijhoff, 1966).

19. Fred Wilson, "Weinberg's Refutation of Nominalism," *Dialogue* 8 (1969), pp. 460–74.

20. Julius R. Weinberg, "The Concept of Relation," in *Abstraction, Relation, and Induction* (Madison: University of Wisconsin Press, 1965), p. 126.

tion. Furthermore, the representative is a sign of the whole, that is, of all the other parts that constitute the whole. These other parts are also sensible, having precisely the same sorts of characteristics that the idea has. There is therefore no problem of one kind of thing making a *toto caelo* different kind of thing known. So Berkeley's radical innovation in ontology solves, or rather dissolves, the skeptical crisis that was implicit in early modern philosophy.

This of course assumes that the representatives in consciousness of ordinary things are objective parts of those things. The brown of which we are conscious is precisely the property brown that characterizes the tree in the quad. Indeed, as Berkeley insists (cf. PC 19), this is precisely what common sense would seem to maintain. Moreover, there is no reason a priori to think that this should not be so. It is simply dogma to hold that the representation in consciousness is an entity that is *not* part of the thing known. It is of course a dogma that receives support from the traditional substance account of knowing, so it is not surprising to find Descartes, Malebranche, and Locke accepting it. There is less excuse for Dennett. To be sure, some representations are not parts of ordinary things—think of afterimages or cases of perceptual error, cases Berkeley himself recognized. But from the fact that some sensible contents are not parts of things, it cannot be concluded that none are. The trick is to distinguish between those which are and those which are not. On Berkeley's view, there is not much of a problem here: it is simply a matter of coming to learn the regularities or patterns among sensible contents. Through experience we become aware that some sensed entities are parts of patterns that define ordinary things, while others do not fit into such patterns. There are no more problems about this than there are problems about learning that smoke means fire. At least, there are no problems of principle. And equally, there is no problem of principle in maintaining that the ideas that represent things are parts of those things. Dennett, in fact, simply takes for granted that representations are not parts of the thing known.

Dennett is also wrong about the homunculus. Ideas or sense impressions are of course intrinsically meaningless. To say that they have meaning, including a semantics, is to presuppose that there is a person who understands them. But there is no reason this person needs to be a wee inner person; it can just as well be taken to be the ordinary person—just as the known can be taken to be the ordinary tree. Hume saw this clearly.

A person is intimately related to his own body, as Hume put it [T, p.

286], and is capable of monitoring and controlling, within limits at least, both his own behavior and his own mental representations. Thus, the patterns that define the system transitions are themselves rule governed. That is, if we have the pattern

(*) all A are B,

then the rulish thought that *A's ought to be B*, or, in symbols,

(**) O (all A are B)

(where 'O' indicates the operator "it is obligatory that"), brings it about that, generally at least, (*) is true.[21] These rulish thoughts bring it about that behavior and thought—reality—conform to their content. Rules of this sort were explored in detail by Hume, both in the context of social norms such as property and promise keeping (his discussion of the latter is particularly important)[22] and in the context of cognition (see his "Rules by which to judge of causes and effects" [T, pp. 173–76]). The set of such standards and rules forms a passably coherent set that constitutes a standard to be lived up to. Each person represents him- or herself as an "I" having both a body and a mental life with a past and a future, an "I" that has both an actual life and an ideal standard for that life, and "I" that is aware of its own behavior and mental life and attempts, often at least, to bring that behavior into line with the standard, the "ego ideal" if you wish, that it sets before itself. This idea of oneself is of course complex. The notion of a self Hume rejects in Book 1 of the *Treatise* is that of the self as a simple substance. But in Book 2 he goes on to point out that for purposes of discussing the passions and our system of moral values and rules, we do need to refer to our idea of the self. This is a complex idea—the self is "that succession of related ideas and impressions of which we have an intimate memory and consciousness" (T, p. 277), "that individual person of whose actions and sentiments each of us is intimately conscious" (T, p. 286); it includes an awareness of the body—he speaks of "the qualities of our mind and body, that is, self" (T, p. 303); and it is, Hume says, an idea of which we are constantly aware: "[T]he idea, or rather

21. Cf. Wilson, "Marras on Sellars on Thought and Language."
22. Cf. Fred Wilson, "Abstract Ideas and Other Rules of Language," presented to the conference on Ideas in the Seventeenth and Eighteenth Centuries, University of Iowa, Iowa City, Iowa, 1989.

impression, of ourselves is always intimately present with us, and our consciousness gives us so lively a conception of our own person that 'tis not possible to imagine that anything can in this particular go beyond it" (T, p. 317). Hume had earlier pointed out that the identity of a person is not that of a simple substance but, rather, teleological, analogous to the sort of unity that we attribute to plants and animals (T, p. 254); the imagination leads us to mistake the succession of related objects for an identical object: we hide the interruption by feigning that the person is a simple substance, "something unknown and mysterious connecting the parts beside their relation" (T, p. 254).[23] Such a substantial self violates the empiricist Principle of Acquaintance and must therefore be exorcised from ontology. But this does not eliminate the self as a complex entity that unites the series of ideas and impressions into a teleological unity.

For us the important point is that this concept of the self is not that of an inner homunculus. It is not the concept of a person that lies inside and controls the real person. It is simply the concept of a person who controls and monitors his or her own behavior and, in many cases, the representations that are part of the person as a cognitive system. It is the *person* who understands, not the inner person, or homunculus. Dennett suggests that the only unity that Hume provides to the self is the glue provided by association and that this is inadequate to account for the person's capacity to understand. However, this is to ignore the role that Hume assigns to the idea of the self in controlling our mental life and behavior. Dennett seems not to have read in the *Treatise* beyond the end of Book 1. If he had, he would have discovered that Hume developed certain themes for which Dennett is now claiming originality.

3. Berkeley's Ontology of Substances

Berkeley also recognizes, I would like to argue, the Humean point that the self is a complex entity that unites the series of ideas and impressions into a teleological unity. In his *Philosophical Commentaries*, he tells us that by "Soul is meant onely a Complex idea made up of existence, willing & perception in a large sense. therefore its is known & it may be defin'd" (PC 154). This concept of the soul as a complex entity is the concept of a person.

23.Cf. Fred Wilson, "Hume's Fictional Continuants," *History of Philosophy Quarterly* 6 (1989), pp. 171–88.

Berkeley came later to distinguish this concept from that of the soul as the substantial mind that, on his view, supports ideas: "The Concrete of the Will & understanding I must call Mind not person, lest offence be given, there being but one volition acknowledged to be God. Mem: Carefully to omit Defining of Person, or making much mention of it" (PC 713). The person as a complex entity can provide the teleological glue that structures our mental life and behavior. There is no need for Berkeley to introduce the substantial mind as an entity that can account for the fact that persons understand. Dennett's scheme thus in no way helps us to understand the role of the substantial mind in Berkeley, or in fact in early modern philosophy in general. In particular, contrary to the Hausmans, it does not help us to understand the Berkeleian move to idealism.

Why, then, does Berkeley have a substantial mind? The complex concept of a person can do the sorts of things that Dennett, Hume, Berkeley, and the Hausmans all need, namely, account for the capacity of persons to understand. What it cannot do, according to Berkeley, is play a certain metaphysical role. To be sure, he apparently begins, as the *Philosophical Commentaries* make clear, with the thought that the concept of the person as complex can do this job. But he changes his mind, again as we have seen the *Commentaries* make clear.

Berkeley makes evident in his last work what he thinks the substantial mind does. In *Siris* he tells us that "It is a doctrine among other speculations contained in the Hermaic writings that all things are One. . . . If we suppose that one and the Mind is the universal principle of order and harmony throughout the world, containing and connecting all its parts, and giving unity to the system, there seems to be nothing atheistical or impious in this supposition" (S 287). And a little later he adds:

[A]lthough such phantoms as corporeal forces, absolute motions, and real spaces do pass in physics for causes and principles . . . , yet are they in truth but hypotheses, nor can they be the objects of real science. They pass nevertheless in physics, conversant about things of sense, and confined to experiments and mechanics. But when we enter the province of the *philosophia prima*, we discover another order of beings, mind and its acts, permanent being, not dependent on corporeal things, nor resulting, nor connected, nor contained; but containing, connecting, enlivening the whole frame, and imparting those motions, forms, qualities, and that order and symmetry, to all those transient phenomena which we term the Course of Nature. (S 293)

Still later we read: "[T]he mind contains all, and acts all, and is to all created beings the source of unity and identity, harmony and order, existence and stability" (S 295). We see two things: first, that *mind, or self-consciousness, is the source of order and unity among the separable entities given in sense experience;* and second, that *this unity derives from the unifying activity of an entity that is itself a unity, one, without separable parts.*

This notion, that the unity of the universe derives from the unity of self-consciousness, goes all the way back at least to one of Berkeley's sources, Plotinus.[24] The materialists, that is, the Stoics, argued that the world consists of matter in motion. The soul is the origin of the motion of the body, but it too is material. Plotinus argued that this was impossible. Matter, as lifeless, cannot move itself; in fact it could not even stay together in a particular configuration: "[B]ody in itself could not exist in any form if soul-power did not; body passes; dissolution is in its very nature; all would disappear in a twinkling if all were body." Indeed, matter "itself could not exist [without soul]: the totality of things in the sphere is dissolved if it be made to depend upon the coherence of a body which, though elevated to the nominal rank of 'soul', remains air, fleeting breath . . . , whose very unity is not drawn from itself" (*Enn*, IV, 7, 3). Soul, as cause, contains within itself the forms or reasons of the things whose temporally ordered diversity it produces. This produced order reflects in time the timeless order implicit in the cause: "If the leading principle of the universe does not know the future which it is of itself to produce, it cannot produce with knowledge or to purpose; it will produce just what happens to come, that is to say by haphazard. As this cannot be, it must create by some stable principle; its creations, therefore, will be shaped in the model stored up in itself; there can be no varying" (*Enn*, IV, 4, 12). Moreover, our consciousness is in the first instance, as indeed the materialists hold, a series of events in time. However, each of these events is related to the others in the series; and they are related moreover to one another as modifications of a single consciousness, a consciousness that is a consciousness of each of them and all of them. "There can be no perception without a unitary percipient whose identity enables it to grasp an object in its entirety" (*Enn*, IV, 7, 6). The conscious self of which the events are the modifications cannot be the series as a whole, since within

24. References are to Plotinus, *The Enneads*, trans. Stephen MacKenna, 4th ed., rev. B. S. Page (London: Faber & Faber, 1969); hereafter, *Enn*, followed by volume, book, and section numbers.

the series the events are successive; but *at any moment the consciousness of those events does not involve a succession:* "[P]rior and past are in the things it [soul] produces; in itself nothing is past; all . . . is one simultaneous grouping of Reason-Principles" (*Enn*, IV, 4, 16). That is, while the consciousness of the series is a consciousness *of* a before and after, *within* that self-consciousness there is no before and after; within the consciousness there is no such relation between the components as there is between the events of which it is the consciousness. The consciousness a self has of itself must lie outside the temporal sequence of events of which it is conscious. Self-consciousness must therefore be an entity outside the temporal changes of the self, an eternal entity to which the events in the temporal sequence are related as modifications.

This position, which is essentially that of Berkeley, continued to be defended long after Berkeley. It was held by T. H. Green,[25] for example, that a whole consisting of separable parts could have no unity; no part of such a whole could provide that unity. Where such a whole did have unity, the latter derived from a timeless self-consciousness that comprehended the whole. Green resisted Mill's notion with respect to the self—shared by Dennett and Hume—that a part could represent the whole, and thereby provide the unity. "To be conscious of it [one's personal history]," Green tells us, "we must unite its several stages as related to each other in the way of succession; and to do that we must ourselves be, and distinguish ourselves as being, out of that succession. . . . It is only through our holding ourselves aloof, so to speak, from the manifold affections of sense, as constant throughout their variety, that they can be presented to us as a connected series, and thus move to seek the conditions of connection between them" (G 92). But Green's argument for this does not so much deny Mill's point as it insists that the *relational structure* of the self presupposes a self that is outside time. According to Green, both selves and material objects have as their basic constituents entities given in sense experience, or, as he calls them, feelings. On this point he is in agreement with Mill and with Hume. "Feelings *are* facts; but they are facts only so far as determined by relations, which exist only for a thinking consciousness and otherwise could not exist" (G 53). Structure can be provided only by a thinking, conscious, self-conscious unity or substance in which the whole as such exists.

It is this metaphysics of structure and not Dennett's metaphysics of

25. *Prolegomena to Ethics* (Oxford: Clarendon Press, 1906); hereafter, G, followed by page number.

understanding to which we should relate Berkeley if we are to appreciate his idealism. In fact the problem of understanding is subsumed by Berkeley within the broader concept of structure.

In the *Philosophical Commentaries* Berkeley returns again and again to the issue of unity and structure. Thus, in PC 71 we learn that by "immateriality is solv'd the cohesion of bodies, or rather the dispute ceases." Space is a structure relating bodies, and so empty space is a meaningless notion: "Space wthout any bodies being in rerum natura, would not be extended as not having parts in that parts are assigned to it wth respect to body from whence also the notion of distance is taken, now without either parts or distance or mind how can there be space or anything beside one uniform no thing?" (PC 96). Again: "The greatness per se perceivable of the sight, is onely the proportion any visible appearance bears to the others seen at the same time; of (wch is the same thing) the proportion of any particular part of the visual orb to the whole. but mark that we perceive not it is an orb, any more than a plain but by reasoning. This is all the greatness the pictures have per se" (PC 204).

If Berkeley is concerned about structure and unity, then he also has an explanation of it. What provides the structure is activity, that is, the will: "We cannot possibly conceive any active power but the Will" (PC 155). "Tis folly to define volition an act of the mind ordering. for neither act nor ordering can themselves be understood without Volition" (PC 635). And this is the same as mind, or soul: "The soul is the will properly speaking & as it is distinct from Ideas" (PC 478a). Power in fact is nothing more than the relation of cause and effect: "Power no simple Idea. it means nothing but the Relation between Cause & Effect" (PC 493). What we observe by sense are only occasions, not causes (PC 856, 853). The causes are the activities that produce the effect consequent upon the cause: "I say there are no Causes (properly speaking) but Spiritual, nothing active but Spirit" (PC 850). These activities are the volitional activities of a substantial soul. "What means Cause as dinstinguish'd from Occasion? nothing but a Being wch wills w^{n} the Effect follows the volition. Those things that happen from without we are not the Cause of therefore there is some other Cause of them i.e. there is a being that will these perceptions in us" (PC 499). Cartesian body, that is, extended substance, is inert. Locke and Newton also make body inert. Moreover, Newtonian space is inert. On Berkeley's view, none of these systems is able to solve the problem of structure. But there is such a problem: the ideas of which we are aware in sense experience display an order that implies active structuring. And sense gives no necessary connection. "Qu: whether possible that those visible ideas wch are now connected with greater extensions could have been connected with lesser extensions. there seeming to be no necessary connexion between those thoughts" (PC 181). In order to account for structure, one needs necessary connections; that in turn requires activity; and that in its own turn implies a substantial mind. *Ideas are in minds because the mind provides the structure that organizes those ideas into structured unities. We thus see that the root of Berkeley's idealism is the attempt to account for the order that we discover among the sense impressions that are presented to us.*

Berkeley begins, basically, with Locke's empiricism. But the substantial mind that creates order is not given in the ordinary awareness through which we are aware of sensible particulars. What he has to do is struggle toward the conclusion that the self that gives order cannot be construed on empiricist lines as a complex entity, "a bundle or collection of different perceptions which succeed one another with an inconceivable rapidity and are in a perpetual flux and movement," as Hume put it (T, p. 252). Berkeley did attempt this: as he put it in the famous passage from his notebooks, "By Soul is meant onely a Complex idea made up of existence, willing & perception in a large sense. therefore its is known & it may be defin'd" (PC 154). But he struggled out of this position: "The substance of Body we know, the substance of Spirit we do not know   it not being knowable. it being purus actus" (PC 701). Or again, "Perception is passive but this not distinct from Idea/therefore there can be no Idea of volition" (PC 756). Ideas are contrasted to acts of thought or volitions (PC 808). Ideas and the will of course go together (PC 841, 842; cf. PC 577); the latter structures the former. But the will is not perceived, nor, therefore, is it the object of understanding (PC 828, 829), that is, understanding in the sense of the empiricism of Locke and Hume, according to which one understands those things given in sense by subsuming them under the matter-of-fact regularities that we learn through experience. When Berkeley suggests that the self can be construed as a complex idea, he is not so much anticipating the Humean conclusion that Dennett recommends to us as struggling to escape the empiricism that he has inherited from Locke and that forbids him any account of structure if he continues to adhere to it.

We thus see that the problem Berkeley is addressing is the traditional one of order, not that of understanding meaningful speech. Once we recognize this, then we see his idealism falling into place. We also see why the inherence account of that idealism, as defended by Allaire, Cummins, and Watson, is substantially correct:[26] it simply appeals to the model of causation that the traditional account of order uses.[27] Properties are in things, that is, inhere in things construed as substances, and the order among those properties is provided by the immanent causal activities of that substance, or by the transeunt causal activities of another substance.[28]

The traditional problem for the inherence reading is PR 49,[29] where Berkeley denies that ideas are predicated of the mind.

> [I]t may perhaps be objected that if extension and figure exist only in the mind, it follows that the mind is extended and figured; since extension is a mode or attribute, which (to speak with the Schools) is predicated of the subject in which it exists. I answer, those qualities are in the mind only as they are perceived by it, that is, not by way of *mode* or *attribute*, but only by way of *idea*. And it no more follows the soul or mind is extended, because extension exists in it alone, than it does that it is red or blue, because those colours are on all hands acknowledged to exist in it, and nowhere else.

If ideas are not predicated of the mind, so goes the objection, then they cannot inhere in it, since, traditionally, inherence has been reflected in language by predication. Berkeley, however, continues the passage to argue that there is no necessary connection between predication and inherence:

> As to what philosophers say of subject and mode, that seems very groundless and unintelligible. For instance, in this proposition, a die is hard, extended and square, they will have it that the word *die* denotes a subject or substance, distinct from the hardness, extension and figure, which are predicated of it, and in which they exist. This I cannot comprehend: to me a die seems to be nothing distinct

26. Richard A. Watson, "Berkeley in a Cartesian Context," *Revue Internationale de Philosophie* 65 (1963), pp. 381–94, points out in detail how Berkeley repeatedly talks as if ideas inhered in substances.

27. Similar points are made in Kenneth P. Winkler, "Unperceived Objects and Berkeley's Denial of Blind Agency," *Hermathena* 139 (1985), pp. 81–100.

28. The connections between order, or relations, and spirit is emphasized by Berkeley in his additions to the *Principles* in the second edition; see E. J. Furlong, "Berkeley on Relations, Spirits, and Notions," *Hermathena* 107 (1968), pp. 60–66.

29. Cf. George Pappas, "Ideas, Minds, and Berkeley," *American Philosophical Quarterly* 17 (1980), pp. 181–94.

from those things which are termed its modes or accidents. And, to say a die is hard, extended and square, is not to attribute those qualities to a subject distinct from and supporting them, but only an explication of the meaning of the word *die*.

Given the abolition of material substance, it is necessary to construe ordinary things as bundles of qualities and to construe predication as reflecting the relation of part to whole. Nonetheless, predication does sometimes reflect the relation of mode to substance, as, for example, when a volition is predicated of a spiritual substance. The point is, of course, that even if predication does sometimes reflect the relation of property to substance, it is clear that Berkeley intends the relation of idea to substance to be other than that of the relation of, say, volition to substance. And that being so, it would seem that the inherence account of Berkeley's idealism is wrong when it insists that that idealism arises precisely because Berkeley construes, if only unconsciously, the relation of idea to mind as that of property to substance.

The correct response should be, I think, to note that Berkeley insists upon distinguishing *two* relations: ideas are *in* spiritual substances, and so are activities; but the latter are in substances by way of mode, whereas the former are in substances in another way. With such a response we recognize, I think, that this distinction reflects a very traditional view of substances. The active form is,[30] traditionally, said to be "predicated of" the substance, while the properties are "present in" the substance. When Berkeley insists upon two relations to the substance, he is simply following this tradition. Where he departs from the tradition is in his insistence that when an idea is "present in" a substance, it is not to be predicated of that substance. The latter is required by his nontraditional account of things as bundles of qualities. But from the fact that being "present in" a substance is no longer reflected in predication, it does not follow that Berkeley is not construing the relation of being "present in," that is, the relation of an idea to a spiritual substance, as the relation of property to substance—with all the ontological freight that implies, including what is necessary to justify the inherence account of his idealism. In particular, for a property to be "present in" a substance *just is* for it to be supported by the informed activity of the substance; inherence is, if you wish, insepa-

---

30. As Winkler, "Unperceived Objects," points out, Berkeley rejects blind agency; that means that the activities of spiritual substances are always informed, or intrinsically directed.

rable from activity.[31] Thus, reading Berkeley as introducing active substances in order to solve the problem of order enables one to meet at least some of the objections to the inherence account of his idealism.

But if Berkeley solves the problem of structure by introducing active substances, he nonetheless still faces problems.[32] There is of course the traditional problem of how we know substances. This he addresses by reviving John Sergeant's thesis about "notions."[33] More deeply, there is the problem of interaction. Berkeley's account of ordinary things as wholes whose parts are sensible particulars, and his idealism, together solve the problem of the interaction of mind and body. He must still, however, deal with the problem of the interaction of substances, since he still has interacting minds. Unlike Leibniz, Berkeley never faced up to the problem of interaction. Without doing so, he has not solved the problem that he tried to solve.

31. This point, too, is emphasized by Winkler, "Unperceived Objects," pp. 87 ff, against various comments by Jonathan Bennett, who accuses Berkeley of using the word 'depend' to blur the difference between "the ownership of ideas" and "what causes ideas to be had by minds" (Bennett, Locke, Berkeley, Hume: Central Themes [Oxford: Clarendon Press, 1971], p. 168).

32. While, as I have been arguing, Berkeley does propose an account of relations as contributed by the substantial mind, I think it is also true that he does not develop the position as systematically as one would hope. As T. E. Jessop has remarked, "Berkeley nowhere develops this view of relations, which seems to imply that relations among 'ideas' are not discovered but instituted by the mental act, or at any rate that activity of relating somehow enters into the content of the relation" (Works II, 106 n. 1).

33. Cf. R. Grossmann, "Digby and Berkeley on Notions," Theoria 26 (1960), pp. 17–30, and Daniel E. Flage, Berkeley's Doctrine of Notions (New York: St. Martin's, 1987).

5

The Substance of Berkeley's Philosophy

Robert G. Muehlmann

In the *Philosophical Commentaries*, the "juvenile" Berkeley enthusiastically sketches out a bundle analysis of finite minds: a mind is constituted of episodes of volition and occurrences of ideas.[1] But it is clear that Berkeley endorses a substance analysis by the

This essay was the winner of the second annual Colin and Ailsa Turbayne International Berkeley Essay Prize Competition (1991). A longer version appeared in *Berkeley's Ontology* (Indianapolis: Hackett Publishing Co., 1992), pp. 170–89.

1. The central entries are PC 577–81 (it is here that Berkeley describes a mental bundle as a "congeries"), but there are supporting entries scattered throughout the notebooks. In the recent secondary literature, see I. C. Tipton's ground-breaking paper, "Berkeley's View of Spirit," in *New Studies in Berkeley's Philosophy*, ed. Warren E. Steinkraus, (New York: Holt, Rinehart & Winston, 1966), pp. 59–71. See also A. C. Lloyd, "The Self in Berkeley's Philosophy," in *Essays on Berkeley*, ed. John Foster and Howard Robinson (Oxford: Oxford University Press, 1985), pp. 187–210. In neither of these articles does the author devote sufficient attention to the development of Berkeley's account of mind within the notebooks, nor do the authors place such developments as are discernible within the broader context of

time the *Principles* appears. As early as PR 2 he says that a mind is "a thing entirely distinct" from its ideas; and numerous additional passages in both the *Principles* and *Dialogues* give voice to the position that finite minds are active *substances* distinct from, but both "causing" (some of) and "supporting" (all of), their ideas. That dramatic change in his position raises the question to which this essay is addressed. Why does Berkeley endorse the substance analysis of mind when he writes the *Principles?*

By the time I am able to provide an answer, I will have shown that this question is not equivalent to its negatively expressed counterpart, obtained by replacing 'endorse the substance analysis' with 'abandon the bundle analysis'. Although it is obvious both that the notebooks' account of mind is inconsistent with the *Principles'* (since the former affirms what the latter denies and conversely) and that Berkeley *does* endorse a substance account of mind in the *Principles,* I show that, in one important sense, he does *not* abandon the bundle analysis. Rather, as I say, he *conceals* it. He conceals it in the sense that nearly all of the philosophical work provided in Berkeley's prepublication bundle, or *congeries,* account of finite mind is camouflaged as work now done by his published substance account; indeed it is difficult to find *any* ontological role, in Berkeley's two major works, that he explicitly and exclusively assigns to finite mental substances. Because he thus conceals the congeries account, I must address a second question. Why does Berkeley conceal the congeries account of mind in the writing of the *Principles* (and *Dialogues*)? The principal answer to this second question also serves as part of the answer to the first.

To quicken the sense of the puzzle raised by the first question, several things are noteworthy. One is that Berkeley is fully aware of the difficulties posed by his introduction of substances into the analysis of mind. He devotes considerable energy, for example, in the attempt to deflect one such difficulty, a difficulty exploited in the "parity argument." This argument can be stated succinctly in ad hominem form: Berkeley's objections to material substances apply, with equal force, to mental substances;

---

his two major works. If these developments are exposed and placed in that broader context, it becomes clear that Berkeley's nominalism (and, consequently, his antiabstractionism) is fatal to substances, whether material *or* mental. It becomes clear, too, that the notebooks' Berkeley not only fully appreciates the significance of this, he also repeatedly and enthusiastically exploits it. Satisfying the antecedent of the preceding conditional is, of course, well beyond the scope of the present essay. I make an effort along these lines in *Berkeley's Ontology.*

and parity of reasoning, therefore, should force him to reject the latter.[2] Nor is this the only difficulty Berkeley addresses. A related one arises within his epistemology.

As Berkeley reads his adversaries, their position is that substances, independently existing things, are not directly perceived; rather, they are known indirectly and inferentially: we directly perceive intervening "phantasms" or "sensible appearances," and then our understanding, our reasoning based on these "appearances," provides us with knowledge of substances. In stark contrast, Berkeley holds, first, that those so-called phantasms and mere appearances are actually real things (or *ideas*, as he prefers to call them when stressing their mind-dependence). He holds, second, that we know real things directly and noninferentially; and he holds, finally, that we also know our selves and our mental operations directly: we know the meanings of 'my self' and 'this volition' without the intervention of ideas and without inference. I have not the space to discuss these three points in detail, but for my purposes here the following will suffice.

While Berkeley devotes a great deal of attention to the first two, he seems to focus insufficient attention on the third. It is given a scant few lines in the first editions of the *Principles* and *Dialogues* and emerges only in a thinly stated doctrine of notions that Berkeley adds to the later editions. Underlying this doctrine, however, is a thesis he does address in some detail, the thesis that particular episodes of volition are *active*—that they are casually efficacious mental operations.[3]

The puzzle raised by the central question is thus magnified by the fact that Berkeley appreciates the difficulties entailed by his introduction of mental substances. But the puzzle becomes more intense when we realize that the notebooks' congeries analysis of mind is firmly grounded in Berkeley's antiabstractionism; that he stresses, particularly in the introduction but also in the main body of the *Principles*, the importance of antiabstractionism to his philosophy; and that the substance analysis of mind, emphasized at PR 2 and elsewhere, nonetheless runs completely counter to his attack on abstract ideas.

As if this were not enough, however, the puzzle is made acute by two additional facts. The first is that it is difficult to see what ontological role

2. Berkeley's effort to deflect this objection is dissected by Phillip D. Cummins in "Hylas' Parity Argument," in *Berkeley: Critical and Interpretative Essays*, ed. Colin M. Turbayne (Minneapolis: University of Minnesota Press, 1982), pp. 283–94.

3. An excellent discussion of Berkeley's theory of causation can be found in Kenneth P. Winkler's *Berkeley: An Interpretation* (New York: Oxford University Press, 1989), pp. 104–36.

is played by the notion of mental substance in Berkeley's philosophy; mental substances *do* play an ontological role, but the role they play, while related to *one* of the traditional roles his adversaries assign to substances, constitutes a revolutionary departure from their analyses. The second fact sharpening the puzzle is that in many places where Berkeley gives voice to the substance account of mind, the notebooks' congeries analysis hovers, inconsistently, in the background. Numerous sections of the *Principles* make this second fact apparent, and we will do well to pay close attention to the more significant ones.

At PR 98 Berkeley says, "[W]hoever should go about to divide in his thoughts or abstract the *existence* of a spirit from its *cogitation*, will, I believe, find it no easy task" (cf. PC 650–52). It will be no easy task because, as Berkeley argues so forcefully in his introduction to the *Principles*, such abstract ideas *cannot* exist.[4] Yet since cogitation consists in the having, the occurrence in a thinker, of ideas, it is hard to see how the distinctness of a mind from its ideas can be squared with Berkeley's assertion at PR 98.

In another significant section, PR 27, Berkeley observes that some philosophers hold that they "can frame the idea of . . . power or active being" and that they have "ideas of two principal powers, marked by the names *will* and *understanding*, distinct from each other as well as from a third idea of substance or being in general, with a relative notion of its supporting or being the subject of the aforesaid powers, which is signified by the name *soul* or *spirit*." But Berkeley then continues by echoing his notebooks' disdain for such philosophers: "This is what some hold; but so far as I can see, the words *will, soul, spirit*, do not stand for different ideas, or in truth, for any idea at all, but for something which is very different from ideas, and which being an agent cannot be like unto, or represented by, any idea whatsoever" (PR 27). The main point of this section is to bring out the fact that our awareness of spirit is not ideational—that being an *agent*, a spirit cannot be represented by something that is *passive*, such as an idea. But for my purposes here, we need only note that implicit in this section is Berkeley's rejection of the traditional substance analysis of spirit—his rejection of the view that a spirit is a "substance or being in general" and that it stands in a relation

---

4. Why does Berkeley hold that the existence of any abstract idea is an "impossibility" (IN 21)? In *Berkeley's Ontology*, pp. 24–76, I argue that the answer to this question lies in his implicit nominalism.

of inherence, of support, to the "principal powers" of will and understanding.[5]

At PR 11 Berkeley dismisses that "much ridiculed notion of *materia prima*, to be met with in Aristotle and his followers"; and, significantly, he says (with emphasis added), "[H]ere I cannot but remark, how nearly the vague and indeterminate description of matter or corporeal substance which the modern philosophers are run into by their own principles, *resembles* that antiquated" notion. The context makes it clear that the notion of a "corporeal substance" depends, as Berkeley puts it, "on that strange doctrine of *abstract ideas*," specifically, on Locke's claim that "the *principium individuationis* . . . is Existence itself, which determines a Being of any sort to a particular time and place incommunicable to two Beings of the same kind."[6] While Berkeley is almost certainly aware of the fact that Locke advances this notion in *opposition* to Aristotle's *materia prima*, he nevertheless objects to it. Berkeley does so because, while he sees that Locke eliminates substance as *individuator*, Locke nevertheless *retains* substance as *substratum* or support: at PR 17 Berkeley says (again, with emphasis added) that this "idea of being in general, *together with* the relative notion of supporting accidents . . . appeareth to me the most abstract and incomprehensible of all other"; and he then argues, in the same section, that Locke's notion of "support" is incoherent because it leads to an infinite regress.

The significance of 'resembles' in PR 11, then, is that it suggests Berkeley recognizes that substances play two roles in his adversaries' philosophies: the notion of a "corporeal substance" is not exhausted by its role as *individuator* but has the additional role of *substratum*. Indeed, the significance of 'resembles' goes beyond even this, for Berkeley recognizes that such substances have a *threefold* role: in addition to the two just mentioned, his adversaries introduce substances as *causal agents*, a notion that Berkeley dismisses, at least with regard to "corporeal substances," with an *independent* series of arguments, in PR 18–19 and 25. Not the least significant part of the puzzle addressed in this essay is the

5. In "Substance, Reality, and the Great, Dead Philosophers," *American Philosophical Quarterly* 7 (1970), pp. 38–49, Michael R. Ayers insists that while PR 27 appears to be an objection to all talk of substance and support, it cannot be an objection to substance *"per se,"* since "Berkeley has just categorically stated that spirit is an incorporeal, active substance, applying to it a traditional definition" of "one simple, undivided, active being" (47). I agree. See note 18.

6. John Locke, *An Essay Concerning Human Understanding*, ed. Peter H. Nidditch, (New York: Oxford University Press, 1975), book II, chap. xxvii, sec. 3.

contrast between (*a*) the fact that Berkeley often *suggests* that minds support their ideas and *says* that minds are agents and (*b*) the fact that mental substances play *neither* of these roles in his philosophy.

It is obvious that mental substances cannot be individuators. In Berkeley's nominalistic ontology, only particular items exist.[7] Consequently, Berkeley can safely dismiss as ridiculous any attempt to identify a mental substance with a *mens prima*, just as he does at PR 11 with *materia prima*. (And, if pressed, he could simply appeal to Ockham's razor.)[8] Of course, though Berkeley has no need of mental substances as atemporal individuators, this does not show that he has no need for them as temporal continuants. Berkeley may introduce mental substances, in other words, in order to account for personal identity. There are good reasons to think, however, that this requirement is viewed by him as a largely theological (rather than as an ontological) requirement, and I return to it at the end.

It is not as obvious that mental substances cannot be causal agents. For one thing, Berkeley consistently describes them as such. The following passage, for example, is not atypical. Berkeley has Philonous say that "I know or am conscious of my own being; and that I my self am not my ideas, but somewhat else, a thinking active principle that perceives, knows, wills, and operates about ideas" (D 233). But while Berkeley in the *Principles* and Philonous in the *Dialogues* frequently make such assertions as these, little effort is devoted to explaining how it is possible for us to have this sort of knowledge, and next to nothing is said about the ontological role this "one individual principle" is supposed to play. The continuation of the above passage is interesting, however, since Philonous advances an argument that one's self must be "one individual principle," although, *note bene*, his argument does not address the question of this

7. In the first of his *Dialogues*, in a context in which Philonous is discussing *qualities* — both determinate: "some degree of swiftness or slowness, some certain magnitude or figure peculiar to each [sensible thing]"; and determinable: "extension in general, and motion in general" — Berkeley has Philonous emphatically declare that *"every thing which exists, is particular"* (D 192). Winkler, *Berkeley: An Interpretation*, p. 30, is thus mistaken when he says that "by 'things' in this context [Berkeley] means all entities capable of *independent* existence" (emphasis added). For more on this, see *Berkeley's Ontology*, pp. 33–36.

8. Berkeley *does* appeal to Ockham's razor as part of his attack on the supposition that there are substantial material *causes*. At the end of PR 19 he says that it "must needs be a very precarious opinion; since it is to suppose, without any reason at all, that God has created innumerable beings that are entirely useless, and serve to no manner of purpose." Berkeley does not appeal to Ockham's razor to dispose of Aristotle's *materia prima* — unless we read his comment at the end of PR 19 as a blanket complaint — because, as the context (PR 11) suggests, he finds this notion beneath contempt.

item's causal agency: "I know that I, one and the same self, perceive both colours and sounds; that a colour cannot perceive a sound, nor a sound a colour; that I am therefore one individual principle, distinct from colour and sound; and, for the same reason, from all other sensible things and inert ideas" (D 233–34). The argument seems to be that since sensible qualities (of one "sensory modality") cannot perceive sensible qualities (of another), there must be some item, not itself a sensible quality (or, presumably, a passion or volition), that does the perceiving, and this can only be a mental substance. Philonous's argument, however, is one for which the notebooks' Berkeley would (and the "mature" Berkeley should) have had nothing but scorn. In the case of immediate perception, the occurrence of a sensible quality (an idea of sense) simply *is* a perceiving; or, to put it differently, an immediate perceiving is not distinct from its object: it *is* its object. Furthermore, since ideas of imagination are sometimes representative of ideas of sense, the former are, broadly speaking, perceptions of the latter. Moreover, mediate perception requires the possibility that, again in an important sense, a sound *does* sometimes "perceive a color": involved in the perception of a sensible object (including that object's color), and in some sense "mediating" it, is the perception of an auditory idea.[9] Finally, even conceding that no idea can perceive another idea, there is no difficulty in accounting for the sense in which *I* perceive a color or sound without supposing that 'I' refers to "one individual principle,"[10] a mental substance: one can hold, as the notebooks' Berkeley does, that 'I' refers to a congeries of ideas (and volitions) and that 'I see this color' constitutes a (partial) "explication" of the meaning of 'I'.[11] Indeed, Berkeley suggests as much in PR 49 when he advances his

9. Cf. the coach example at the end (D 204) of the first dialogue.

10. In "Hylas' Parity Argument," p. 291, Cummins holds that Berkeley's attempt here to derail the parity argument can be defended against its principal criticism, namely, that Berkeley "argues from what is experienced (the empirical self and its ideas) to an unexperienced entity (the individual active principle or substance) on the basis of a premise (one idea cannot perceive another) whose truth cannot be established from the data of experience." But while Cummins is right to point out it "is a profound mistake to represent Berkeley as permitting no metaphysical premises," this does not alter the fact that Berkeley never explains why this particular unexperienced entity, introduced by a different metaphysical "premise," must exist—why the "furniture of the world" must include individual active mental substances in addition to "their" volitions and perceptions. While the *empirical self*, invoked in that passage from the third dialogue, can be described as "one and the same self," what is the point of describing the unexperienced substance in this way? The answer is surprising. But wait.

11. In the body of his *Treatise* Hume found no difficulty in advancing a substance-free account of mind. See *A Treatise of Human Nature*, ed. L. A. Selby-Bigge and Peter H.

antisubstantialist account of the meaning of 'a die is hard, extended and square'.

Shortly before advancing the above argument Philonous says, "My own mind and my own ideas I have an immediate knowledge of"; and shortly after this, he tells Hylas "you neither perceive matter objectively, as you do an inactive being or idea, nor know it, as you do your self by a reflex act" (D 232). From these two assertions it is safe to conclude that knowledge of the self and its volitions is not inferential and that nothing intervenes—there is no *tertium quid*—between the "reflex act" and the mind and its operations that act makes known. But what is this reflex act and what sort of entity is its target? Berkeley provides no answer.

The end of the later passage (cited above from D 233–34) is designed to reinforce Berkeley's claim at PR 2 that a mind is entirely distinct from its ideas. And it is noteworthy that he does not say here that a mind is distinct from its volitions. Indeed, when he explains, at PR 27, why we cannot have ideas of our minds, the explanation rests entirely on the fact that our *episodes of volition* are active: ideas, being passive, cannot represent them. Now, Berkeley holds that causation is *activity*, but it is particular episodes of volition, not mental substances, that play this causal role. If a mind is constituted, in part, of episodes of volition, then the mind can safely be described as an "agent" or "active principle"; but it is nonetheless clear that causal agency resides, *fundamentally*, in individual episodes of volition. Moreover, since *only* such episodes are causes, a mental substance could not, in any case, cause one of its own episodes of volition without first *willing* it.

Finally, Berkeley also dismisses the support role of substance, explicitly with regard to material substance and also with regard to mental substance. Seeing this requires an examination of several additional passages, and in the course of this examination, while working up to an explanation of how minds are supposed to support ideas, we discover additional evidence both that the notebooks' analysis hovers in the background and that Berkeley takes some pains to conceal this.

Nidditch (New York: Oxford University Press, 1978), pp. 251–63. For a response to many of the standard objections to this account, see Nelson Pike, "Hume's Bundle Theory of the Self: A Limited Defense," *American Philosophical Quarterly* 4 (1967), pp. 159–65. To be sure, Hume himself found something troubling in his account (see *Treatise*, appendix, pp. 635–36), but no satisfactory explanation has been found for his lament that "my account is very defective." For a critical review of some attempts to do so, as well as an intriguing new attempt, see Wayne Waxman, "Hume's Quandary Concerning Personal Identity," *Hume Studies* 18 (1992), pp. 233–53.

The two most significant sections for my purposes are PR 49 and PR 91. The former, like PR 27, is about minds, but it is much more explicit in its import. Berkeley insists at PR 49 that sensible qualities are *not* in the mind "by way of mode or attribute"; rather, "they are in the mind *only* as they are perceived by it, that is, . . . *only* by way of *idea*" (the italics on 'only' are added). This is Berkeley's answer to an objection he anticipates, an objection *premised on* the very substance account of mind he seems to have endorsed earlier in the *Principles*. The objection is that on the Scholastic-Cartesian account,[12] a mind is a subject of prediction, and thus Berkeley's introduction of a substance into his analysis of mind entails the absurdity that sensible qualities are predicable of minds. Berkeley puts that objection this way: "[I]f extension and figure exist only in the mind, it follows that the mind is extended and figured; since extension is a mode or attribute, which (to speak with the Schools) is predicated of the subject in which it exists" (PR 49). Again, if Berkeley has introduced a Scholastic-Cartesian mental substance into his analysis of finite minds, it is hard to see how PR 49 can be squared with such an introduction.[13]

In this connection, it is also worth noting that there are many passages in which a substance analysis of mind seems to have been, not reintro-duced—for until the end of the notebooks, Berkeley seems never to have taken this as a serious philosophical possibility—but rather, *injected*. The very first mention of mental *substance* at PR 7, for example, begins with the sentence "From what has been said, it follows, there is not any other substance than *spirit*, or that which perceives." But the continuation in this section alludes to the argument of PR 49 when Berkeley says that "for an idea to exist in an unperceiving thing, is a manifest contradiction; for to have an idea is all one as to perceive: that therefore wherein colour, figure, and the like qualities exist, must perceive them; hence it is clear there can be no unthinking substance or *substratum* of those ideas" (PR 7). The allusion to the argument of PR 49 resides in the fact that Berkeley does

12. For the Aristotelian-Scholastics, a mind is part of the *substantial form*, the *substantia secondae*, of a body, but for Descartes, a mind is a substance distinct from a body. When I speak, then, of the Scholastic-Cartesian account of mind, my intention is to stress that the account of mind Berkeley attacks is a Cartesian hybrid growing out of a crack in the Aristotelian-Scholastic bedrock.

13. In "Berkeley's Idealism," *Theoria* 29 (1963), pp. 229–44, Edwin B. Allaire gives an ingenious reading of PR 49 in which he tries to do just this. However, in "Berkeley's Idealism Revisited" (in *Berkeley: Critical Essays*, ed. Turbayne, 197–206, esp. 198–200), he retracts this reading of PR 49 while nevertheless defending the inherence interpretation as a valuable analytical tool. See also Allaire's contribution to this volume, Essay 1, as well as Fred Wilson's, Essay 4.

not conclude here that ideas must be in a mental substratum. He seems deliberately to conclude only that they cannot be in a material substratum[14] and that their mind-dependence rests rather on the fact that "to have an idea is all one as to perceive." Indeed, this last statement itself alludes to PR 49, where Berkeley says sensible qualities "are in mind . . . only by way of idea"; and his emphasis on 'substratum' in PR 7 is amplified at PR 49 when he asserts, not with respect to bodies but, rather, with respect to *minds:* "As to what philosophers say of subject and mode, that seems very groundless and unintelligible." As Berkeley well knows and as the remainder of PR 49 makes clear, 'subject' refers to the linguistic correlative of the ontic 'substance', and he is thus saying that talk of mental substances and their modes is "groundless and unintelligible."

We can turn now to the second important section, PR 91. In this section, Berkeley gives what appears, *at first glance,* to be an argument for the mind-dependence of sensible objects based on the premise that sensible qualities must inhere in mental substances. That is, he *seems* to argue in this way: "Qualities need a support, a substance in which to exist. But the only substances available are minds. Hence, qualities must be supported by minds, they must be in minds."[15] Here, from PR 91, is the passage in question:

> It were a mistake to think, that what is here said derogates in the least from the reality of things. It is acknowledged on the received principles, that extension, motion, and in a word all sensible qualities, have need of a support, as not being able to subsist by themselves. But the objects perceived by sense, are allowed to be nothing but combinations of those qualities, and consequently cannot subsist by themselves. Thus far it is agreed on all hands. So that in denying the things perceived by sense, an existence independent of a substance, or support wherein they may exist, we detract nothing from the received opinion of their *reality,* and are

14. Cf. Phillip D. Cummins, "Berkeley's Manifest Qualities Thesis," Essay 6 in this volume (esp. 123). In "The Role of Perceptual Relativity in Berkeley's Philosophy," *Journal of the History of Philosophy* 29 (1991), pp. 397–425, I argue in detail that Berkeley makes a similar move in the first of his *Dialogues:* he holds, as he does three years earlier in the *Principles,* that the argument from perceptual relativity shows *only* that sensible qualities cannot be in material substances. To put it differently, I argue—*pace* the standard interpretation—that Berkeley does *not* use the fact of perceptual relativity to establish the mind-dependence of sensible qualities. Cf. also Alan Hausman and David Hausman, Essay 4 in this volume (esp. 54).

15. Allaire, "Berkeley's Idealism," p. 235.

guilty of no innovation in that respect. All the difference is, that according to us the unthinking beings perceived by sense, have no existence distinct from being perceived, and cannot therefore exist in any other substance, than those unextended, indivisible substances, or *spirits*, which act, and think, and perceive them.

Beyond that *first glance*, a careful reading of this passage reveals no argument, implicit or explicit, based on a Scholastic-Cartesian inherence pattern. The passage suggests in fact that Berkeley is making a note here only of his agreement, in respect of "the reality of sensible things," with the "received principles." He is saying that, in *his* philosophy, the dependence of sensible things on minds does not strip sensible things of their reality; and he suggests that it does not do so, because "it is agreed on all hands," *first*, that sensible qualities "have need of a support, as not being able to subsist by themselves." Let us call this, the requirement demanded by the dependent nature of sensible qualities, the *support condition*. The *first* point of agreement, then, between Berkeley and his adversaries, is the support condition.

On the "received principles," the support condition is satisfied within a substance-mode account of bodies. On this account, sensible qualities are modes; they are dependent items that, if they are to exist, must *inhere in* existentially independent items or substances. On the "received principles," as Berkeley well knows, it is in *that* sense that "sensible qualities . . . have need of a support." But in what sense of 'support' does *Berkeley* hold that sensible qualities have such a need? In other words, how does Berkeley, within his own philosophical system, satisfy the support condition?

There is no direct answer to that question in PR 91, but Berkeley does answer it directly in PR 49. Before turning to that, however, it is worthwhile to pause briefly and examine the *second* point of agreement between his and the "received principles." This point is that "the objects perceived by sense, are allowed to be nothing but combinations of those qualities, and consequently cannot subsist by themselves." But in point of fact not every materialist would "allow" this *second* point. It is certain that no Aristotelian-Scholastic philosopher would agree that a sensible object is nothing but a collection of sensible qualities. Moreover, as Berkeley well knows, such philosophers would certainly also disagree with his implication here that the sensible qualities we normally attribute to a body must be in a substance *simpliciter:* they hold that *these* sensible qualities must be in a *material* substance. Berkeley's intentions in this passage are thus unclear: one cannot help feeling that irony is at play in PR 91 (not an uncharacteristic Berkeleian strategy) or that Berkeley is deliberately obscuring his own position. In view of what we have seen to this point, the latter alternative is at least as likely as the former.

If we turn from the *second* point of agreement and examine the *first* more carefully, however, that second alternative becomes a virtual certainty: in PR 91 Berkeley *is* deliberately concealing the congeries analysis of mind. At PR 49 he declares as "very groundless and unintelligible" the materialists' talk of "subject and mode"; and the sentences preceding this declaration make it clear that he is talking about minds. The example he uses to illustrate this, however, is not a mind but a body: "For instance, in this proposition, a die is hard, extended and square, they will have it that the word *die* denotes a subject or substance, distinct from the hardness, extension and figure, which are predicted of it, and in which they exist. This I cannot comprehend." Berkeley then presents us with his own analysis of a die: "[T]o me a die seems to be nothing distinct from those things which are termed its modes or accidents. And to say a die is hard, extended and square, is not to attribute those qualities to a subject distinct from and supporting them, but only an explication of the meaning of the word *die*." These passages and numerous others (PR 1, to cite just one example) make it clear that, for Berkeley, a sensible object is just a collection of sensible qualities: an inventory of the sensible qualities of bodies exhausts their analyses. Berkeley holds that the support condition is satisfied within his account by requiring that sensible qualities always be members of such combinations as constitute individual bodies.[16] But this means, of course, that the sense in which sensible qualities "have need of a support" is quite different from the sense of 'support' countenanced by the materialists—quite different from the sense of 'support' that Berkeley finds unintelligible and groundless. Thus, again, in PR 91 we find Berkeley craftily disguising his real position.

His real position is that sensible qualities—and those collections apart from which they are inseparable—need to be "supported" by minds because they, *in addition* to being inseparable from collections or combinations, are *also* inseparable from *sensations*.[17] This position is suggested by what Berkeley says at PR 5; it is greatly amplified in the first of his

---

16. More accurately, Berkeley's position is that sensible qualities cannot exist apart from the *proper* objects of immediate perception.

17. Historically, this interpretation is first advanced by Thomas Reid. See Phillip D. Cummins, "Berkeley's Ideas of Sense," *Nous* 9 (1975), pp. 55–72.

Dialogues (D 176–78 and 191–92); and although he does not say as much in PR 91, what he does say presupposes either that sensible qualities are sensations or, at least, that sensible qualities depend for their existence on being perceived.[18]

At the end of the long passage from PR 91 cited above, Berkeley calls attention to a difference between the position that he advocates and the position of those accepting the "received principles"; and this difference is crucial: sensible things have no existence apart from being perceived and *therefore* cannot exist apart from spirits. In other words, Berkeley explicitly argues that *because* the *esse* of sensible things is *percipi*, sensible things cannot exist apart from minds. The argument of PR 91, then, is not an argument for the mind-dependence of sensible things based on the inherence pattern. It is not, to say the same thing differently, an argument for idealism based on the support condition that the materialists would find agreeable. Rather, if there is an argument here at all, it is an argument that presupposes idealism, an argument that assumes idealism has been antecedently established.

Now, I do not mean to suggest here that any of this proves that Berkeley has *not* introduced a Scholastic-Cartesian mental substance into his analysis of mind by the time he publishes the *Principles;* indeed, it seems clear that he *has*. Although this introduction generates difficulties, is embarrassing, and is inconsistent with several key sections, and al-

---

18. In "Substance, Reality, and the Great, Dead Philosophers," Michael R. Ayers points out that Berkeley "is liable to be misread as if he objects to the concept of substance *per se*, although his language makes it plain that he is not in fact doing so" (p. 49). It is, indeed, plain that Berkeley uses 'substance' in talking about minds, and plain too that he describes mental substances in the traditional ways (PR 27 and 135). But let me emphasize once again that my argument is not directed at demonstrating a Berkeleian rejection of "the concept of substance *per se*"; rather, I am raising the question about what role, beyond this *merely nominal* one, the concept of mental substance plays in Berkeley's philosophy. My conclusion, that it plays none of the traditional roles, is not a possibility Ayers considers, even though it is consistent with his observations that in the Aristotelian tradition "ontological and causal priority go together" and that the causal role played by Berkeley's mental substance is not "the usual explanation of activity by essences" (p. 48). While Ayers tells us what the causal role of mental substance is not, he does not explain what it is; and as for its ontological role (the role of "immaterial support"), while he alleges that it "can be made clear and intelligible by identifying" *supporting* with *perceiving* (p. 47), Ayers in fact provides no explanation how the Berkeleian conversion of 'support' (or 'inherence') into 'perceiving' is to be understood. In *Berkeley's Ontology* I have argued, in effect, that the right explanation resides in Berkeley's construing an object of immediate perception as a sensation (his argument for this is the first major argument presented in the *Dialogues:* the heat-pain argument) and then relies on the assumption, shared by all his contemporaries and predecessors, that sensations are mental, that is, that sensations cannot exist apart from sensory awareness.

though Berkeley has gutted it of much of its ontological significance—for he certainly believes he can establish idealism as well as his theory of causation without it—Berkeley nevertheless has not only introduced mental substances and emphasized their distinctness from ideas, but he has also taken great pains to conceal his underlying congeries analysis of mind. Why?

As I mentioned at the outset, this is really two questions: Why does Berkeley introduce mental substances? And why does he conceal the congeries analysis? Part of the answer to the first question is, I think, that Berkeley needs a way to distinguish minds from sensible objects if he is to vouchsafe his commitment to common sense, in particular if he is to secure the *bare possibility*[19] that the plain person's bodies can exist independently of the plain person's mind. Moreover, the required method must, at the same time, not compromise his idealism. This is a very tall order. Berkeley certainly thought it could be filled; and, indeed, he came very close to filling it.

Having nearly completed his notebooks, Berkeley reasoned, I submit, in the following way. On the one hand, if my mind is nothing but a congeries of ideas and volitions, and if some of these ideas are bodies—that is, "houses, mountains, and rivers" (PR 4) or "the furniture of the world" (PR 6)—how can *any* sense be given to the notion that such bodies might exist apart from my mind? To be sure, such bodies can exist apart from my volitions, since I am not the causes of them. Moreover, since causes are distinct from their effects (PC 780), even if my volitions did produce bodies, it would be logically possible for bodies to exist apart from me. But if a mind is constituted, even in part, by its ideas, it would seem that my ideas *cannot* exist apart from my mind.[20] On the other hand, if my mind can be described as "entirely distinct" from its ideas,[21] then it is at least logically possible that some of my ideas, those which constitute bodies, might exist apart from my self.[22] Thus the attraction of a substance analysis of mind.

19. I stress this because the distinction between a mental substance and an idea of sense (an object) can provide only a necessary condition of the truth of realism. (That Berkeley is fully aware of this is clear from his response, at PR 48, to the intermittency objection of PR 45: the response is simply that the "foregoing principles" do not *entail* intermittency.) To provide a sufficient condition, Berkeley needs an additional argument, an argument he thinks he finds in his proof of God's existence.

20. This appearance is deceptive, as Hume recognized. See *Treatise*, p. 207.

21. Berkeley never says that a mind is distinct from its *volitions*.

22. While Berkeley several times asserts that minds are entirely distinct from their ideas, he *never* asserts that ideas are entirely distinct from minds. How could he? The latter is inconsistent with his idealism. This fact is connected to a controversial point of interpreta-

We should note that if this interpretation is correct, Berkeley has introduced mental substances for a purpose that has nothing directly to do with the analysis of mind. He introduces them, rather, to shore up the claim that his philosophy is not in opposition to the plain person's "vulgar" realism.[23] The upshot is astonishing: the revolutionary departure from his adversaries' general notion of substance is that Berkeley introduces *mental* substances to secure the reality of *material* things![24] Of course, from the perspective of "the modern philosophers," Berkeley's maneuver here is, far from being revolutionary, completely absurd. But Berkeley is nothing if not bold.

Yet although the problem of securing commonsense realism is almost certainly on his mind, Berkeley has another reason for introducing mental substrata—one that, in his view at least, is even more important than saving realism: the substance analysis of mind is required to placate the *theologian*-philosophers. This second answer to my first question also provides an answer to the second question: the congeries analysis must be concealed because it cannot be easily squared with theological dogma. The evidence for this is, in the nature of the case, rather thin. Nevertheless, I think it is convincing.

Return, once again, to Berkeley's notebooks. There is a "memo file" in these notebooks, and toward the end one finds the following entries:

> I must not Mention the Understanding as a faculty or part of the Mind, I must include Understanding & Will etc in the word Spirit by wch I mean all that is active. I must not say that the Understand differs not from the particular ideas, or the Will from particular Volitions. (PC 848)

---

tion: are Berkeley's ideas acts of perceptual awareness (or features of those acts), or are they objects of awareness? Winkler examines this controversy with some care in *Berkeley: An Interpretation*, pp. 291–300; I examine Winkler's argument in *Berkeley's Ontology*, pp. 229–33; and the issue comes up again in Charles J. McCracken's quarrel with Margaret Atherton (Essays 13 and 14 in this volume).

23. According to the inherence account, advanced by Edwin B. Allaire more than two decades ago in "Berkeley's Idealism," Berkeley requires a mental substance in order to vouchsafe *idealism*. For more on this, see the editor's Introduction and Essays 1 and 4 in this volume.

24. It might be urged that in Berkeley's ontology only *God* is a mental substance in anything like the traditional sense of 'substance'. I agree. Since God is required to secure the reality of bodies, however, the result is the same: mental substances are introduced to secure the reality of material things.

The Spirit, the Mind, is neither a Volition nor an Idea. (PC 849)
I must not give the Soul or Mind the Scholastique Name pure act, but rather pure Spirit or active Being. (PC 870)

In these late entries Berkeley has reached the decision that will shape his description of mind in the *Principles*. Despite all of the entries arguing against the existence of mental substances, Berkeley now reminds himself that he "must" downplay the congeries analysis (PC 848) and incorporate a substance, "the Mind" (PC 849) or an "active Being" (PC 870), into his ontology.

There is no entry in the immediate context that explains why Berkeley thinks he must do this. From a series of entries occurring just a bit earlier, however, the right explanation nearly leaps off the page: Berkeley is here reminding himself to avoid theological difficulties when he publishes the *Principles*, difficulties that are sure to follow from any explicit endorsement of the congeries analysis. At the beginning of this series (PC 713–15), Berkeley has written the following memo, similar in content to the ones above: "The Concrete of the Will & understanding I must call Mind not person, lest offence be given, there being but one volition acknowledged to be God. Mem: Carefully to omit Defining of Person, or making much mention of it" (PC 713). In the next entry (PC 714) he gives voice to his rejection of mental substrata: "You ask do these volitions make one Will. w^t you ask is meerly about a Word. Unite being no more." And this is followed immediately (PC 715) by an urgent memo: "N. B. To use utmost Caution not to give the last Handle of offence to the Church or Church-men." Berkeley describes himself as having been "distrustful at 8 years old and Consequently by nature disposed for these new Doctrines" (PC 266). Having so boldly insisted at PC 714 that we should eschew the temptation to "unite being"—that we should eschew the temptation to postulate a single item to which individual episodes of volition are connected and from which they emanate—a Berkeley with that eight-year-old's temperament might well have ignored this urgent memo. It is no "juvenile" Berkeley who writes the notebooks, however, but the mature man of twenty-two that boy became. And *this* man, the notebooks' Berkeley, is fully prepared to heed those less bold but more discretionary memoranda. Indeed, since he is himself grooming to become one of these very "Church-men," the memo at PC 715 is not only prudent, it is understandably urgent.

It seems clear, then, that Berkeley's introduction of mental substances is motivated primarily by the desire to account for personal identity in a way consistent with religious dogma. If a mind is simply a collection of mental episodes (of episodes of perception, passion, and volition), it is hard to see how this can account for the theological concept of a *soul*—a concept that seems to require an ontological ground in a continuously existing item. Berkeley says about ideas that they are "fleeting indeed, and changeable" (D 258), but if the same be said of the contents of a substanceless mind, then—notwithstanding that he can give an account of the continuance or identity of minds similar to the one he advances for bodies (at, e.g., D 247–48), that is, a relational account in which there is no item that endures or is "strictly" identical through time—he will indeed have given the "Handle of offence to the . . . Church-men"

I conclude that Berkeley makes no use of the substance analysis of mind in securing any of his central metaphysical doctrines, that the principal use to which he puts it resides in vouchsafing commonsense realism, and that the even more pressing need for it derives from extraphilosophical prudence. Berkeley speaks freely of minds as substances, despite the inconsistency between this analysis and the preferred congeries account of mind—an inconsistency so cleverly concealed—in order to avoid exposing an offensive opening to the theologians. What is most remarkable in all of this is Berkeley's mastery of the arts of deflection and camouflage. Indeed, he succeeded so exceedingly well that generations of theologians, as designed, but also generations of commentators on his philosophy, have been thoroughly misled.

6

Berkeley's Manifest Qualities Thesis

Phillip D. Cummins

B erkeley's constructive presentation of immaterialism is built around a dualism of sensibles and spirits. Sensibles are perceived; they do not perceive. Spirits perceive; they are not themselves perceived. Spirits are substances and causes; sensibles are neither substances nor causes. Nothing is both a sensible and a spirit.[1] It is worth emphasizing what Berkeleian sensibles do not do. Most thoughtful persons would have no trouble listing many examples of things they sense that they consider to perceive and act. For Berkeley, however, sensibles

This essay was the winner of the first annual Colin and Ailsa Turbayne International Berkeley Essay Prize Competition (1990). It was first published in the *Journal of the History of Philosophy* 28 (1990), pp. 385–401.

1. Berkeley's official dualism of spirits and sensibles and the implicit monism it conceals are discussed in my "Berkeley's Unstable Ontology," *Modern Schoolman* 67 (1989), pp. 15–32. The role of the manifest qualities thesis in his metaphysics is there touched upon, but not examined in detail.

neither perceive nor perform any other mental activity. Moreover, they are inactive; that is why no sensible is ever a cause. It is worth considering his arguments for these claims, since examining the key principle upon which they rest reveals much about his philosophy.

1. Senseless Inactive Sensibles

Berkeley endorses inferences from sensibles to perceivers and thinkers. However, although he employs arguments from states of sensibles to unsensed thoughts had by subjects logically distinct from those sensibles, he does not permit assigning such thoughts to the sensibles themselves. He is emphatic in claiming sensibles neither perceive nor think. Sensibles are senseless. To see why this is significant, consider an example. From watching someone fill in a crossword puzzle, one can, according to Berkeley, reasonably infer a process of thinking, but one cannot assign that thinking to the sensible whose behavior leads one to infer the thinking. To conclude from what one perceives that the item being perceived is thinking, albeit imperceptibly, is for Berkeley a fundamental error. The numerical difference between the thinker one infers and the sensible one observes must always be preserved. This claim is problematic. If a sensible's observed states can support inferences to imperceptible thoughts, why can it not be the very subject having those thoughts? If Berkeley is simply stipulating that by 'spirit' he means nonsensible perceiver, he is entitled to the conclusion that spirits cannot be sensed and sensibles cannot be spirits. One is free, however, to challenge his stipulation. Notice, too, that it would not preclude sensibles that perceive or think; such perceiving or thinking sensibles could not, by Berkeley's definition, be called spirits, but that is beside the point. Were there sensibles that perceived or thought, Berkeley's refusal to call them spirits could simply be ignored. Clearly, then, an argument is needed to establish the impossibility of perceiving or thinking sensibles and so prove that sensibles are senseless.

The materials for such an argument are found in PR 148, where Berkeley writes, "A human spirit or person is not perceived by sense, as not being an idea; when therefore we see the colour, size, figure, and motions of a man, we perceive only certain sensations or ideas excited in our own minds: and these being exhibited to our view in sundry distinct collections, serve to mark out unto us the existence of finite and created spirits like ourselves. Hence it is plain, we do not see a man, if by *man* is meant that which lives, moves, perceives and thinks as we do."[2] The argument seems to be that the person who lives, perceives, and thinks (the perceiver) cannot be identified with any sensible human body, because the latter is a collection of sensible qualities and because "when . . . we see the colour, size, figure, and motions of a man, we perceive only certain sensations or ideas excited in our own minds." No sensation or group of them, presumably, can be identified with a perceiver. The argument, with its seeming reduction of perceived human bodies to sensations or ideas, has strong idealistic overtones. The same seems to be true of Berkeley's argument for the essential inactivity of sensibles.

An important assumption in Berkeley's philosophy is that whenever there is change, there is a cause of that change. If something comes to be, there is a cause by means of which it comes to be. A second assumption is that an indispensable condition for being a cause is being active. The former assumption is implied in PR 26: "We perceive a continual succession of ideas, some are anew excited, others are changed or totally disappear. There is therefore some cause of these ideas whereon they depend, and which produces and changes them." The second assumption is at work in the preceding section, which begins: "All our ideas, sensations, or the things which we perceive, by whatsoever names they may be distinguished, are visibly inactive, there is nothing of power or agency included in them. So that one idea or object of thought cannot produce, or make any alteration in another." This passage contains the following enthymematic argument: (1) No sensibles (the things we perceive) are active. (2) All causes are active. Therefore, (3) no sensibles are causes. Further, (4) no sensibles cause any other sensibles. The phrase "visibly inactive" anticipates the proof that sensibles are inactive with which PR 25 continues: "To be satisfied of the truth of this, there is nothing else requisite but a bare observation of our ideas. For since they and every part of them exist only in the mind, it follows there is nothing in them but what is perceived. But whoever shall attend to his ideas, whether of sense or reflexion, will not perceive in them any power or activity; there is therefore no such thing contained in them." Here are two arguments, one for the conclusion that sensibles lack power or activity, the other for a key premise in the first. The former is as follows: (1) All sensibles (ideas) have

2. Berkeley contrasts perceiving a spirit with having one marked out by what we do perceive and rejects the possibility of doing the former. 'Mark out' seems to mean "provide an observational ground for an inference to what cannot itself be perceived."

in them only what they are perceived to have. (2) No sensible is perceived to be active. Therefore (3) no sensible is active. Let us call this the manifest qualities argument, or MQA, since the crucial premise (the manifest qualities thesis, or MQT) is the first premise, which I interpret as the claim that a sensible has no qualities besides those which it is perceived to have. The latter is an argument for MQT. Berkeley says of sensibles, "For since they and every part of them exist only in the mind, it follows that there is nothing in them but what is perceived." I reconstruct this as follows: (a) Whatever exists only in the mind has only those qualities it is perceived to have. (b) Sensibles and all their parts exist only in the mind. Therefore, (MQT) sensibles have only those qualities they are perceived to have. Premise a is an implied premise that links premise b ("they and every part of them exist only in the mind") to MQT ("there is nothing in them but what is perceived").[3] Let us for now ignore the argument for MQT, with its strongly idealistic overtones, and consider instead MQT's role in MQA.

Both the appeal to observation in MQA and the inference drawn from it on the basis of MQT are controversial, perhaps even contrary to common experience. If one were asked whether any of the things one perceives by sense are active, one's affirmative answer would be supported by a long list of active beings whose activities one claims to perceive. Such a list would include, besides humans, various species of animals, perhaps even plants.[4] Fires, winds, and other nonliving agents of change might also be included. The activity of such things seems to be observable. And even if this is not the case, that is, even if one could never truly perceive more than the effects of the activity of a sensible thing, just as one never perceives the actual thinking of a thinking thing, the inference from (2) *no sensible is perceived to be active* to (3) *no sensible is active* still seems arbitrary and willful. Conceding, for example, that the activity of a fox one sees to be moving is distinct from the moving and is not itself seen does not commit one to the conclusion that the moving fox is inactive. Why can

3. In an editorial note, *Works* II, 51 n. 1, T. E. Jessop says the statement "[S]ince they and every part of them exist only in the mind, it follows that there is nothing in them but what is perceived" expresses a modern axiom. To me it seems to be a controversial enthymeme whose implied major premise is that whatever exists only in the mind is only what it is perceived to be.

4. To my knowledge no one has examined in depth the status of animals in Berkeley's philosophy and, specifically, whether for him one can infer animal perceivers or thinkers from the sensible bodily states of animals, as one presumably can infer human perceivers from their sensible bodily states. Perhaps we need to take seriously the possibility that Berkeley was defending his own special version of the Cartesian "beast machine" hypothesis.

a sensible not have a quality it is not perceived to have? Why accept MQT?[5]

To better grasp the central issue, it helps to distinguish three quite different cases. Consider, first, a sensible quality, say redness, that is sometimes perceived by sight, and an object seen on some occasion that is not on that occasion seen to be red. Here the question is whether the visual object, or rather the part of it that is seen, is red even though it is not seen to be red. Second, suppose one sees but does not touch a sensible object. Could the seen object have a quality, for example heat, that cannot be perceived by sight? Finally, consider a quality that is stipulated to be inherently imperceptible. Consider, for example, thought or perception, which according to Berkeley cannot be perceived. Here the question is whether a perceived object can have a quality that is by nature imperceptible. In the first case, the claim that a visual object is not seen to have a visual quality at least seems relevant to the question whether it has or lacks that quality; in the second and third cases, however, where the issue is whether a perceived object has some quality that is in principle imperceptible (third case) or imperceptible by a specific mode of sensing (second case), it seems a non sequitur to argue from one's not perceiving a sensible to have a quality to its lacking that quality. One's failure to perceive an imperceptible quality when perceiving a sensible seems inconclusive evidence that it lacks that quality. (Imagine someone arguing that an apple has no odor because he or she looked at it and saw no odor). This is by no means a moot point, since Berkeley himself tends to portray the activity of spirits as unconditionally imperceptible. What, then, is to be made of MQA? It turns on MQT, an initially rather implausible claim, for which Berkeley does offer an argument, one that apparently employs the idealistic claim that sensibles exist only in the mind.

It would be premature to claim that the language of Berkeley's argu-

---

5. In section 2 of his *Essay Towards a New Theory of Vision* (NTV), Berkeley asserts as well established and commonly held the thesis that distance is never immediately seen (see *Works* I, 171). Subsequently he maintains without explicit argument that what is immediately seen is at no distance whatsoever from its perceiver. See NTV 41 and 45 (*Works* I, 186–88), for example. The question, why cannot a visual, an immediate object of sight, be at some distance from its perceiver even though its distance is not immediately seen? can be generalized as the following questions: First, can an object of immediate perception have a quality that is perceivable but that it is not immediately perceived to have? Second, can an object of immediate perception have an imperceptible quality? For a discussion of these questions as they pertain to distance, see my "On the Status of Visuals in Berkeley's New Theory of Vision," in *Essays on the Philosophy of George Berkeley*, ed. Ernest Sosa, (Boston: Reidel, 1987), pp. 165–94; hereafter, Sosa.

ment for MQT is sufficient to show his commitment to idealism. In the passage in which the argument is presented, Berkeley uses 'idea' instead of 'sensible' or 'sensible object'. His key claim is that since ideas and all their parts exist only in the mind, "there is nothing in them but what is perceived." One needs to consider various interpretations of 'idea' in order to see whether one can render MQT plausible without holding, in some strong idealistic sense, that sensibles exist only in the mind.[6] Berkeley attaches a variety of senses to the word 'idea' in the course of the *Principles* and *Dialogues*. Four seem especially relevant to the question whether and why a sensible cannot have unperceived qualities:[7] (1) To be an idea is to be an object of immediate perception. (2) To be an idea is to be a collection of sensible qualities or a member of such a collection. (3) To be an idea is to be something that can exist only when perceived. (4) To be an idea is to be of the same nature as a feeling or sensation of pleasure or pain. The first two are compatible with a realistic interpretation of Berkeleian sensibles, according to which they are physical objects or momentary states that collectively form physical objects. The latter two are idealistic, inasmuch as they impose a necessary connection between sensibles and perceivers. The first task is to ascertain whether MQT can be established from principles governing realistic accounts of sensibles.

2. Immediate Perception

It is not uncommon to use verbs of sensory perception—seeing, for example—in an extended or relaxed sense. Looking across a large room

6. An indirect realist might hold that material things are perceived insofar as they are represented in consciousness by effects they produce. On this view sensibles (understood as those effects) might be held to exist only in or as elements of consciousness. Idealism, as I am using the term, characterizes sensible objects as elements of consciousness, even though it might challenge the supposed causal linkage between sensibles and material objects. For the idealist, a sensible cannot exist when unperceived or outside consciousness. Two other comments: First, idealism is not to be equated with immaterialism, the denial of material substances. Second, Berkeley must hold that an idealistic account of sensibles does not presuppose indirect realism. Were it to do so, his basic principle for rejecting the existence of material substances would presuppose the existence of such substances.

7. Berkeley sometimes uses 'idea' simply to mean sensible object (sensible). That sense cannot be of relevance to the present discussion. If by 'idea' one simply means *sensible*, one can hardly argue that no sensible is a perceiver, because it is merely an idea. A similar problem holds for the argument that sensibles cannot be active. Berkeley also says he calls sensibles ideas because they are inactive and senseless; obviously, this sense presupposes the soundness of the arguments under consideration and so cannot be employed to secure it.

at reddish coals in a fireplace, one can say one sees the coals are hot without misusing 'see' or saying something false. This way of speaking provokes no intellectual discomfort even though one might concede, if challenged, that strictly speaking one feels, rather than sees, heat. 'Mediate perception' is frequently used by philosophers for cases in which we say we see, hear, or smell, respectively, what strictly is not or cannot be seen, heard, or smelled. 'Immediate perception' is correspondingly employed when seeing, hearing, feeling, smelling, and tasting are understood very strictly. Many philosophers, including Berkeley, have investigated the distinction between immediate and mediate perception. He is among the most restrictive with respect to what can be immediately perceived.[8] He writes, for example: "By a sensible object I understand that which is properly perceived by sense. Things properly perceived by sense are immediately perceived"(TVV 9). In *Three Dialogues Between Hylas and Philonous* the following agreement is reached:

HYLAS. . . . by *sensible things* I mean those only which are perceived by sense, and that in truth the senses perceive nothing which they do not perceive immediately: for they make no inferences. . . .
PHILONOUS. This point then is agreed between us, that *sensible things are those only which are immediately perceived by sense.* You will farther inform me, whether we immediately perceive by sight any thing beside light, and colours, and figures: or by hearing, any thing but sounds: by the palate, any thing beside tastes: by the smell, beside odours: or by the touch, more than tangible qualities.
HYLAS. We do not. (D 174–75)

Subsequently Philonous offers a criterion for what is immediately perceived by any given sense: "In short, those things alone are actually and strictly perceived by any sense, which would have been perceived, in case that same sense had then been first conferred on us" (D 204).

What is mediate perception, if strictly speaking, it is not perceiving? One answer: "Beside things properly and immediately perceived by any sense, there may be also other things suggested to the mind by means of those proper and immediate objects. Which things so suggested are not

8. See "The Concept of Immediate Perception in Berkeley's Immaterialism," in *Berkeley: Critical and Interpretive Essays,* ed. Colin M. Turbayne, (Minneapolis: University of Minnesota Press, 1982), pp. 48–66, in which Georges Dicker distinguishes a variety of senses of immediate and mediate perception in Berkeley's writings.

objects of that sense, being in truth only objects of the imagination, and originally belonging to some other sense or faculty" (TVV 9).[9] In the *Dialogues* Berkeley has Philonous put his position as follows: "I grant we may in one acceptation be said to perceive sensible things mediately by sense: that is, when from a frequently perceived connexion, the immediate perception of ideas of one sense suggests to the mind others perhaps belonging to another sense, which are wont to be connected with them" (D 204).[10] Since in this passage Berkeley allows a sense for 'mediate perception', so that a contrast between perception and immediate perception can be drawn, we can formulate the question to be considered as follows: Can an immediately perceived object have a quality it is not immediately perceived to have? The next step is to inquire whether Berkeley's insistence that immediate perception is infallible, so that perceptual error is restricted to mediate perception, yields a negative answer. That Berkeley did insist upon the infallibility of immediate perception is undeniable; in the *Dialogues* he writes, of one who misperceives: "His mistake lies not in what he perceives immediately and at present (it being a manifest contradiction to suppose he should err in respect of that) but in the wrong judgment he makes concerning the ideas he apprehends to be connected with those immediately perceived: or concerning the ideas that, from what he perceives at present, he imagines would be perceived in other circumstances" (D 238). It is quite clear from this and other passages that for Berkeley immediate perception is infallible in at least two ways:[11] first, if someone immediately perceives on some occasion, then an object of perception exists; second, if at some time someone immediately perceives the object of perception to have some quality, then the object has that quality at that time.

These two principles do not imply MQT; they do not, individually or

9. Berkeley errs, surely, in making the object of mediate perception always an object of another sensory mode. When I hear a series of notes and identify it as Beethoven's Fifth Symphony, both what I immediately perceive and what I mediately perceive are sounds. Correcting Berkeley on this point does not significantly alter his contrast between what is perceived and what is suggested.

10. Dicker, "The Concept of Immediate Perception," is careful to distinguish Berkeley's sense of mediate perception as involving suggestion from his sense of it as involving inference. Since my interest is in the epistemological and ontological implications of immediate perception and not in the nature and epistemological status of mediate perception, I have not here concerned myself with the genuineness or ultimacy of the further finer distinctions Dicker draws.

11. Note Philonous's claim at D 238 that when an oar in water is perceived as crooked, what is immediately perceived by sight is crooked; and compare PR 88.

conjointly, preclude an immediately perceived sensible having a quality that is not immediately perceived. Did Berkeley implicitly augment them with a third principle of immediate perception, MQT restricted to immediate perception, according to which, if some object has a quality and is immediately perceived, then its perceiver immediately perceives the object to have the quality in question?[12] The principle would have to be formulated carefully, so as to be restricted to nonrelational qualities. For example, Berkeleian sensibles are produced either by God or some other spirits. Neither spirits nor their causal activities can be perceived. Berkeley thus holds that sensibles can stand in imperceptible relations to imperceptible perceivers. Consequently, MQT must be restricted to nonrelational qualities and, if only for the sake of argument, activity, perception, and thought—the problematic qualities—must be construed as nonrelational. So understood, MQT, if defensible, would provide a warrant for Berkeley's argument that since sensibles are not perceived to be active, they are not active.[13] The real question is, On what basis could MQT for immediate perception be defended?

The goal here is to find a position that can provide a basis for MQT as a fundamental principle of immediate perception. One route to it would be to find a position on immediate perception that Berkeley explicitly holds and to show that it yields MQT. Another route would be to find an unstated position that yields MQT and is compatible with other main tenets of Berkeley's philosophy; it could then be characterized as one of his implicit assumptions. The candidate to be considered next is of the second type. It is a model for immediate perception that is thought to provide justificatory grounds for the first two principles of the infallibility of immediate perception and might be thought to validate MQT as well. It is the awareness model, or what I call the E-relation model (existence-

12. Dicker, "The Concept of Immediate Perception," pp. 49–50, in characterizing an epistemological sense of immediate perception, portrays it as infallible in the first two senses, but seems to leave open the question whether an immediately perceived object can have a quality not revealed by immediate perception. Dicker ignores there the issue of the model for immediate perception, which is the basis for its infallibility, and whether that basis establishes the infallibility of immediate perception in the third sense. Compare my "On the Status of Visuals," pp. 186–87 no. 10, and Jessop's editorial note cited in note 3 above.

13. To preserve the relevance of appeals to what we do and do not immediately perceive, we will suppose that prior to the argument neither Berkeley nor his opponents have stipulated or proven that activity is imperceptible in principle. This permits one to ask, first, is any sensible immediately perceived to be active? and second, what can validly be inferred about the activity or inactivity of an immediately perceived sensible if it is not immediately perceived to be active?

implying model) for the intentionality of sense perception.[14] Immediate perception is frequently understood to be mere awareness; its objects are said to be given. Awareness is contrasted with intentional relations, whose objects may fail to exist; unlike such relations it requires the existence of both a conscious subject and an object of awareness. In awareness, on this theory, the mind plays no productive role, so the object of awareness, considered solely as an object of awareness, is in no way determined or altered by the perceiver. It is given to consciousness, not made or conditioned by consciousness or any other faculty of the perceiver. Nothing besides the given object adds anything that could partially or fully determine what the object is immediately perceived to be. That is why what is immediately perceived exists and has the qualities it is immediately perceived to have. Construing immediate perception as E-relational awareness makes the first two principles of the infallibility of immediate perception appear self-evident.

Nevertheless, one need not ascribe the awareness model to Berkeley in order to explain his commitment to MQT, because it does not succeed in warranting that thesis. The awareness model, that is, does not guarantee that what is immediately perceived or given is given in its entirety and with all of its qualities revealed. Just because awareness adds nothing to and in no way determines or conditions its object, it need not reveal all of its object's qualities. Even though, on the awareness model, what is immediately perceived cannot fail to exist and cannot fail to be what it is perceived to be, it does not follow that it cannot be more than what it is perceived to be.[15]

3. Sensibles as Collections of Sensible Qualities

Berkeley consistently holds that a sensible object is either a sensible quality or a collection of sensible qualities. For my purposes we can ignore

14. See my "Reid's Realism," *Journal of the History of Philosophy* 12 (1974), pp. 317–40, esp. pp. 319–21.

15. In his "Berkeley and Immediate Perception," in Sosa, pp. 195–213, George Pappas convincingly argues that a phenomenalistic account of perceptual knowledge based on the distinction between immediate and mediate perception does not by itself commit one to a radical realism regarding the objects of immediate perception. That is correct. However, the conclusion I draw is that since Berkeley was committed to MQT and it cannot be established on the principles governing immediate perception, there is more to Berkeley's immaterialism than phenomenalism founded on the distinction between immediate and mediate perception.

the first alternative and concentrate on the thesis that a sensible object is only a collection of sensible qualities. On this approach it might seem natural to let the identity conditions for individual sensible objects be set by their constituent qualities. This raises the possibility that analyzing sensible objects as collections of sensible qualities can secure MQT. A given collection of qualities is numerically different from any collection including more or less or different qualities. If some object is analyzed as a collection of qualities, so that it exists only if its constituent qualities are suitably united, then it is numerically different from anything constituted by a different collection of qualities. A sensible object, that is, a thing composed of a collection of sensible qualities, would be numerically different from a thing consisting of the same sensible qualities and one or more unperceived qualities. A sensible thing thus could have an unperceived quality only by being numerically different from itself. But that is impossible. An abstract illustration may help make clear the point of this argument. Let q_1, q_2, q_3, and q_4 be numerically different sensible qualities, so that the collection $[q_1, q_2, q_3]$ is numerically different from the collection $[q_1, q_2, q_3, q_4]$. Let q_4 be an unperceived quality. If some object, X, is analyzed as the first collection, so that it exists if and only if q_1, q_2, and q_3 are suitably united, then it is numerically different from the thing consisting of the collection $[q_1, q_2, q_3,$ and $q_4]$. Therefore, X cannot have the unperceived quality, q_4. The same conclusion can be reached for any unperceived quality. On this line of argument, if sensible objects are united collections of sensible qualities, it follows that a sensible object perceived at any given time can have—while remaining itself—no additional quality and therefore no additional unperceived quality.

The thesis that a sensible object is merely a collection or combination of sensible qualities can be understood in several quite different ways. Minimally, Berkeley takes over Locke's account of sortal concepts, according to which whatever item exhibits all of the properties that collectively define a sort or kind is classified as a member of that sort or kind. Being a lion is having or instantiating a specific collection of qualities. However, Berkeley also characterizes individual sensible objects as being nothing more than collections of coexisting qualities. The doctrine relevant here is open to numerous interpretive questions. One concerns whether and how sensibles, defined as collections of qualities perceived by different senses at different times, can be objects of immediate perception. Illustrating the difficulty is this passage from the *Dialogues:* "When I hear a coach drive along the streets, immediately I perceive only the sound; but from the experience I have had that such a sound is connected with a coach, I am said to hear the coach. It is nevertheless evident, that in truth and strictness, nothing can be *heard* but *sound:* and the coach is not then properly perceived by sense, but suggested from experience" (D 204).[16] One is inclined to classify a coach as a sensible object, but what Berkeley says here, as well as his definition of sensible objects as "those only which are immediately perceived by sense," precludes that possibility. 'Sensible object', used strictly, applies only to the quality or qualities (immediately) perceived by a single sense at a single time. Of course, Berkeley commonly implies that houses, mountains, rivers, apples, and cherries are sensible objects, even though they are characterized by qualities of more than one sense, so clearly he has a looser sense as well.[17] The ground that justifies treating a group of qualities collectively as a single individual thing presumably would be lawful connections that permit one to anticipate (mediately perceive) one or more qualities of the sensible upon (immediately) perceiving others.[18] MQT receives no support if sensibles are understood in the loose sense, since, as Berkeley himself notes, one can see a red-hot iron bar without perceiving its solidity (D 204). It might seem, however, that the first, or strict, sense could be linked to MQT, it being held that no sensible in the strict sense has any quality it is not perceived to have and that the objects lawfully linked together so as to yield sensible objects in the loose sense are all sensibles in the strict sense. On this line of argument, a case can be made that no sensible is active provided it can be proven that no sensible in the strict sense is active, that is, provided one can establish MQT for sensibles in the strict sense.

Does the identity-conditions argument given above hold when restricted to sensibles in the strict sense? No. Consider a visual, V_1, an immediately seen object comprising extension, color, and shape. The

16. The coach example first appeared in print in NTV 46.

17. See PR 1, PR 4, and D 249.

18. Provided one keeps firmly in mind that it is the lawful connections that bind diverse qualities into individual things, one will see that nothing in the broad sense of sensible objects prevents their having imperceptible qualities. As noted earlier, Berkeley allows inferences from immediately perceived states of affairs to the activities of minds as well as to other qualities of the same sensible and to other sensibles and their qualities. Clearly, he owed, but did not provide, his readers a carefully worked out account of how these inferences differ. What Berkeley could consistently do was impose constraints on the qualities one could perceive (anticipate, infer) in mediate perception, making them only those which are immediately perceived at one time or another. For an account of individuals as collections of inferable qualities, the empirical generalizations that support those inferences, and the notional activity of the mind in mediate perception, see Daniel E. Flage, *Berkeley's Doctrine of Notions* (New York: St. Martin's Press, 1987), pp. 192–208.

problem with the identity-conditions argument is that it overlooks the real ground for the existence and identity of the complex sensible object. The three qualities stand in some unifying relation in virtue of which they constitute a single object of sight. V_1 (the visual) exists, not because q_1 (extension), q_2 (color), and q_3 (shape) exist, but because they exist as a single whole, that is, because they are united by some connection or relation. That being so, there seems to be no good reason why the three immediately perceived qualities that constitute V_1 cannot also be united to an unperceived fourth quality so as to constitute another thing.[19] One could, of course, stipulate that by V_1 is meant only the individual sensible object formed by the union of q_1, q_2, and q_3, so that q_4 would not be a property of V_1. That, however, would not solve the real problem. One could still speak intelligibly of a composite comprising both the three qualities that are immediately perceived and a further quality that is not. V_1 would simply be a proper part of the more complex object. To infer that there is no object V_2 consisting of V_1 and a fourth quality, because V_1 is not seen to have the fourth quality, would be a mistake unless there were some special reason the three immediately seen qualities could not have to an unseen fourth quality the thing-making or unifying relation they have to one another.

When a sensible is portrayed as a collection of sensible qualities, it becomes difficult to see the point just made. It is crucial to remember that sensibles may be defined in terms of sensible qualities either as a collection of sensible qualities *at least one of which is immediately perceived* or, instead, as a collection of qualities *all of which are immediately perceived*. The first definition does not rule out the possibility of a sensible object that includes a quality that is not immediately perceived. The second

---

19. If the connection, or relation, that by uniting a group of qualities makes them a sensible object is just coperception (being perceived simultaneously), an unperceived quality could not be part of a sensible object. However, the relation of coperception could hardly be the constitutive relation in virtue of which several qualities become a sensible object. If it were, then all qualities perceived at one time would be parts of a single sensible object. On such a view, there could be but one sensible object in one's visual field at one time, a view Berkeley surely would reject. Another point worth making is that while this position might preclude a sensible object with an unperceived quality, it does not preclude an object consisting of both unperceived and perceived qualities. The definitional illusion soon to be discussed in the main text would again need to be overcome. Of course, were Berkeley able to prove that there can be no uniting principle besides coperception for perceived qualities, then there would be a substantive ground for denying sensibles with unperceived qualities. I have benefited greatly from discussions with my colleague Richard Fumerton about the uniting relation and the constraints that could be placed on its terms.

definition does and thus gives the illusion of supporting MQT, since a sensible just is the qualities immediately perceived on some occasion. The support is illusory, however, because the second definition does not by itself preclude an object that consists of several perceived qualities combined with one or more unperceived qualities, an object collection that would differ from its sensible component only in being more complex. The second definition only stipulates that such a mixed object could not be called a sensible object. That is of no philosophical importance so long as there is no proof ruling out objects that combine perceived and unperceived qualities.

4. Sensible Qualities as Sensations

In the last two sections it has been argued that MQT cannot be generated from principles governing either of the two senses of 'idea' that are compatible with realistic accounts of sensible objects and their qualities. Consequently, we have no good reason to ignore the strongly idealistic language occurring in those passages, quoted above, in which Berkeley argues for the senselessness and inactivity of sensibles. The next task is to explicate his claim that sensibles can be nothing more than they are perceived to be because they exist "only in the mind."

Berkeley's position, I propose, is that MQT holds for sensible qualities and the objects they compose because sensible qualities, in his view, are sensations. Because they are sensations, sensible qualities are always exactly what they are perceived to be and can only combine to form objects (real wholes) with other sensible qualities. One of Berkeley's famous metaphysical principles is that the only thing like an idea is an idea; I propose that another of his implicit metaphysical principles is that the only thing that can unite with an idea to compose a sensible object is another idea. What gives plausibility to this principle is that sensible qualities are ideas in the fourth sense; that is, they are sensations. The paradigms for sensations are feelings of pleasure and pain, and two intuitions about pleasure and pain guide the interpretation. The first is that a feeling of pleasure or pain is not more, less, or other than what it is perceived to be; it has no qualities that are not felt when it is felt. The second is that the only complex objects of which such feelings can be parts are objects of consciousness. A feeling of pleasure or pain cannot unite with an unperceived entity to form a genuine whole; it and other sensations, entities of the same nature as itself, may coexist or compose a complex object, but all such complex objects are objects of consciousness; no feeling of pleasure or pain or any other sensation can unite with unperceived qualities or objects. What precludes a mixed sensible object, which combines sensed qualities with unsensed qualities, is not the unifying or collecting relation, or connection, but the nature of sensed qualities. A complex thing including a sensation cannot include a nonsensation. My suggestion, then, is that when Berkeley asserts MQT in PR 25, saying of ideas of sense, that "since they and every part of them exist only in the mind, it follows there is nothing in them but what is perceived," his confident pronouncement is founded on his implicit characterization of sensible objects as sensations that exist only in consciousness. And, I submit, when in PR 87 he explicitly links MQT to sensations, saying that "colour, figure, motion, extension and the like, considered only as so many *sensations* in the mind, are perfectly known, there being nothing in them which is not perceived," the model for what a sensation is, is a feeling of pleasure or pain.

There is substantial evidence that Berkeley characterizes sensibles as sensations understood on the model of feelings of pleasure and pain. The first intimations of this characterization can be found early in both the *Principles* and *Three Dialogues*. In the *Principles*, after introducing the term 'idea' in PR 1 and contrasting ideas to perceivers in PR 2, Berkeley without explanation begins using the expressions "sensations or ideas" and "ideas or sensations" where one would anticipate merely "idea." His "or" in such contexts is the 'or' of reformulation; the two terms put in apposition are considered to be equivalent.[20] By PR 5 he is employing 'sensation' unaccompanied, as in this passage: "Hence as it is impossible for me to see or feel anything without an actual sensation of that thing, so is it impossible for me to conceive in my thoughts any sensible thing or object distinct from the sensation or perception of it." Berkeley indicates that he regards 'idea' and 'sensation' to be more or less interchangeable in the contexts in which he is most concerned with stating and defending immaterialism: "The things, I say, immediately perceived, are ideas or sensations, call them which you will" (D 215). In the *Three Dialogues*, there is evidence not only that sensible qualities are called sensations but also that sensations are understood in terms of feelings of pleasure and

---

20. The 'or' of reformulation is explained and illustrated in Randolph Quirk and Sidney Greenbaum, *A Concise Grammar of Contemporary English* (San Diego: Harcourt Brace Jovanovich, 1973), pp. 278–81.

pain. At the beginning of the *Dialogues* Berkeley argues that sensible qualities of various kinds cannot exist unperceived. For some qualities his main argument for this thesis is that they cannot be distinguished from feelings of pleasure and pain. Moreover, when Hylas attempts to secure a distinction between the object sensed and the sensation, Berkeley concludes his denial of the distinction with an explicit modeling of the status of other sensible qualities on the status of pain. He has Philonous assert: "Besides, since you distinguish the *active* and *passive* in every perception, you must do it in that of pain. But how is it possible that pain, be it as little active as you please, should exist in an unperceiving substance? In short, do but consider the point, and then confess ingenuously, whether light and colours, tastes, sounds, etc. are not all equally passions or sensations in the soul" (D 197). In short, there is abundant evidence that Berkeley understood sensible qualities as sensations.[21]

An important advantage of the sensation interpretation of sensible qualities is that it immediately secures *esse est percipi*. There are innumerable passages in which Berkeley asserts that neither sensible objects nor sensible qualities can exist unperceived, that is, that sensibles are ideas in the third sense. If sensible qualities are understood as on a par with feelings of pleasure and pain, one can understand why Berkeley took his principle to be virtually self-evident. Many philosophers insist it is a necessary truth that pleasure and pain cannot exist unsensed.[22] Thus, the interpretation that warrants using 'idea' in the fourth sense for sensible objects and qualities also warrants using it in the third sense.

My interpretation is that Berkeley secures MQT by holding that the nature of sensible qualities precludes their combining with unperceived qualities. Their nature prevents their standing in the required relation. One can find at least one other case in which the nature of sensibles is said

21. For additional evidence that Berkeleian sensible qualities are best interpreted as sensations, see my "Berkeley's Ideas of Sense," *Nous* 9 (1975), pp. 55–72.

22. For example, John W. Cook, in "Hume's Scepticism with Regard to the Senses," *American Philosophical Quarterly* 5 (1968), pp. 1–17, writes (p. 3): "What I have suggested is that it would be so patently senseless to suppose that a pain might continue to exist unfelt that no philosopher could think that this is a contingent matter." Cook quotes on this point Thomas Reid, who, in his *Essays on the Intellectual Powers of Man* (Cambridge: MIT Press, 1969), asserts (p. 27): "Pain, when it is not felt, has no existence. It can be neither greater nor less in degree or duration, nor any thing else in kind, than it is felt to be. It cannot exist by itself, nor in any subject, but a sentient being. No quality of an inanimate insentient being can have the least resemblance to it." There are philosophers, however, who do consider unfelt pains a genuine possibility. Hume and G. E. Moore come to mind.

to block their standing in a relation to another entity. In PR 7 Berkeley offers an argument that spirits alone are substances:

> From what has been said, it follows, there is not any other substance than *spirit*, or that which perceives. But for the fuller proof of this point, let it be considered, the sensible qualities are colour, figure, motion, smell, taste, and such like, that is, the ideas perceived by sense. Now for an idea to exist in an unperceiving thing, is a manifest contradiction; for to have an idea is all one as to perceive: that therefore wherein colour, figure, and the like qualities exist, must perceive them; hence it is clear there can be no unthinking substance or *substratum* of those ideas.[23]

Note that the crucial claim is not that the sensible qualities cannot exist unperceived; it is that they cannot exist in an unperceiving thing. Berkeley uses it to block the possibility that sensible qualities, even though they must be perceived to exist, exist as qualities *of* an unperceiving and unperceived substance. Despite his introductory comment linking his denial of substances other than spirits to what has gone before, Berkeley did not earlier explicitly lay the foundation for this argument. Before PR 7 he emphasized that sensible objects cannot exist unperceived; only here does he insist that they cannot exist in an unperceiving thing. The argument is that to *have* a sensible quality (an idea) just is to perceive it, which an unperceiving substance cannot do. Consequently, to propose that an unperceiving substance has a sensible quality or a combination of them is to propose an implicit contradiction. (The argument is analogous to Berkeley's argument that for a sensible to exist is for it to be perceived, so that to propose a sensible existing unperceived is to propose an implicit contradiction.) The crucial question is why having a sensible quality must be understood as perceiving it. Since Berkeley emphasizes that the qualities he specifies are ideas, the answer would seem to be that sensible

---

23. This argument obviously is not strong enough to prove that minds (spirits) are the only substances. For one thing, it does not prove that sensibles are not substances; at best it establishes that there cannot be nonperceiving substances in which sensibles exist. For another, it does not prove there are no nonperceiving nonsensible substances that produce or resemble sensibles. Finally, it does not preclude the possibility of nonsensible nonperceiving substances that have absolutely no relation to sensibles. Berkeley's subsequent arguments focus on the second of these alternatives. His earlier characterization of sensibles and their qualities was meant, I think, to rule out the first. The third alternative is not explicitly examined in the *Principles*.

qualities are ideas in some sense that restricts having an idea to perceiving it. If sensible qualities are understood to be sensations, the argument has some force, since having a sensation of pain and feeling pain seem to be one and the same. Here, then, is an argument that sensible qualities cannot stand in a relation (being had by an unperceiving thing), an argument that turns on what they are and that gains plausibility is sensible qualities are interpreted as sensations on a par with feelings of pleasure and pain. Given this, it is plausible that Berkeley might argue for MQT on the ground that sensible qualities are merely sensations.[24]

It remains to be shown that merely holding sensible objects to be ideas in the third sense of 'idea' is insufficient to secure MQT. The reason is the same as that which defeated the identity-conditions argument considered above in section 3. For the sake of discussion, assume that sensible qualities and objects are characterized as ideas because they are held to be incapable of existing unperceived. Assume, further, that the dependence of a sensible quality on perception is necessary. The following specious argument against the activity of sensibles can be built around this idealistic principle: Sensibles are collections of sensible qualities. Sensible qualities are immediately perceived. Sensible qualities cannot exist unperceived. If sensible qualities cannot exist unperceived, then sensible objects cannot have qualities they are not immediately perceived to have. Activity is not a quality a sensible object is immediately perceived to have. Therefore, sensibles are inactive. The considerations that deflated the identity-conditions argument equally deflate this one. Given that two or more sensible qualities become a sensible object in virtue of a thing-making relation that collects or connects them, securing MQT requires eliminating the possibility of a sensible (a group of immediately perceived qualities) that is part of a more complex object (one that includes both

24. There is a radical version of idealism that can also generate both the argument of PR 7 and MQT. It involves two principles: first, every quality or combination of qualities must inhere in a substance; second, *being perceived* just is inhering in a substance. This is idealism because the thesis that sensible qualities and objects cannot exist unperceived is a consequence of the two principles. The argument of PR 7 would be that assuming a sensible quality inhering in an unperceiving substance is a contradiction because *inhering in* just is being perceived and no unperceiving substance could perceive. The argument for MQT would be that for a sensible object to have an unperceived quality would be for one or more sensed qualities to form a combination with one or more unsensed qualities. An unsensed quality, however, is impossible. Every quality must inhere in a substance, and inhering in is being perceived. One problem with this approach is that there seems to be no reason for accepting the second principle unless one already accepts the mind-dependence of sensible qualities. It assumes, not yields, idealism.

perceived and unperceived or imperceptible qualities). The idealistic principle that sensible qualities cannot exist unperceived does not preclude this alternative. It would be odd, perhaps, but not inconsistent, to hold that sensible qualities cannot exist unsensed yet also hold that they combine with imperceptible qualities to form things, some parts or qualities of which can, and other parts or qualities of which cannot, exist unperceived. The idealistic principle—sensible qualities cannot exist unperceived—does not as such imply MQT. The argument given above fails because there is no reason to accept its crucial premise, that if sensible qualities cannot exist unperceived, then MQT is true.

The sensation interpretation of sensible qualities has it that the nature of sensible qualities determines the principles that can be truly asserted of them. According to it, because sensible qualities are sensations on a par with feelings of pleasure and pain, neither they nor any combination of them can exist unperceived, exist in an unperceiving thing, be other than they appear to be, or combine with unsensed qualities to form objects that are not wholly perceived. According to it, the inactivity and senselessness of sensibles can be established because they are not perceived to perceive, think, or be active and because (MQT) they have only those qualities that they are perceived to have. The manifest qualities thesis is warranted for Berkeley not because sensibles are immediately perceived, are collections of sensible qualities, or cannot exist unperceived, but because sensibles are sensations, that is, because they are the kind of things they are.

There is consensus that essential to Berkeley's metaphysics is his immaterialism, his rejection of material substance. Whether his immaterialism rests upon idealistic principles is a central interpretive issue, perhaps the most important interpretive issue. In this essay I have argued that Berkeley insisted that sensibles do not perceive, think, or act, and relied on the manifest qualities thesis to secure that conclusion. I have also argued that principles compatible with a nonidealistic interpretation of Berkeleian sensibles are insufficient to secure MQT, whereas at least one idealistic interpretation of sensibles, the sensation theory, does provide a foundation for it. This essay, therefore, is an argument that Berkeley's immaterialism is inherently idealistic.

7

Berkeleian Idealism and Impossible Performances

George Pappas

Berkeleian idealism minimally consists of three theses that, on the face of it, are independent of one another, namely: (1) each perceiving entity, whether finite or infinite, is a spirit; (2) each perceived entity, whether simple or complex, exists if and only if (or perhaps when and only when) it is perceived; and (3) everything that exists is particular—that is, there are no universals *in re* or in the mind of any perceiver or anywhere else. Perhaps, under a certain interpretation, Berkeley took the nominalist thesis expressed in (3) to entail or at least strongly to support (2). I touch on that possibility, albeit briefly, below. My primary concern in this essay is with thesis 2.

Scholarly attention regarding thesis 2, the *esse est percipi* thesis, has been considerable, but I think we may safely say that three primary questions have been addressed. First, how shall we interpret the thesis? Berkeley's actual texts support more than one reading, and the differences between readings are not trivial. Second, is the thesis supposed to be some sort of necessary truth? Most commentators have thought the answer to this question is yes, and this not without reason, for Berkeley writes as if he so regarded the thesis. Third, what exactly are the arguments Berkeley proposes in behalf of the thesis? There have been almost as many answers to this last question as there have been writers on the subject. In this essay I do not break with this grand tradition; I propose a new account of what I think is afoot with Berkeley's central argument for the *esse est percipi* thesis. The account to be given has certain affinities with the performative account of Descartes' cogito that Hintikka has discussed,[1] so I call the account to be provided here the performance analysis of Berkeley's master argument for *esse est percipi*. The roots of the present account, though, are not in Hintikka but rather in an interpretation once presented by Marc-Wogau.[2]

Thesis 2, What?

Thesis 2 speaks of perceived entities, and for Berkeley, one might say, all perceived entities are ideas. So a natural reading of thesis 2 would be this:

A. Each idea exists if and only if it is perceived.

Of course, if A is true, then any idea cluster is also an entity that exists if and only if it is perceived, since every idea in every idea cluster is perceived, given A, and surely a sufficient condition for perceiving a cluster of entities is that one perceive every element in the cluster. Thus, A readily gives way to a more specific claim:

B. Each idea and each idea cluster exists if and only if it is perceived.

Statement A, and by implication B, are suggested by various passages in the *Principles*. For example, Berkeley tells us that a spirit or mind is not "any one of my ideas, but a thing entirely distinct from them, wherein they

1. Jaakko Hintikka, "Cogito, Ergo Sum: Inference or Performance?" in *Descartes*, ed. Willis Doney (New York: Doubleday, 1967).
2. K. Marc-Wogau, "Berkeley's Sensationalism and the *Esse Est Percipi* Principle," in *Locke and Berkeley*, ed. C. Martin and D. Armstrong (New York: Doubleday, 1968).

exist, or, which is the same thing, whereby they are perceived, for the existence of an idea consists in being perceived" (PR 2). Related comments occur at many other places in the *Principles* (e.g., see PR 7, 45, 48) making it seem that *A* and thus *B* are natural readings of the text.

However, there are reasons to resist taking *A* or *B* as the meaning of thesis 2. One is that from the *Three Dialogues* especially, but also from places in the *Principles*, it is clear that Berkeley is talking about what he calls sensible qualities and sensible objects, that is, perceivable qualities such as colors, sounds, and shapes, and ordinary macro-objects such as trees and tables. In the second of the *Three Dialogues*, Philonous, speaking for Berkeley, says, "To me it is evident, for the reasons you [Hylas] allow of, that sensible things cannot exist otherwise than in a mind or spirit" (D 212). Throughout this book Berkeley uses the term 'sensible thing' variably, to denote either sensible qualities or sensible objects or both; and existing in a mind is, for Berkeley, the same thing as being perceived by a mind. Or, consider this passage: "Some truths there are so near and obvious to the mind that a man need only open his eyes to see them. Such I take this important one to be, to wit, that all the choir of heaven and furniture of the earth which compose this mighty frame of the world, have not any subsistence without a mind, that there being is to be perceived or known" (PR 6). These passages, and others like them, indicate that neither *A* nor *B* is an accurate reading of thesis 2.

Quite independent of the texts, another reason for rejecting *A* and *B* is, to put it paradoxically, that each is so *obviously* true. Of course the *esse* of an *idea* is *percipi*. Such a claim would have been regarded as true, merely in virtue of the meanings of the constituent terms, by nearly every philosopher in Berkeley's period, including all those Berkeley cites as materialists. No one would have found such a claim disputable or controversial. Yet Berkeley took himself to be making an important discovery in coming on the truth of thesis 2; and we know that thesis 2 was and ever has been controversial at best.

Let us think of a sensible-quality cluster either as any group of two or more sensible qualities that happen to be perceived simultaneously, typically by means of the same sense modality, such as two different colors adjoining one another, or as two or more sensible qualities that are linked together whether or not simultaneously perceived, such as the particular shape and color of some object. Then we may formulate thesis 2 more accurately as

> *C.* Each sensible quality, sensible-quality cluster, and sensible object is an entity that exists if and only if it is perceived.

Notice that *C* is far from truistic; unlike *A* and *B*, it is debatable at best. Indeed, on the face of it, *C* seems clearly false. So, for this very reason, *C* is better suited to serve as expressing the thesis Berkeley thought he was discovering, the "simple though amazing truth" that each nonperceiving entity exists if and only if it is perceived.

Statement *C* makes no mention of possible perception; instead, the *esse* of each sensible thing is reckoned as actually being perceived. There are passages, however, where Berkeley speaks of possible or hypothetical perception, for instance, in the *Philosophical Commentaries*, where he says:

> Existence is percipi or percipere (or velle i.e. agere) the horse is in the stable, the Books are in the study as before. (PC 429, 429a)

> Bodies taken for powers do exist w^n not perceiv'd but this existence is not actual. W^n I say a power exists no more is meant than that if in ye light I open my eyes & look that way I shall see it i.e. ye body &c. (PC 293a)

Passages such as these suggest that *C*, too, is in need of amendment, so that what follows the biconditional is a disjunction, giving us

> *D.* Each sensible quality, sensible-quality cluster, and sensible object is an entity that exists if and only if either it is perceived or it would be perceived if such-and-such conditions were to obtain.

The expression 'such-and-such conditions', of course, denotes various things, for example, someone's looking in a certain direction or auditorially attending at a certain time.

Although *D* does comport with some texts, I doubt if it is Berkeley's considered view. The reason has to do with God and God's perceptions. Berkeley holds that all sensible qualities not being perceived by some finite perceiver are nonetheless at all times perceived by God. For example, Philonous says, "[I]s there therefore no difference between saying, *there is a God, therefore he perceives all things:* and saying, *sensible things do really exist: and if they really exist they are necessarily perceived by an infinite mind: therefore there is an infinite mind, or God"*

(D 212; emphasis in original). Here the first view expressed is what some of Berkeley's opponents are supposed to hold, whereas the second is Berkeley's own. In fact, here Berkeley endorses the stronger thesis that every sensible thing not perceived by God at all times it exists; a fortiori, each existing sensible thing perceived by a finite being is still perceived by God.

We should, then, side with C rather than D as expressive of the import of thesis 2. Passages in which D seems indicated are relatively few and mostly in the early *Philosophical Commentaries* entries; references to God and his perceptions are many and spread through the mature works. Moreover, we know on independent grounds that the existence and perceptual activity of God is of critical importance in Berkeley's philosophy; so his insistence that God perceives all sensible things at all times, something Berkeley repeats several times, is also apt to be a matter he took to be of central significance.[3]

Semantic Status of C

Thesis 2, here taken as given by C, is usually reckoned a necessary truth, at least as Berkeley saw the matter, for Berkeley almost says as much. For example, he seemingly tells us that the denial of C is a contradiction. He writes, "[T]o what purpose is it to dilate on that which may be demonstrated with the utmost evidence in a line or two, to anyone that is capable of the least reflection? It is but looking into your own thoughts, and so trying whether you can conceive it possible for a sound, or figure, or motion, or color, to exist without the mind, or unperceived. This essay trial may make you see, that what you contend for is a downright contradiction" (PR 22). In the *Dialogues* the sentiment is repeated: "[I]t is absolutely impossible, and a plain contradiction to suppose any unthinking being should exist without being perceived by a mind" (D 244). Elsewhere Berkeley speaks not of contradictions but rather of repugnancies, but his point seems to be the same. He says: "But why should we trouble ourselves any farther, in discussing this material *substratum* or support of figure and motion, and other sensible qualities? Does it not suppose they have an existence without the mind? And is not

3. The contention made here that Berkeley himself held that God is a perceiver is, of course, perfectly consistent with the claim made by some commentators to the effect that Berkeley's God is not really a perceiver.

this a direct repugnancy, and altogether inconceivable?" (PR 17; emphasis in original). Other passages are not so clear. There are places where Berkeley seems to hedge a bit and to maintain that the denial of C is *either* a contradiction *or* meaningless. Consider PR 24, which I here quote in full.

> It is very obvious, upon the least inquiry into our own thoughts, to know whether it be possible for us to understand what is meant, by the *absolute existence of sensible objects in themselves, or without the mind*. To me it is evident those words mark out either a direct contradiction, or else nothing at all. And to convince others of this, I know no readier or fairer way, than to entreat they would calmly attend to their own thoughts: and if by this attention, the emptiness or repugnancy of those expressions does appear, surely nothing more is requisite for their conviction. It is on this therefore that I insist, to wit, that the absolute existence of unthinking things are words without a meaning, or which include a contradiction. This is what I repeat and inculcate, and earnestly recommend to the attentive thoughts of the reader. (emphasis in original)

This passage, it should be noted, comes immediately after Berkeley has presented his most well-known and notorious argument for C. This is the so-called master argument, to be discussed below, in which Berkeley argues that no one can conceive a sensible object existing unperceived, so that no such object exists unperceived. In other words, he is summing up what he thinks he has established by the argument of the preceding section. This, it seems to me, is some evidence that Berkeley is at least not sure that the denial of C is a contradiction, and it also goes some way toward showing that it is an open question whether Berkeley regarded thesis 2 as a necessary truth.

The foregoing passage is not the only place where Berkeley treats the denial of C as meaningless. In considering and responding to an objection to C he makes the same point, claiming that a person who finds that he cannot conceive a sensible thing existing unperceived "will acknowledge it is unreasonable for him to stand up in defence of he knows not what, and pretend to charge on me as an absurdity, the not assenting to those propositions which at bottom have no meaning in them" (PR 45). It is true that Berkeley sometimes says that the denial of C is impossible, that is, that the existence of an unperceived sensible thing is an impossibility. However, lest we think that he thereby took C to be a necessary truth, we should note how Berkeley talks about the impossibility of matter.

At the end of the second dialogue Berkeley has Philonous acknowledge that the impossibility of matter's existence is not based on its being somehow contradictory. Philonous continues:

> Now in that which you call the obscure indefinite sense of the word *matter*, it is plain, by your own confession, there was included no idea at all, no sense except an unknown sense, which is the same as none. You are not therefore to expect that I should prove a repugnancy between ideas where there are no ideas; or the impossibility of Matter taken in an *unknown* sense, that is no sense at all. My business was only to show, you meant *nothing*; and this you were brought to own. So that in all your various senses, you have been shown either to mean nothing at all, or if anything, an absurdity. And if this be not sufficient to prove the impossibility of a thing, I desire you will let me know what is. (D 225–26; emphasis in original)

As this passage makes clear, Berkeley is prepared to infer the impossibility of a sensible thing's existing unperceived from the fact that the denial of C is meaningless or empty. However, such an impossibility would not be any sort of logical or conceptual impossibility. For the meaninglessness in question would derive not from the demonstrated repugnancy between ideas but rather from the fact that there is no idea of an existing unperceived sensible thing.

Of course, the last-quoted passage speaks of matter, and not of unperceived sensible things. But I assume that Berkeley would draw the same inference regarding the latter as with the former provided the same point about meaninglessness holds.

Even if the lack of meaning is the correct way to construe the denial of C for Berkeley, one might wonder how that fact can be used in support of C. After all, as we recall from discussions of the verifiability theory of meaning a few decades ago, if a proposition is meaningless, then so is its denial. Thus, C would be meaningless provided that its denial was— hardly a comforting result for Berkeley. I return to this question later, following a discussion of Berkeley's arguments for C. For now I take it that some evidence has been provided for the claim that C is not, for Berkeley, a necessary truth if the denial of any necessary truth is or implies a contradiction.

The Arguments for C

I believe that Berkeley has three distinct arguments in behalf of thesis 2, or C. The first is presented in a capsule and unsatisfactory way in the first dozen sections of the *Principles* and is repeated in a more satisfactory way in the *Three Dialogues*. The two points that drive the argument are (1) that each sensible quality is an idea and (2) that each physical object is a collection of sensible qualities. From these a species of phenomenalism follows, namely, that each sensible object is a collection of ideas. Then, from the truism that no idea exists when not perceived, it is supposed to follow that no sensible thing or physical object exists when not perceived, nor does any sensible quality so exist. By reasoning given earlier, it would also follow that no sensible-quality cluster exists when not perceived, so that C would be established.

The claim that each sensible object is a collection of sensible qualities is defended on the grounds that there is no material substance in which such qualities might inhere. The *Principles* version of the argument is not satisfactory, because its first premise (that each sensible quality is an idea) is not at all argued for, but instead is assumed from the very start. That premise, surely, is no truism, yet Berkeley opens the *Principles* by baldly asserting it without justification. He must have realized that this was a serious problem, for he devotes the bulk of the first dialogue to an elaborate argument for this very premise. There he uses a variety of perceptual relativity and other arguments to show of each sort of sensible quality (sound, taste, color, figure, motion, and so on) that it is an idea.

There is much of interest in this argument, and a great deal can be said about its various elements. I will limit myself to a few observations. First, neither of its main premises, those that I say drive the argument, is a necessary truth. Moreover, very little that is essential to the arguments for those respective premises qualifies as a necessary truth. Consider the relativity arguments used in support of the first premise, that every sensible quality is an idea. Premises to the effect that objects appear different under different conditions are contingently true, if true at all. Or consider the case for the second premise, that each sensible object is a collection of sensible qualities. This is defended partly on the grounds that there are no material substances, and I showed earlier that when Berkeley claims that such entities are impossible, he means only that the concept of matter is meaningless, not that it is contradictory. These considerations strongly indicate that even if sound, this first argument does not establish the necessity of *C*. Thus, we should not construe Berkeley as committed to the necessity of *C*, or thesis 2, on the basis of this argument.[4]

Another often overlooked argument for *C* depends on the rejection of abstract ideas. Specifically, there is some evidence that Berkeley accepted the claim that if there are no abstract general ideas, then the *esse est percipi* thesis is true. We know that in the introduction to the *Principles* Berkeley attacks the claim that such ideas exist; this is couched in the form of an attack on some doctrines attributed to Locke. Thus, we would have the following simple argument (the no-abstraction argument):

(1) If there are no abstract general ideas, then the *esse est percipi* thesis [i.e., thesis 2 in the form of *C*] is true.
(2) There are no abstract general ideas.
(3) Hence, the *esse est percipi* thesis is true.

Whether Berkeley actually presents this argument, as I think, depends on whether he actually asserts or otherwise endorses its first premise. I have presented evidence for this claim elsewhere, and so will not rehearse it here.[5] In some ways more interesting is how Berkeley did (or could) defend this premise. I believe the arguments for it rest on comments Berkeley makes about conceivability, especially this: "[C]an there be a nicer strain of abstraction than to distinguish the existence of sensible objects from their being perceived, so as to conceive them existing unperceived?" (PR 5). One point made in this passage seems to be this:

(1a) One can conceive a sensible object existing unperceived only if one can conceive an abstract idea.

But we also know from the master argument (to be discussed below) that Berkeley accepts the claim that

4. It is true that Berkeley sometimes speaks of the concept of matter as being inconsistent, or as including or involving a direct contradiction. Although I cannot argue for it here, my view of these passages is that in all cases Berkeley is referring to a contradiction between the supposition of matter and the truth of the *esse est percipi* thesis. If I am right, then, Berkeley is hardly in a position to use the alleged inconsistency in the concept of matter in an argument for *C*.

5. See my "Abstract Ideas and the '*Esse* Is *Percipi*' Thesis," *Hermathena* 139 (Winter 1985), pp. 47–62. For related discussion, see Margaret Atherton, "Berkeley's Anti-Abstractionism," and Martha Bolton, "Berkeley's Objection to Abstract Ideas and Unconceived Objects," both in *Essays on the Philosophy of George Berkeley*, ed. Ernest Sosa (Dordrecht: Reidel, 1987).

(1b) if one cannot conceive a sensible object existing unperceived, then the *esse est percipi* thesis (= *C*) is true.

It is clear that

(1c) if there are no abstract ideas, then one cannot conceive of an abstract idea.

Given what I here refer to as a *de re* reading of the term 'conceives', these three statements imply the first premise of the no-abstraction argument. And it is clear that a *de re* reading is appropriate, since Berkeley speaks always of conceiving actual objects unperceived, not of conceiving that some sensible object in fact exists unperceived.

De re conception of the sort I have in mind can be clarified by contrasting it with *de re* belief. In the latter case, we say that a person believes of some entity E that it is F (has the property F). Thus, John may believe of the man on the corner that he is a spy. We could have a perfectly analogous notion of *de re* conception. John may conceive of the differential equation vexing him at the moment that it is of type T. And this notion of *de re* conception would be, perhaps, the normal way of thinking of the matter, on a par with *de re* belief. But it is not what Berkeley makes use of, because for him there is no predication included within the *de re* conceiving. Instead, one conceives the thing itself. The analogy would be with non-propositional direct perception of an object, as when we say, "John perceives O." In such a case, the perceptual verb takes a grammatical direct object as complement. The same holds for the sort of *de re* conceiving made use of by Berkeley. Let us call this nonpropositional *de re* conception *pure*: whatever is the character of one's mental state when one conceives a cup-on-a-table, rather than conceiving *that* there is a cup on a table, or when one conceives a white cup, rather than conceiving that a cup is white.

There is, then, Berkeleian support for the first premise of the no-abstraction argument. And there is certainly support for the second premise as well. I will not review here the arguments against abstract ideas in the introduction to the *Principles* except to say that Berkeley distinguishes different kinds of abstract ideas, and only some of them are held to be entities whose existence would be logically impossible. In particular, the sort of abstract idea relevant to the truth of premise 1 is the abstract idea of existence; it is this sort of idea that is relevant, moreover, to the truth of (1a). It is, thus, the sort of abstract idea Berkeley must minimally reject in premise 2 of the no-abstraction argument. However, although Berkeley finds such an abstract idea the most incomprehensible of all abstract ideas (PR 81), he presents no argument to show that such an idea cannot exist. So, again, the no-abstraction argument would not commit Berkeley to the conclusion that C, the *esse est percipi* thesis, is a necessary truth.

The third argument Berkeley presents for C is the so-called master argument of PR 22–23 and the first dialogue. This argument, too, makes important use of the notion of conceivability. Berkeley is willing to allow that if one *can* conceive a sensible object existing unperceived, then the *esse est percipi* thesis, or C, is false. He notes that this sort of conception cannot be achieved or carried out, and so he concludes that the *esse est percipi* thesis is true. Here is the *Principles* version of the argument:

> I am content to put the whole upon this issue; if you can but conceive it possible for one extended movable substance, or in general, for any one idea or anything like an idea, to exist otherwise than in a mind perceiving it, I shall readily give up the cause: And as for all that *compages* of external bodies which you contend for, I shall grant you its existence, though you cannot give me any reason why you believe it exists, or assign any use to it when it is supposed to exist. I say the bare possibility of your opinion's being true, shall pass for an argument that it is so. (PR 22)

This passage sets up a part of the argument; it is continued in the next section.

> But say you, surely there is nothing easier than to imagine trees, for instance, in a park, or books existing in a closet, and no body by to perceive them. I answer, you may so, there is no difficulty in it: but what is all this, I beseech you, more than framing in your mind certain ideas which you call *books* and *trees*, and at the same time omitting to frame the idea of anyone that may perceive them? But do not you your self perceive or think of them all the while? This therefore is nothing to the purpose: it only shows you have the power of imagining or forming ideas in your mind; but it doth not shew you can conceive it possible, the objects of your thought may exist without the mind: to make out this, it is necessary that you conceive them existing unconceived or unthought of, which is a manifest repugnancy. When we do our utmost to conceive the

existence of external bodies, we are all the while only contemplating our own ideas. But the mind taking no notice of itself, is deluded to think it can and does conceive bodies existing unthought of or without the mind; though at the same time they are apprehended by or exist in it self. (PR 23)

In the first of these passages, Berkeley speaks of conceiving a possibility: conceiving the possibility of a sensible object existing unperceived. If one can do this conceiving, he tells us, he will grant the falsity of the *esse est percipi* thesis. But, he says in the second passage, we cannot do this conceiving, because to accomplish it we would have to conceive an unperceived but existing sensible object, and this is a manifest repugnancy. We can represent what he is saying in a simple argument:

Master Argument, First Version

(1) If one can conceive the possibility of a sensible object existing unperceived, then the *esse est percipi* thesis is false.
(2) One can conceive the possibility of a sensible object existing unperceived only if one can conceive a sensible object existing unperceived.
(3) But one cannot conceive a sensible object existing unperceived.
(4) Hence, one cannot conceive the possibility of a sensible object existing unperceived.

Notice that one cannot pass directly from (4) to an affirmation of the *esse est percipi* thesis, since doing so commits an elementary blunder: (4) is the denial of the antecedent of premise 1. However, the argument can be continued if Berkeley accepts the principle that what is inconceivable is impossible, as it seems he does.[6] Thus:

(5) If something is inconceivable, then it is impossible.
(6) Hence, a sensible object existing unperceived is impossible (from 1, 4, and 5).

---

6. Kenneth P. Winkler says, "One of Berkeley's most deeply held beliefs is that conceivability and possibility coincide: a state of affairs is conceivable, he thinks, if and only if it is possible." See George Berkeley, *A Treatise Concerning the Principles of Human Knowledge*, ed. Winkler (Indianapolis: Hackett Publishing Co., 1982), p. xvi. If Winkler is right, then Berkeley also accepts that if a state of affairs is inconceivable, then it is impossible, for this is implied by the principle Winkler cites.

From (6) it follows that it is not possible that a sensible object exists unperceived, in which case the *esse est percipi* thesis comes out as a necessary truth.

In this version of the master argument we construe Berkeley as seeking a certain *de dicto* conception, reflected in the antecedent of premise 1, and claiming that a necessary condition for attaining this conception is that one achieve or be able to achieve a certain *pure de re* conception, noted in the consequent of premise 2, in which one conceives the sensible object itself. There is, however, another reading of those passages, one in which the apparent *de dicto* conception—conceiving the possibility of a sensible object existing unperceived—just *is*, for Berkeley, the sort of *pure de re* conception here described. The rationale for this reading is straightforward: PR 22, containing the apparent *de dicto* notion, in effect lays down a challenge, to which section 23 is a response. The very thing one is challenged to do in PR 22 is claimed capable of accomplishment in PR 23. This suggests that Berkeley does not have in mind two different sorts of conception but just one, namely, *pure de re* conception. Exactly the same challenge pattern occurs in the *Dialogues:*

PHILONOUS. . . . I am content to put the whole upon this issue. If you can conceive it possible for any mixture or combination of qualities, or any sensible object whatever, to exist without the mind, then I will grant it actually to be so.

HYLAS. If it comes to that, the point will soon be decided. What more easy than to conceive a tree or house existing by itself, independent of, and unperceived by, any mind whatsoever? I do at this present time conceive them existing after that manner. (D 200)

The master argument suggested by this second reading of the relevant passages is considerably simpler:

Master Argument, Second Version

(1) If one cannot conceive a sensible object existing unperceived, then the *esse est percipi* thesis (=C) is true.
(2) One cannot conceive a sensible object existing unperceived.
(3) Thus, the *esse est percipi* thesis, or C, is true.

Of these two readings, and two resulting arguments, I believe the second is the more plausible as an interpretation of what Berkeley wants. I do not have conclusive evidence militating in favor of this reading, but still there is some. It emerges later, after the second version of the master argument has been investigated more fully.

De Re Conceivability

Why can one not conceive a sensible object existing unperceived, as alleged in premise 2? We know Berkeley's answer: when one tries to accomplish this feat, one is *eo ipso* conceiving that very object. The natural response is that this makes no difference; the object still exists *unperceived* despite the fact that someone *conceives* it. Berkeley is usually represented as responding to this point with the claim that, no, by *conceiving* the object one thereby *perceives* it. Hence, the object does not exist unperceived. And of course the point is general: no matter who tried to engage in this sort of conception, he or she would in that very process conceive, and thus perceive, the object in question.

If this is Berkeley's reasoning, it certainly seems that he has made an elementary blunder, namely, as many commentators have pointed out, that of conflating conceiving and perceiving. These two mental operations are quite distinct, and Berkeley's argument runs them together.

I doubt if Berkeley is guilty of quite such a notorious error. The reasoning used in defense of premise 2 does not require so wide a claim as

(2a) All conception is perception.

At most the reasoning requires the more modest claim that

(2b) all *pure de re* conception is perception.

In fact, it seems that even (2b) is too strong; Berkeley needs only something such as

(2c) All *pure de re* conception of sensible objects is perception.

This claim, though perhaps implausible, is less so than (2a).

Even so, why would Berkeley have accepted (2c)? In PR 23 he claims that when one tries to conceive a sensible object existing unperceived, one ends up conceiving one's own ideas. He makes the same point, through

Hylas, in the *Dialogues:* "But now I plainly see that all I can do is frame ideas in my own mind. I may indeed conceive in my thoughts the idea of a tree, or a house, or a mountain, but that is all" (D 200). So, Berkeley is prepared to accept the view that

(2d) if one has a *pure de re* conception of a sensible object, then one *de re* conceives an idea.

If we assume that the idea attended to is not an abstract idea, as indeed Berkeley would, then it is easy to see why he would infer (2c) from (2d). Berkeley holds that perceiving *just is* the having of the right sorts of ideas, and given this and (2d), (2c) follows directly.

We can be more specific. What (2d) and the claim that perceiving just is the having of the right sorts of ideas show is that

(2e) if one has a *pure de re* conception of a sensible object, then one perceives an idea.

Nevertheless, what Berkeley seems to require is something different, namely,

(2f) If one has a *pure de re* conception of a sensible object, then one perceives that object.

What is needed is some way to relate these last two statements to each other.

The reasoning Berkeley seems to be using in the passages quoted from the *Principles* and *Dialogues* is that *de re* conception of a sensible object inexorably involves perceiving an idea, and the perception of that idea is, as well, the perception of that object. Then, consider trying *de re* to conceive a sensible object existing unperceived. By (2d) one thereby *de re* conceives an idea, and thus, by (2e), one perceives that idea. But then, given the points just made, perception of that idea just is perception of the sensible object in question, in which case it does not qualify as unperceived. Thus, premise 2 of the second version of the master argument is established.

With this reasoning, we still have Berkeley making a serious mistake regarding conception and perception, for we have him accepting the claim that

(2g) if one has a *pure de re* conception of a sensible object, then one perceives an idea, and perception of this idea constitutes perception of that sensible object.

Given (2g), Berkeley has no way to distinguish effectively between imagining an object and perceiving it.[7] But we can see why he is driven to such a conclusion, at least in a way that we could not with (2a). The theory of ideas, that is, the theory that perception not only includes but is actually constituted by the having of appropriate ideas, together with the view that *de re* conceiving of objects requires that one have appropriate ideas, leads directly to this result. In this respect, acceptance of (2g) on Berkeley's part is not quite the egregious error that acceptance of (2a) would be.

Impossible Performances

On the account presented thus far, we see that for Berkeley any attempt to have a *pure de re* conception of an unperceived existent sensible object is doomed to fail. The reason is clear: the very attempt to engage in this sort of conception guarantees its own failure. The sense of 'guarantees' here is worth noting. The very event or activity of attempting *de re* to conceive an unperceived existent sensible object *is* the perception of that object. The attempt, then, is self-defeating. We can even to some extent see why Berkeley speaks of contradictions in this context. For suppose one does attempt the relevant conception. Then one would be *de re* conceiving an existent sensible object, and that very object, *ex hypothesi*, would be unperceived. But *de re* conception of that object, given (2g), is perception of that object. Such an object would thus be both perceived and unperceived. Small wonder that Berkeley speaks of impossibility in this context.

But notice where the impossibility lies. The proposition expressed by 'Person S *de re* conceives an existent but unperceived sensible object' does not of itself imply a contradiction. Instead, it is the conjunction of this proposition and (2g) that implies a contradiction; hence, this conjunction is inconsistent. From this, of course, we cannot infer that either conjunct is inconsistent. Indeed, we know the contrary. We have just noted that the

7. On this point, see I. C. Tipton, "Berkeley's Imagination," in *Essays on the Philosophy of George Berkeley*, pp. 85–102.

first conjunct does not imply a contradiction, and surely (2g) is contingent. Thus, the 'cannot' in premise 2 of the second version of the master argument is not a logical 'cannot'.

What, then, shall we say of that premise? A clue is provided by a passage from the second dialogue: "The things, I say, immediately perceived are ideas, or sensations, call them what you will. But how can any idea or sensation exist in, or be produced by anything but a mind or spirit? This indeed is inconceivable; and to assert that which is inconceivable is to talk nonsense: is it not?" (D 215). Here we find that, as Berkeley sees it, inconceivability implies nonsense or meaninglessness. So were we to consider premise 2, we would infer that the proposition expressed by 'Some sensible object exists but is unperceived' would count as meaningless.[8] It is this that lies behind premise 2.

However, should we not then say that the proposition expressed by 'No sensible object exists unperceived,' which is equivalent to C, is also meaningless on the grounds, mentioned earlier, that if a proposition is meaningless then so is its denial? To help answer as Berkeley might, it is useful to look again at the end of the second dialogue:

PHILONOUS. Now in that which you call the obscure indefinite sense of the word *matter*, it is plain, by your own confession, there was included no idea at all, no sense except an unknown sense, which is the same as none. . . . My business was to shew that you meant *nothing*; and this you were brought to own. So that in all your various senses, you have been shewed either to mean nothing at all, or if any thing, an absurdity. And if this be not sufficient to prove the impossibility of a thing, I desire you will let me know what is. (D 225–26)

Here we find that Berkeley infers impossibility from meaninglessness. Hence, he would also infer this same impossibility from *de re* inconceivability, since the latter implies the meaninglessness of the relevant proposition. Thus, it is impossible that matter exists, and it is impossible that some sense object exists unperceived. Both follow, as Berkeley sees it, from respective inconceivabilities.

Yet to say of something that it is impossible that it should exist is to say that the proposition asserting the existence of that thing is logically false.

8. In the passage just quoted, Berkeley infers lack of meaning from *de dicto* inconceivability. I am here assuming that he would draw the same inference from *de re* inconceivability.

Is Berkeley, then, simply entirely muddled on all this? Yes and no. Yes, because it is a confusion to run together the alethic modalities with meaninglessness. Logical impossibility is quite distinct from, and does not follow from, lack of meaning. If Berkeley has made this error, he is certainly confused. But it is not clear that he has; rather, he does seem to be groping toward some alternate modality and does seem quite aware of this. Consider these remarks from the second dialogue:

HYLAS. But I am not so thoroughly satisfied that you have proved the impossibility of matter in the last most obscure abstracted and indefinite sense.
PHILONOUS. When is a thing shewn to be impossible?
HYLAS. When a repugnancy is demonstrated between the ideas comprehended in its definition.
PHILONOUS. But where there are no ideas, there no repugnancy can be demonstrated between ideas.
HYLAS. I agree with you.

These remarks come from the same passage quoted just above, in which Berkeley goes on to infer impossibility from meaninglessness. He is there speaking of matter, but what he says carries over directly to the case of *esse est percipi*. We cannot have the relevant ideas, because the *de re* conception in which we would have to engage in order to get them is self-defeating.

We are now in a position to see why the second version of the master argument is preferable to the first: the first would have had us searching for some logical necessity attaching to the *esse est percipi* thesis (C). But we have found that Berkeley's actual arguments on the point lead elsewhere, to something weaker than logical necessity. A focus upon the second version of the master argument helps to bring these points out more clearly. In fact, in the end the examination of the second version of the master argument sheds light on the first. For consider again premise 1 of the first version, namely:

> If one can conceive the possibility of a sensible object existing unperceived, the *esse est percipi* thesis is false.

We noted earlier that the antecedent of this conditional is best read in a *de dicto* manner: what cannot be conceived is that it is *possible that* some sensible object exists unperceived. We noted that Berkeley infers impossibility from inconceivability, and so we said that the *esse est percipi* thesis would come out as a necessary truth on the first version of the master argument. But we now see that this is a mistake, if we take the necessity to be logical, as we did earlier. For as we notice in the second premise of the first version of the master argument, *de re* conceivability is reckoned a necessary condition for the appropriate *de dicto* conceivability, and Berkeley takes the former to imply something other than logical impossibility. So even the first version of the master argument does not show that the *esse est percipi* thesis, or *C*, is a necessary truth for Berkeley, not even when one assumes that inconceivability implies impossibility.[9]

What these considerations show or at least support is that the *esse est percipi* thesis, or *C*, is not understood by Berkeley to be a logically or conceptually necessary truth. Instead, its necessity consists merely in the fact that the attempt to conceive its denial requires that one successfully complete an act of *de re* conception, which conception in this particular case is peculiar in that it is always self-defeating.[10]

---

9. Another reason to prefer the second version of the master argument over the first was given earlier, namely, that the challenge Berkeley issues and then responds to seems to use just one notion of conceivability.

10. Earlier versions of this essay were read at the University of Illinois (Urbana), the meetings of the Australasian Association of Philosophy in Brisbane, and the University of Western Ontario. I acknowledge helpful comments and criticism from David Schwayder, Steven Wagner, Robert McKim, Lloyd Reinhardt, André Gallois, Robert Imlay, Martha Bolton, and David Raynor.

PART II

Volition, Action, and Causation

8

Berkeley's Problem of Sighted Agency

Robert G. Muehlmann

D espite its cardinal importance for his philosophy, Berkeley has remarkably little to say about volition. In the *Principles* and *Dialogues* he clearly uses the concept in a number of different contexts having to do with causation. But in neither of these works do his pronouncements on volition approach anything like an adequate explication. He assumes with little discussion that we all know what volition is—that we are all in some sense immediately acquainted with particular episodes of the operation of the will—and that it is obvious, or nearly so, that volitions, and thus agents, are the only things possessing causal efficacy. Part of the reason for the paucity of his account is, no doubt, that he takes episodes of volition to be *sui generis*, "simple" givens: items whose natures are known fully but that are incapable of being analyzed in terms of anything else.

An earlier version of this essay appeared in *Berkeley's Ontology* (Indianapolis: Hackett Publishing Co., 1992), pp. 78–97.

Yet the *sui generis*, or simple, nature of an item, especially an item so central to Berkeley's case, neither justifies nor explains his silence about it. For if, as Berkeley insists, we *know* such items, then some sort of account of them must be possible. The sort of account needed would begin with "our (easily describable) knowledge of their similarities to and differences from other things—of their position, so to speak, on the conceptual map."[1] As Hume put it with regard to such simple items as love and hatred, although it is "impossible we can ever, by a multitude of words, give a just definition of them," nonetheless "we can pretend to a description of them by an enumeration of such circumstances, as attend them."[2] A basic account, in other words, ought to provide us with an analysis, an "enumeration," of the relations between the *sui generis* givens and other items in the world—for example, the relations of volition and desire or volition and (bodily) action. If our accounts of simple items are to approach adequacy, of course, they need to go beyond this basic expectation: they need additionally to consist in "the acceptance or rejection of, emphasis or deemphasis on, various analogies between them and such other things."[3]

In his published works Berkeley's account of volition never approaches adequacy—indeed, he barely manages to supply us with the beginnings of an account, for he fails to satisfy even the basic expectation just mentioned. But if we grant that the nature of volition may be explicable in some such ways as these, why does Berkeley neglect to provide one? Catherine Wilson rightly observes that "where a theory seems sketchy, incoherent, or mostly absent, as Berkeley's theory of the will does, it is precisely there that we ought to devote some effort, for the evasion is likely to be hiding something of importance."[4] What, then, is Berkeley hiding?

1. Panayot Butchvarov, *The Concept of Knowledge* (Evanston, Ill.: Northwestern University Press, 1970), p. 224.
2. David Hume, *A Treatise of Human Nature*. ed. L. A. Selby-Bigge and Peter H. Nidditch (New York: Oxford University Press, 1978), p. 277. There is no doubt that Hume would have applied these comments to volition as well. Although the Humean account of volition is scattered throughout the *Treatise*, it is nonetheless much richer than Berkeley's. See J. Bricke, "Hume's Volitions," in *Philosophers of the Scottish Enlightenment*, ed. V. Hope (Edinburgh: Edinburgh University Press, 1984), pp. 70–90.
3. Butchvarov, *The Concept of Knowledge*, p. 224. An eighteenth-century account of volition more closely approaching adequacy in this fuller sense—in marked contrast to the paucity of Berkeley's or the haphazard nature of Hume's—can be found in Thomas Reid's *Essays on the Active Powers of the Human Mind* (1788), ed. Baroch A. Brody (Cambridge: MIT Press, 1969), esp. essay 2.
4. See Essay 10 in this volume, p. 196.

Although there is nothing in his published works that helps to answer this question, in his earliest recorded thoughts on this subject, the notebooks of 1707–8,[5] Berkeley manages to say a good deal about volition. We can thus hope to find an explanation for the paucity of Berkeley's account of volition by examining the notebooks' entries in which he addresses himself to the basic expectation—by examining entries in which he reflects on volition: on its intentionality and on its relations to ideas, desires, and sensations.[6] One entry of particular importance contains an emphatic rejection of the concept of a "blind agent" (PC 812). Since a discussion of this concept must be at the heart of Berkeley's account of volition, the entry provides us with a convenient point of focus.

A blind agent is one that acts without a goal in mind, and *blind agency* is thus volition with no intrinsic direction, volition that produces some thing or event without intention. Are there any blind agents? Is blind agency possible? The notebooks' Berkeley is convinced that the answer to both questions is negative, and consequently, he recognizes his obligation to advance an account of volition that will vouchsafe this conviction, vouchsafe *sighted* agency. Whatever may be the merits of the notebooks' account, Berkeley fails to address this issue in the *Principles* and *Dialogues*. Not surprisingly, this more specific failure is of a piece with the paucity of Berkeley's account of volition generally. The upshot of this essay is an explanation of both.

It is worth stressing before I begin that Berkeley's notebooks are just that: a set of notes, not a finished work. While many of the doctrines espoused here are also to be found in the *Principles*, many more have been abandoned by the time Berkeley first publishes. The work is exploratory, and many entries seem to be devoted to the working out of problems. Such is the case, I contend, with my title issue. I show that several doctrines

5. Berkeley's notebooks were first published by A. C. Fraser in 1871 under the cumbersome and inaccurate title *Commonplace Book of Occasional Metaphysical Thoughts*. A. A. Luce gave them the more apt title *Philosophical Commentaries*. The work originally consisted of a two-volume set of often thematically organized prepublication notes bound together in reverse order (*Works* I, 3). If Berkeley did the binding, it is easy to understand why they were so bound: almost all of the mature thoughts are contained in the second notebook (PC 400–888); and binding the two volumes so would have given Berkeley easier access to the most useful entries when preparing works for publication a year or so later. In order to emphasize this fact I refer to the two volumes simply as 'notebooks'.

6. The explanation I advance in this essay is that Berkeley discovered that any account of sighted volition would be difficult to reconcile with certain central theses of his philosophy. The following two essays in this volume (Essays 9 and 10) discuss other, perhaps more serious difficulties with Berkeley's scanty account.

dear to the good Bishop's heart are ones that make it difficult for him to vouchsafe sighted agency within his system. And I present reasons to conclude that the omissions in his published work stem primarily from his reluctance to address the complexities of the issue. Section 1 examines one series of entries in which Berkeley explores the relations between hedonic sensation, idea, and volition; section 2 examines an overlapping, but different, series in which he endorses, and attempts to account for, sighted agency; and section 3 draws together the results of these examinations.

1. Sensations, Ideas, and Volitions

In the earlier of his two notebooks (PC 1–399), Berkeley addresses himself to the following position of Locke's: "That which in the train of our voluntary actions determines the *Will* to any change of operation is some present uneasiness, which is, or at least is always accompanied with that of *Desire*."[7] Entries throughout the notebooks in one way or another are occupied with this position, which Berkeley reads as asserting both that (*a*) hedonic sensations determine our episodes of volition and that (*b*) they do this by affecting, or acting on, "the Will," the faculty of volition. Berkeley's antiabstractionism, so forcefully expressed in the introduction to the *Principles*, probably predates, but in any case pervades, the notebooks: it can be found both early (e.g., PC 53a) and late. Hence it is not surprising that his objection to (*b*), on the penultimate page (PC 871), is that the Will and the Understanding "are both Abstract Ideas, i.e. none at all."

Some of the earliest entries exhibit Berkeley's negative reaction to (*a*): at PC 146, for example, he sarcastically asserts that on Locke's view, "doctrines of Liberty, prescience etc explain'd by Billiard balls." The objection is that Locke here treats volition, not as an active power, but as a passive effect;[8] and though Berkeley later presses home this objection, his next entries on the subject have to do with the doctrine's theological implications. At PC 357 and again, verbatim, at PC 423, he asks "if uneasiness be necessary to set the will at work. Qu: How shall we will in

---

7. John Locke, *An Essay Concerning Human Understanding*, ed. Peter H. Nidditch (New York: Oxford University Press, 1975), book II, chap. xxi, secs. 71, 282–83; hereafter, *Essay*, followed by book, chapter, and section numbers.

8. Berkeley is no doubt aware that Locke does not always treat volition in this way. See *Essay*, II, xxi, 5, with which Berkeley's familiarity must certainly have been intimate.

Heaven." This line of thought culminates at PC 610, where, drawing on the unstated premise that uneasiness is a hedonic sensation that "God & the Blessed Spirits" cannot feel—although, in some sense of course, they can *know* (cf. PC 675 and D 240-41)—Berkeley concludes: "That God & Blessed Spirits have Will is a manifest Argument against Lockes proofs that the will cannot be conceiv'd put into action without a Previous Uneasiness."

Berkeley returns to the more fundamental objection of PC 146 when he gives his own account of causation,[9] arguing that finite minds are the causes of things that happen from within: by the exercise of our volitions we cause the existence and order of our ideas of imagination and some of our bodily movements (PC 548). While Berkeley seems to think that there is no difficulty in holding that ideas of imagination involve our volitional activity, he worries throughout his notebooks about the *relation* between volition and hedonic sensation, on the one hand, and between volition and perception or idea, on the other.

Again, given Berkeley's antiabstractionism, it is not difficult to see why he should be so worried. Consider a normal case of perception: under a very bright light, I decide to look at my hand; I raise it; and focusing on its vivid but pleasing shape, I see my hand before me. There is a certain gestalt to this complex fact: many of its distinguishing features seem to be inseparably "mixed and blended" (cf. IN 7) together. And yet, it is easy in this case to distinguish (i) perception ('see'), (ii) volition ('deciding', 'raising', 'focusing'), and (iii) hedonic sensation ('vivid', 'pleasing'). In the early sections of the *Principles* Berkeley tacitly appeals to the inseparability of (i) and (iii); and in the first of the *Dialogues*, the appeal is explicit, forming the cornerstone of his first argument. But if anything is crystal clear in Berkeley's deep ontology, it is that the middle member (ii) of this triplet is radically different from either of the others.

In the notebooks Berkeley is already making a fundamental distinction between mental events, a distinction that will carry over into his published works; and he is working on the terminology with which to describe it.[10] Throughout this entire six-year period—from the beginning of the notebooks in 1707 to the publication of the *Dialogues* in 1713—Berkeley holds that any given episode of volition is numerically distinct from the occur-

9. The following PC entry numbers are relevant to Berkeley's position on causality: 461, 499, 548, 562, 611–13, 699, 712, 780, 829, 850, 855–56.
10. See the following PC entry numbers: 478, 478a, 523, 621, 644, 674, 684, 699, 712-13.

rence of its product: causes are distinct from their effects.[11] but beyond the merely numerical there are enormous additional differences between volitions and other sorts of mental entities. These other sorts are always, on Berkeley's view, the sensational/ideational effects of volition; they are what he later comes to call ideas. Volitions are active, he holds, while ideas are passive: a volition is always a cause or a potential cause, while an idea is always an effect.[12] More generally, a volition is always exercised, while an idea, whether of sense or imagination, is always suffered or enjoyed— always accompanied by hedonic sensation. Finally, Berkeley also holds that while we can have ideas of ideas by using one idea to stand for another, we can have no ideas of volitions. Instead, volitions are known "notionally."[13] In sum, sensations (pains and pleasures), as well as their necessary attendants, ideas of sense and imagination, on the one hand, and volitions, on the other, are radically heterogeneous.[14] In short, they differ *toto caelo*.

Return now to the case of seeing my hand. As I said above, its distinguishing features seem to be inseparably "mixed and blended" together, but Berkeley insists that hedonic sensation and perception are inseparably tied and at the same time insists not only that volition and

11. Berkeley stresses these differences repeatedly in the notebooks, as well as in the published works. The central text is PR 25–30.

12. Although Berkeley does not discuss it anywhere, he probably also holds that a volition can be an effect, as when we decide that an achievable desire we have is immoral and that therefore we should will its opposite, thus willing to will. And while PC 616 might be read as evidence that the notebooks' Berkeley rejects this, I do not think the entry supports that conclusion.

13. Berkeley's position on nonideational awareness, his doctrine of notions, is not solidified until he writes the *Dialogues*. See Kenneth P. Winkler, *Berkeley: An Interpretation* (New York: Oxford University Press, 1989), pp. 278–84; hereafter, W, followed by page number. The first edition of the *Principles* uses the terms 'idea' and 'notion' interchangeably, though, as Winkler points out, "even there the word 'notion' often suggested something that did not merely reproduce ideas impressed on the senses" (W, p. 279). It is significant, I think, that Berkeley had very early considered a sharp demarcation between sensuous and nonsensuous awareness. Moreover, the manuscript of the first edition of the *Principles* has the words 'or notion' crossed out at PR 140 (see Jessop's footnote at *Works* II, 53). PC entry numbers relevant to the distinction are 576, 643, 663, 706, 756. The need for such a sharp distinction does not become pressing for Berkeley until the *Principles*, and even here he is reluctant to draw it.

14. In *An Essay Towards a New Theory of Vision*, Berkeley argues for the heterogeneity of visual and tangible extension, but this heterogeneity thesis is weaker than the thesis regarding the heterogeneity of volitions and ideas: while visual and tangible extension differ in all else, they resemble in respect of their passivity, their causal inefficacy. In contrast, ideas and volitions have *nothing* in common.

perception are distinguishable but also that they are radically distinct. The question that confronts him, then, is how he can have it both ways: how can he hold that some of the items so "mixed . . . and blended together" (IN 7) are inseparable, while others are separable? Thus, the notebooks' worry about the relation between volition, sensation, and perception.

Now, Berkeley's use of 'perception' and 'idea', in the second of the two notebooks, is undergoing a steady development toward the terminology he will settle upon in the *Principles*. His predecessors had often used 'idea' to cover any mental event. Descartes, for example, used *'cogitatio'*, or *'thinking'*, in this way and, in particular, had treated episodes of volition as modes of thought. At PC 478a Berkeley rejects this practice and, shortly afterward, asks himself "whether it were not better not to call the operations of the mind ideas, confining this term to things sensible?" (PC 490). At PC 572, probably using 'perception' to cover ideas of sense and imagination, he says, "I Defy any man to Imagine or conceive perception without an Idea or an Idea without perception." But at PC 582 Berkeley corrects this: "The having Ideas is not the same thing with Perception. a Man may have Ideas when he only Imagines. But then this Imagination presupposeth Perception."

Despite this development, however, the notebooks' Berkeley does not make the sharp distinction, in terminology at any rate, between ideas of sense and ideas of imagination. Indeed, he often uses both 'perception' and 'idea' interchangeably to cover all ideas. But the *distinction* is in the notebooks as, for example, at PC 499: "What means Cause as distinguish'd from Occasion? nothing but a Being wch wills w^n the Effect follows the volition. Those things that happen from without we are not the cause of therefore there is some other Cause of them i.e. there is a being that wills these perceptions in us." This entry contains an embryonic version of an argument that will reappear in the published works, an argument that depends heavily on the distinction between ideas of sense and ideas of imagination, however it is designated.[15] "Those things that happen from without," which Berkeley will come to call ideas of sense, are not things that we finite minds can produce. And this is a central premise, both in the notebooks and in the *Principles*, and *Dialogues*, of the argument for God's

---

15. At PC 41 we find the earliest version of this argument: "Nothing corresponds to our primary ideas w^{th}out but powers, hence a direct & brief demonstration of an active powerfull being distinct from us on whom we depend. etc." By 'primary ideas w^{th}out' Berkeley almost certainly means what he will later call ideas of sense.

existence. In the published works, Berkeley sharpens the argument by settling the terminology: ideas of imagination are the products of our volitions; and he argues that ideas of sense are the products of God's.

The first sentence of PC 499 (including the question) can be read as asserting that there are two necessary conditions for causality—a being willing the effect and the effect following upon the willing—and that these two conditions are jointly sufficient. However, the entry is almost certainly asserting something more significant: since finite minds are not capable of willing "w^n the Effect follows the volition,"[16] the implication of PC 499 seems to be that only the volitions of the deity are necessarily connected to their effects. In other words, Berkeley implies that, for finite volitions, there is no necessary connection between them and their objects; the occurrence of a finite volition is a cause that does not necessitate (cf. PC 461 and 699).[17] Nor is this the only entry with that implication. However, the fact that a finite volition has no necessary *causal* connection to its effect does not prevent one from holding that it is connected in some other way. In particular, while God (or even one's own bodily incapacity) could easily intervene to prevent the occurrence of an object upon the occasion of a volition, one is not thereby barred from holding that a finite volition is, nevertheless, intrinsically directed toward its effect. However, Berkeley's inclination is to deny even this.

Although, as noted, there are clear notebooks' moves toward the settled terminology of the published works, it is usually unsafe to take the notebooks' use of 'perception' to stand for only what Berkeley will come to call ideas of sense. Indeed, unless the context strongly suggests otherwise, one is most often right in reading both 'perception' and 'idea' as referring to any kind of mental episode *except* volition and our (notional) awareness of volition. Both are so used, I think, in PC 833: "It seems there can be no perception, no Idea without Will, being there are no ideas so indifferent but one had rather Have them than annihilation, or annihilation than them. or if there be such an equall Ballance there must be an equal mixture of pleasure & pain to Cause it. there being No ideas perfectly void of all pain & uneasiness But w^t are preferrable to annihilation." Berkeley

16. At PR 28 Berkeley writes, "It is no more than willing, and straightway this or that idea arises in my fancy." Similarly, upon willing to move parts of our bodies, "straightway" they move (but see note 27). Only when the goals are more remote can we make sense of a finite mind's willing "w^n the Effect follows the volition."

17. The belief, first advanced by John Stuart Mill, that "Berkeley makes a mistake [in his account of causation] Hume was later to expose"—namely, that volitions have real power or efficacy—is examined and rejected by Winkler. See W, pp. 106–17.

is here giving voice to a consequence of the activity analysis of minds he has settled upon—an analysis that identifies a mind with a (determinate and unique) series of volitions. At PC 791 he writes: "While I exist or have any Idea I am eternally, constantly willing, my acquiescing in the present State is willing." PC 833, read in connection with PC 791, concludes that the occurrence of a solo passive perceiving is impossible because we would always prefer the idea (thus paying attention to it) to the annihilation of our selves. In other words, he seems to be claiming that (1) the occurrence of a solo passive perceiving would annihilate the mind. On top of this, however, Berkeley may also be claiming that an "indifferent" idea, one "perfectly void of all pain & uneasiness," would go unattended and that, if so, (2) the idea would be annihilated.

We should note, on the one hand, that if either of these is Berkeley's intention, we have a fairly clear example of a position he later abandons: in the *Dialogues* Philonous seems to reject the conclusion of PC 833, arguing that in the immediate perception of sensible qualities we are entirely passive (D 197). Whether the position expressed in PC 833 is really abandoned in the *Dialogues'* argument or just ignored in that context is a question to which I return in section 3.

The notebooks' Berkeley is concerned to stress the connection between volition and idea, and he very shortly does just this: "It seems to me that Will & understanding Volitions & Ideas cannot be severed, that either cannot be possibly without the other" (PC 841). "Some Ideas or other I must have so long as I exist or Will. But no one Idea or sort of Ideas is essential" (PC 842). PC 842 draws on (1) in that "so long as I exist or Will" suggests a finite mind is identical, essentially, with episodes of volition. An entry that anticipates (2) is PC 692, where Berkeley writes that "in proportion to the Pleasure & pain Ideas are attended with desire, aversion & other actions wch include volition."[18] One might reasonably take it from PC 692, then, that if one's ideas were diminished to total "indifference," that is, to ideas void of any pleasure or pain, they would be "annihilated." Either way PC 833 is read, however, Berkeley clearly holds that ideas can never be ignored: they are either enjoyed or suffered. Does the fact that, whether of sense or imagination, an idea cannot be ignored entail that a volition is involved in our awareness of it?

---

18. The suggestion of the entry as a whole is that ideas, being suffered or enjoyed, must always be in the presence of volitions; and this provides Berkeley with an argument for the mind-dependence of ideas, since "volition is by all grant'd to be in Spirit." PC 692 is thus of great importance, since it gives voice to an embryonic version of the first dialogue's heat-pain identification argument. See my *Berkeley's Ontology*, pp. 193–94.

Berkeley's affirmative answer to this question is explicit in PC 692 and is repeated at PC 812 and 841. The first two entries jointly suggest that since any idea is enjoyed or suffered, an idea compels our attention, thus exercising our will. In other words, they conclude (3) all ideas require volitions. PC 841 seems to repeat this point while adding (4) all volitions require ideas. Conclusion 3, then, is derived from the connection between idea and hedonic sensation, but why does Berkeley advance (4)? The answer may be found if we examine another series of entries where Berkeley is worried about how to secure the intentionality of volition.

2. Guiding Ideas

Kenneth Winkler examines some of the entries in this other series in what appears, at first sight, to be an entirely unrelated context. The context of Winkler's examination is what can be called Berkeley's realism, that is, his bundle analysis of deity-sustained objects. Even more specifically, Winkler is working toward a reading of Berkeley's position in which some major criticisms of Berkeley's argument for the theocentric side of this analysis, that is, Berkeley's argument for God's existence, are to be demolished.[19] We can safely ignore that broader context in this paper and focus instead only on what Winkler calls, following Locke, "the denial of blind agency."

In the substance tradition, *agency* is the causal efficacy of an *agent*, an organism that is capable of goal-directed action. For human beings, of course, it is a phenomenological fact that we often exercise our volitions with goals in mind: our agency seems to be *directed*. An agent whose volitions were not directed would be a *blind* agent. Can there be a blind agent? In the teleological system of Aristotle, inanimate objects tend to be treated as if they were: the Stagirite can be read, no doubt uncharitably, as holding that while rocks are not conscious beings, they fall to earth because they *want* to be at the center of the universe. More generally, in the Aristotelian-Scholastic system, the "natural movements" of bodies are often caused by volitions of which they are not conscious.

With the rise of the experimental and mathematico-geometrical sciences in the seventeenth century, Aristotelian teleologism, including this

---

19. Criticisms advanced by Jonathan Bennett and endorsed by George Pitcher and I. C. Tipton. For references, see W, p. 205–16.

conception of blind agency, tends to be treated with scorn. To explain the behavior of rocks, "billiard ball" causation is deemed sufficient; and while it is permissable to invoke volitional causes in the explanation of human behavior, such causes must always have a conscious content, they must be guided by the human mind, they must be directed toward goals, they must be naturally attached to their effects—in a word, they must be *sighted*.

Berkeley shares his affirmation of sighted agency with almost all of his immediate predecessors and contemporaries. To cite just two examples: Descartes holds that in willing "there is always a particular thing which I take as the object of my thought";[20] and Locke writes, "If you say that the judgement of the understanding, or cogitation, is not one of the 'requisites for acting'. Please consider whether, while you want in this way to make a man free, you are not simply making him a blind agent."[21] In the notebooks, Berkeley takes up Locke's concern here.[22] Indeed, the first entry I examined, PC 146, is part of Berkeley's response[23] to a position stated in Locke's *Essay* that Berkeley finds inconsistent with the above passage, among others.[24] In contrast to that context, Berkeley is with Locke here in denying that there can be a blind agent. PC 812 gives voice both to the theocentric side of Berkeley's realism and, with emphasis, to that denial: "The propertys of all things are in God i.e. there is in the Deity Understanding as well as Will. He is no Blind agent & in truth a blind Agent is a Contradiction." Unfortunately, there is no notebook entry in which Berkeley exposes the inconsistency he finds in this concept.

Now, in the published works Berkeley denies that sense perception is intentional and affirms that resemblance is the ground of representation. He is silent, however, about the intentionality both of notions and of volitions. It seems clear, nevertheless, that the notebooks' Berkeley wants

20. *The Philosophical Writings of Descartes*, ed. John Cottingham, Robert Stoothoff, and Dugald Murdoch (Cambridge: Cambridge University Press, 1985), vol. 2, p. 26; cited at W, p. 207.

21. E. S. De Beer, ed., *The Correspondence of John Locke* (Oxford: Oxford University Press, 1982), vol. 7, p. 408; cited at W, p. 208.

22. Locke's concern with blind agents is closely tied to the problem of free will, as the passage above suggests. Berkeley's interest in this issue is also tied to that problem, as PC 146 makes clear. However, for the most part I ignore this issue and focus on the more fundamental ones.

23. Only a small part, indeed, since Berkeley returns to this issue again and again, particularly in the latter of the two notebooks. In addition to the entries already cited, see PC numbers 587, 599, 611–15a, 616, 628, 629, 630, 645, 653, 672a, 674, 707, 708, 743, 777, 815, 820.

24. See note 8 above.

to vouchsafe the intentionality of volition—to vouchsafe sighted agency. Since he does not pursue the issue in either the *Principles* or the *Dialogues*, two entries we have already examined, PC 841 and 842, might be taken as the culmination of his account.[25] It might be held, in other words, that Berkeley feels PC 841 secures sighted agency by intimately connecting volitions to ideas (the intentionality of which is a matter of similitude).

There are, however, several reasons to be troubled by this reading. I have already shown that the two entries are connected to the issue of the "annihilation" of either mind or idea. Read in this first connection, the two entries present us with no interpretive difficulty; in particular, at PC 842 Berkeley is saying that a finite mind has to have some ideas or other in order to exist (to will), but that there is no sort of idea (e.g., an idea of a determinate color) that is necessary: *an* idea is essential, but no particular sort is. However, if we read these two entries in the second connection, that is, if we connect these two entries to the problem of sighted agency, the meaning of PC 842 becomes more obscure.

To see this, consider Berkeley's own example of moving one's hand: reading PC 841 as an affirmation of sighted agency, it would seem that the willing of my hand's motion must be accompanied by a quite specific and determinate idea, an idea of my hand moving. In all such cases, this is not going to be an idea of sense but, rather, an idea of imagination. Let us call such an idea, the idea directing a particular episode of volition, a *guiding idea*. A guiding idea could be a constituent, perhaps the content, of a desire or aversion accompanying a volition;[26] but even if it is not such a constituent, a guiding idea is never an idea of sense. For although an idea of sense may be involved in the "whole fact of willing," this cannot be the idea to which the volition must be intimately related. For this idea of sense occurs only if the volition is successful; and in any case, the moving of my hand (which, on Berkeley's view, of course, *just is* this idea of sense) is something that, at best, is *produced* by my volition—"We move our Legs our selves. 'tis we that will their movement" (PC 548)[27]—and thus can play no role in giving sight to the volition. But if this is so—if moving our limbs requires that a determinate idea, a guiding idea, of the yet-to-be-realized movement be in intimate relation to the volition that produces

---

25. Cf. W, p. 208.

26. The only entry in which Berkeley talks about the relation between desire or aversion and volition is PC 692, and here he says of the former only that they "include volition."

27. Berkeley never explains how it is possible, given that (the movements of) "our Legs" are *ideas of sense* (whether visual or tactual [proprioceptive]), that we, as opposed to God, are their causes. For an exploration of this problem, see the next two essays in this volume.

that movement—why does Berkeley say, in the second sentence of PC 842, that "no one Idea or sort of Ideas is essential"? If PC 842 is part of Berkeley's response to the problem of sighted agency, we would expect him to say that one sort of idea *is* essential, namely, an idea of imagination or, even more specifically, a guiding idea.

The most natural reading of PC 842, as I have already stressed, is one that connects this entry, as well as PC 841, to the issue of annihilation—an issue motivated either by (1) Berkeley's antisubstantialist notebooks' account of mind or (2) his attempt to ground the mind-dependence of ideas. Perhaps we can bypass the above problem if we suppose that while PC 841 is connected, PC 842 is *not* connected to the concern over sighted agency; and we could then read "sorts of ideas" in a straightforward way as being ideas of particular sorts of things (colors, odors, or even bodies).

But there remains a larger problem that can easily be seen if we first recall the radical distinction Berkeley makes between the will and the understanding or, as he prefers to stress in most of the notebook entries, between *a* volition and *a* perception (or idea). We would normally be inclined to say that, of any desire we can achieve, the object of the desire (some yet-to-be-realized state of affairs) is also the object of the volition that is prompted by that desire. And yet, Berkeley implies that this is false: "We see no variety or difference betwixt the Volitions, only between their effects. Tis One Will one Act distinguish'd by the effects. This will, this Act is the Spirit, operative, Principle, Soul etc." (PC 788). Since the object of a desire does not yet (or, at least, is not believed to) exist, it (typically) cannot be identical to the object of the volition prompted by that desire: the first sentence of PC 788 implies that only if the object of a volition exists can we distinguish that volition from others. (On this reading, the remainder of the entry is designed to secure the unity and the continuant nature of a finite mind.)

This reading of PC 788 is supported by PC 780, where Berkeley writes that "the effect is contained in ye Cause is an axiom I do not Understand or believe to be true." Here, in PC 780, Berkeley may well be thinking primarily of the sort of causation he will construe as entirely a matter of the lawfulness of ideas of sense, holding that there is no causality between such ideas because they contain no intrinsic activity. (Ideas are passive both in the sense that we are passive in the "reception" of them *and* in the sense that they contain no activity.) But with regard to finite volitions, Berkeley was aware that, though truly causal because active, they do not contain their effects within them. (Cf. my earlier examination of PC 499.) PC 788, then, can plausibly be read as asserting that an episode of volition differs from another such episode, if we consider them in themselves, only numerically. Considered in itself, a volition contains nothing internal to it that reveals or indicates its effect. In other words, it has no intrinsic intentionality: it neither contains its effect within it, by way of similitude, nor is intrinsically directed toward either its effect or some thing that represents its effect. Rather, the intentionality of a volition resides entirely in an external relation to the effect it brings about: an episode of volition "has" an object only because it is productive of one.

However, if nothing in an episode of volition is indicative of its object, volitions, at least intrinsically, must be "blind." This, then, is the puzzle. If parts 3 and 4 of the point of PC 841 (and PC 692) are to solve the problem of sighted agency, why has Berkeley undercut this solution shortly before (and after) giving it?

Now, one way to resolve this difficulty is to provide a different reading for the first sentence of PC 788.[28] The entry as a whole, according to this second reading, gives voice to a concern about securing the unity of God's will, similar to the concern expressed at PC 712; and the first sentence may then be read as saying that we finite minds see no variety or difference between the volitions *of others* (including God's), but only between the effects. On this reading, there is no inconsistency between PC 788 and PC 841, because Berkeley could hold that there are intrinsic differences between volitions of others even if we cannot observe them, and this is precisely what he can be held to be advancing at PC 841.

This second reading seems to me less plausible than the first, however, if only because it makes Berkeley's point in the opening sentence of the entry to be of little or no significance: clearly, we do not see others' volitions *at all*, and from this alone it follows that we do not see any differences between their volitions. In addition, it is at least not obvious that in PC 788 Berkeley's concern is about God's will; indeed, the surrounding entries seem to be focused not on the volitions of God (or others) but on the volitions *within* an agent (cf. PC 777 and 791).

At PC 743 Berkeley writes that "I think Judicium includes Volition I can by no means distinguish these Judicium, Intellectus, indifferentia, Uneasiness so many things accompanying or preceding every Volition as e.g. the motion of my hand." Of this entry, Winkler (W, p. 209) makes the following suggestion: "Here Berkeley is not disputing Locke's denial of blind agency, though he is unhappy with Locke's claim that judgement

28. The following interpretation of this entry was suggested by Kenneth Winkler. See note 37.

precedes volition, which suggests that the two are distinct. Berkeley wants to strengthen the denial by emphasizing the intimacy of the connection between will and understanding." Although he does not employ the concept of a guiding idea, Winkler appears to read Berkeley as stressing, in PC 841 and elsewhere, the intimacy of the connection between a volition and its guiding idea in order to secure the intentionality, the sightedness, of the former. And while I think he is right in this reading, Winkler displays no recognition of the problematic nature of Berkeley's stance. I close this section with a look at some of the problems, but before doing so, it is worth noting what the problem is not.

If a mind at a given moment is an episode of volition along with a guiding idea, *whether or not* the guiding idea is intimately connected to the volition, then that mind can be said to be a sighted agent: its agency resides, at any given moment, in an episode of volition; and its sightedness resides in the related, however loosely, guiding idea. Berkeley's problem, then, is primarily a problem with sighted *agency*, with sighted volitions, rather than a problem with sighted *agents*. It becomes the latter problem both because Berkeley needs to insist on a radical distinction between volitions and ideas and because he is convinced that "a blind Agent is a Contradiction" (PC 812).

How, then, can a volition and an idea be *intimately* related? A bundle of sensible qualities is intimately related to a (hedonic) sensation because the former is necessarily connected to the latter; and even ideas of imagination are suffered or enjoyed. But no finite volition, on Berkeley's view, is necessarily connected to any such sensational or imaginational congeries. What, then, makes this relation, the relation between a volition and its guiding idea, a more intimate one? It cannot be simply a matter of fact, for example, that every time I have a volition that results in the raising of my arm, I also have the appropriate guiding idea. For if this is all there is to it, then there is no contradiction involved in the supposition that I might will to raise my arm by means of the guiding idea that my leg should raise or, what is worse, that I might will to raise my arm without having any guiding idea at all. Indeed, only a *necessary* connection between volition and guiding idea can ground the impossibility of such an event; only a necessary connection can secure Berkeley's claim that "in truth a blind Agent is a Contradiction" (PC 812). Can *this* be the stance Berkeley is taking at PC 841?

If Berkeley holds that any particular judgment *includes* both an idea and a volition, then of course the judgment is not distinct from "its" volition, but this is no bar to holding that the idea "in" that judgment may well be distinct from its associated volition. Perhaps this is the only point being made at PC 743, that while both idea and volition are, of *de dicto* necessity, part of judgment, there need be no *de re* necessity in the connection between a volition and its guiding idea. Nevertheless, this seems clearly *not* to be the point stressed at PC 841, where Berkeley's wording suggests that volition and (guiding) idea are necessarily connected.

It is tempting to suppose that Berkeley would unpack this in the following way. The expression 'I am currently willing' is necessarily incomplete: volition—just as much as, for example, desire or belief—always has a determinate *content*. Berkeley could hold, in other words, that (the notion of) a volition void of content is an illicit abstraction, that an episode of volition always has, as an essential component, a guiding idea. However, given his commitment to a radical distinction between volitions and ideas—they are *toto caelo* different—it would be difficult for Berkeley to argue this way. At the very least he would have to "soften" the distinction between volition and idea.[29]

This is not, of course, the only problem that looms. Berkeley seems to hold that we are the causes, via our volitions, of all our ideas of imagination. But suppose now that I will to raise my arm. To do so I must have an idea of imagination, a guiding idea, of my arm's movement. The fatal question, then, is one quite independent of the relation between volition and guiding idea: Since every idea must have a cause, what is the cause of my guiding idea? One answer would be to say that *I* am its cause. But what is the analysis of the referent of 'I'? Throughout most of his notebooks Berkeley seems committed to the view that 'I' refers not to a distinct mental substance but rather to a "congeries" (PC 580) of ideas and volitions. By the end of the notebooks and in his published works, however, Berkeley has introduced a mental substance as the referent of 'I'. But in either case—whether a mind is a congeries or a substance—if episodes of volition are the only items with causal efficacy (i.e., if the efficacy of a mind is entirely a function of the efficacy of its volitions), the guiding idea attached to my original volition must be caused by a second volition; and since this second volition must itself be sighted and can be so only if

29. For example, he could say that the reason there are no ideas of volitions is not that there is nothing in common between these two sorts of items—not that they are *toto caelo* different—but rather that since all ideas (even guiding ideas) are passive, no idea can represent the "active ingredient" of a volition, the item "in" the volition that grounds its causal efficacy.

attached to a second guiding idea, there must be a third volition to produce the second guiding idea, and so on.

One way to avoid this regress requires commitment to substantialism—to a radical distinction between my mind and its volitional (and ideational) episodes;[30] and in the *Principles* and *Dialogues*, of course, Berkeley makes this commitment. But to halt the regress, this commitment is not sufficient: he must additionally commit himself to a fundamental distinction between *agent* and *episode* causality: he must hold that *I* am the cause of my volitions in a way (inexplicably) different from the way my volitions are the causes of my bodily movements.[31]

3. The Source of the Omission

The fact that Berkeley returns so often, with queries, changes of position, and memoranda, to the relations of volition, perception, and sensation suggests that he found something, indeed several things, troublesome; and one of these troublesome things is, clearly, the relation between volition and hedonic sensation. Winkler makes little or nothing of Berkeley's worry about this relation, nor does he make anything of its connection to the notebooks' passages he examines in which Berkeley seems to be endorsing sighted agency (e.g., Winkler does not apply his reading of PC 743 to PC 788). Both of these seem to me shortcomings of his account. The fact is that Berkeley reviews all of these relations jointly; indeed, PC 743, which Winkler does cite, draws all three together. Berkeley's denial of blind agency is therefore not simply, as Winkler would have it, the affirmation of "a commonplace of seventeenth century philosophy of mind" (W, p. 207). Winkler writes:

> I want to emphasize not only the fact that Berkeley issues the denial [of blind agency] in his notebooks, but also its commonplace character, because Berkeley does not make the denial explicit in either the *Principles* or the *Dialogues*. It fails to appear, though, not because he abandons it, but because he takes it for granted. My

30. Another way out is less promising: I am not the cause of at least one of my guiding ideas. Of course, if I am not the cause of my original guiding idea (i.e., the initial idea of my arm's raising), then its cause must be God. But if so, what then becomes of my vaunted freedom?

31. This seems to be Thomas Reid's solution. See note 3 above.

evidence for this is its enthusiastic acceptance in the notebooks, its re-appearance in works published after the *Dialogues* and the illumination it provides for several texts in the *Dialogues* and the *Principles*, quite apart from the problem of unperceived objects. (W, p. 210)

I think Winkler is right to stress the reappearance of the notebooks' denial in later works[32] and right also in his assessment of its import (W, pp. 211–16).

However, there is something odd about the points preceding it: if Berkeley accepts the denial of blind agency because of its commonplace character and thus simply and silently takes it for granted in the *Principles* and *Dialogues*, why is his acceptance of it in the notebooks "enthusiastic"? If sighted agency is such a commonplace, enthusiasm would seem to be inappropriate. Winkler does not see anything odd in this, but had he done so, he might have reviewed the entries in question and discovered that Berkeley's notebooks' acceptance of sighted agency is more accurately described by the word 'troubled' than by the word 'enthusiastic'. Berkeley does not just endorse the denial of blind agency, he works his way up to it. And this suggests that while he feels a need to accommodate the denial within his philosophy, he worries about how to make that accommodation, about how to make a place for sighted agency within a context that contains several powerful doctrines in blinding collusion. To be sure, Berkeley can happily take advantage of the fact that the denial of blind agency is a commonplace of seventeenth-century philosophy, but this provides us only with a shallow explanation of his neglect.

Perhaps this shallow explanation is the best we can do. But the examination just completed suggests a deeper explanation than Winkler's for Berkeley's silence on this issue in the *Principles* and *Dialogues*. The generic explanation is one to which I have just alluded, namely, that Berkeley remains troubled: sighted agency is not mentioned in these two works, not because Berkeley takes it for granted, but rather because

32. In "Berkeley's Denial of the Denial of Blind Agency: A Reply to Kenneth P. Winkler," *Hermathena* 139 (Winter 1985), pp. 145–52, Stanley Tweyman disagrees (Winkler's thesis first appeared as "Unperceived Objects and Berkeley's Denial of Blind Agency," in ibid., pp. 81–100). Tweyman argues that PR 27 and PR 28 give voice to a Berkeleian *affirmation* of blind agency; but if the thesis of the present essay is correct (see immediately below), we should not be surprised to find Berkeley (implicitly) affirming in one place what he (implicitly) denies in another.

within his concept of volition he has found no way to accommodate it. But we can advance a more specific explanation.

The intimate relation between volition and idea expressed at PC 841 can be read in either of two ways. On the first, Berkeley is asserting not only (4) all volitions require ideas but *also* (3) all ideas require volitions. The second reading capitalizes on the ambiguity of "either" and "other": Berkeley may be saying, not that neither volitions nor ideas can be without the other, but rather only that volitions cannot be without ideas. In other words, this second reading has Berkeley asserting only (4).[33]

If we take the first reading, a more specific explanation suggests itself. For Berkeley *abandons* (3) in the *Principles* and *Dialogues*: he repeatedly tells us in both works that we are, in the immediate perception of "the proper objects of sense," entirely passive.[34] In this he *returns* to a position stated emphatically in the first notebook: "Whatsoever has any of our ideas in it must perceive, it being that very having, that passive reception of ideas that denominates the mind perceiving. that being the very essence of perception, or that wherein perception consists" (PC 301). As with this entry, in the *Principles* Berkeley avoids calling attention to his rejection of (3) by framing it not as a disclaimer about volitions but only as a disclaimer about ideas: "All our ideas, sensations, or the things we perceive, by whatsoever names they may be distinguished, are visibly inactive, there is nothing of power or agency included in them. To be satisfied of the truth of this, there is nothing else requisite but a bare observation of our ideas" (PR 25).[35] By the time he writes the *Dialogues*, however, Berkeley has come to see that his case for idealism cannot be secured without *directly* rejecting (3).

In the first of the *Dialogues*, Berkeley has Hylas advance this "materialist" distinction: "The sensation I take to be an act of the mind perceiving; beside which, there is something perceived; and this I call the *object*" (195). He then has Philonous argue that there is no volition involved in the immediate perception of a tulip's odor. In other words, he argues that *some* ideas do not require volitions: "[I]n the very perception

33. This second reading was suggested by Winkler. See note 37.
34. In a different sense, of course, (3) is not abandoned, since all ideas require volitional causes, which, if not those of finite minds, are God's.
35. Berkeley's underlying assumption here is that ideas of sense are *wholly presented:* if we are acquainted with no power or agency when we perceive them, then they contain no power or agency. The implications of this assumption are carefully explored by Phillip D. Cummins in "Berkeley's Manifest Qualities Thesis," Essay 6 in this volume.

of [odors,] light and colours [we are] altogether passive" (197). Note that this tulip-smelling argument begins by replacing the act/object distinction with an act*ion*/object distinction. As many have pointed out,[36] this replacement of 'act' with 'action' illicitly bypasses Hylas's distinction (a distinction borrowed from Descartes), but if Berkeley insists on (3), then even if he is permitted to make this replacement, the argument will fail. For if every idea is accompanied by a volition, nothing prevents his adversaries (consistently, *nota bene*, with Berkeley's own radical distinction between volitions and ideas) from holding that, in immediate perception, a sharp distinction can be drawn between an *act* (the volition) and the object (the idea). And if the first reading of PC 841 is correct, Berkeley may well have felt that abandoning (3) would call attention to (4); and since he sees no painless way to secure (4), he cautiously avoids anything that will bring further attention to it.

If the second reading is correct, this more specific explanation, at least in part, must be abandoned. On either reading, however, (4) remains problematic, since it is difficult to square with the radical distinction Berkeley wants to draw between volitions and ideas. I do not think the problems are insuperable, however. In the first place, in the context of his tulip-smelling argument Berkeley could insist that while there are always volitions that *accompany* ideas, the odor of the tulip is not the *object* of accompanying volitions. He could hold, in his own words, that such volitions are not *ingredients* in the immediate perception of the odor. To put it differently, Berkeley could hold that the only items necessarily connected to volitions are guiding ideas and that the objects of volitions are only those ideas of sense of which, resembling their intrinsic guiding ideas, the volitions are productive. Of course, inserting this into the context of the tulip-smelling argument would unnecessarily complicate the issue between Hylas and Philonous. Indeed, the complications might prove to be rhetorically suicidal. Moreover, such an insertion would compromise the distinction between ideas and volitions, and Berkeley would then feel required to address it more directly when he argues for God's existence. This last point leads us to the second place.

Having identified guiding ideas and distinguished them from ideas of other sorts, Berkeley would have to "soften" his distinction between

---

36. See, for example, Daisie Radner's "Berkeley and Cartesianism," *New Essays on Rationalism and Empiricism, Canadian Journal of Philosophy*, supp. vol. IV (1978), pp. 165–76, esp. p. 167, where Radner writes that the "flaw in the [tulip-smelling] argument, the confusion of mental act (state) with mental activity (production or initiation) is obvious."

volitions and ideas. But while conceding that ideas and volitions have something in common (their content), he could continue to hold that only volitions are active and in this way preserve his argument for God's existence. Moreover, the concession might have an additional virtue: if volitions and ideas can resemble in content, Berkeley can sidestep the embarrassing question raised earlier, namely, What is the cause of a guiding idea? (If a guiding idea is an idea of imagination, then the agent must be its cause. But an agent can only bring about an idea of imagination by means of another episode of volition, and this seems to entail a vicious regression. Cf. the "strange Mystery" of PC 599.) For he could hold that a guiding idea is not something separate from the volition of which it is the content; indeed, he could hold that it is not, strictly speaking, an idea (of imagination) at all and thus requires no cause. Again, of course, all of this would complicate his argument in a way he might have felt to be rhetorically counterproductive. In any event, while Berkeley may have felt he could resolve the difficulties he seems to struggle with in his notebooks, it seems equally probable that, with such difficulties in mind, he simply shied away from a thorough analysis of volition and, in particular, avoided explicitly repeating his notebooks' denial of blind agency.

If the examination undertaken in this essay is essentially correct, the problem of sighted agency must have been a very vexing one for Berkeley, one with which he struggled to provide a satisfactory solution, and thus one that, when penning his major works, he prudently consigned to silence.[37]

37. Kenneth Winkler was commentator on an earlier version of this essay delivered at a conference on Berkeley's Metaphysics, the University of Western Ontario, March 14, 1992. In addition to gratitude for specific suggestions indicated in earlier notes, I must thank Professor Winkler, as well as the other participants at the conference, for motivating further revisions of major portions of this essay.

9

Berkeley and Action

Robert Imlay

I

Systematic problems with Berkeley's theory of action are well known and hardly require to be rehearsed in detail. The fundamental problem from which the others in one way or another have their origin consists in the tension between a metaphysics that would make God the cause of my bodily movements *qua* sensations and a theory of action that at times at least would make actions the causal result of my willing.[1] If we opt for the first alternative and at the same time ascribe to Berkeley the independently plausible view that bodily movements brought about by me constitute an essential element of most, if not all, of my actions, then we seem forced to conclude that in reality I do nothing. I am condemned

---

1. PR 29–30, PC 433. For his commitment to interactionism, see PR 147 and PC 548.

not so much to will but, insofar as I do will, to will impotently![2] The only genuine agent is God, who employs my body to carry out his designs. He, as a result, must bear the responsibility for what occurs when I, as we should normally wish to say, have, for example, sinned.

The second alternative is hardly more attractive. If we allow for genuine causal interaction between my will and certain movements of my body, then insofar as Berkeley, as already noted, identifies the latter with sets of sensations, my passivity in the face of such entities (PR 29 and D 214)—another key Berkeleian contention—is revealed to be an illusion. And if I am the cause of some of them, how can I be sure that I, instead of God, am not the cause of the rest? Berkeley's main proof for the existence of God, depending as it does on my passivity in the face of my sensation, is exposed to the assault of the skepticism he so despises.

Is there any other way out of this impasse, which instead of at least permitting the metaphysical to complement the moral renders them incompatible? For it seems safe to assume that Berkeley, like Kant after him, would regard responsibility for our actions as a necessary condition for any genuine morality. I noted at the beginning in describing the first alternative—the metaphysical one—that it deprived me of agency only if we took it in conjunction with the altogether plausible view that bodily movements brought about by me constitute an essential element of most, if not all, of my actions. To describe a view as plausible, however, is not the same thing as to describe it as true. And perhaps more pertinent, it is not the same thing as to ascribe it to Berkeley. Despite the latter's contention that it is he, as opposed to Locke and the "materialists," who is on the side of common sense (PR 34–42)—a rich source, one would have thought, of plausible views—such a contention is relative; it allows for cases where both Berkeley and his "materialist" opponents reject a plausible view in the name of science or whatever. Thus both they and Berkeley reject what at first blush appears to be the case, namely, that the so-called secondary

2. Berkeley may have something like this in mind at PC 107. The marginal sign '+' is present, however, and this often signifies a retraction. It is in any case worth noting that I should continue to will impotently, even if God brings about what I will. It is not successful but efficacious willing that is at issue here. And by hypothesis it is not my will but God's, albeit occasioned by mine, that is efficacious. The situation, interestingly enough, parallels the one we find in epistemology; when I have adequate evidence for p and p furthermore is true, I still may not know p, because, even if I believe it, I may not believe it on the evidence at hand. Perhaps I'm just superstitious. The lack of evidential efficacy corresponds to the same lack in the realm of intentions and has analogous results.

properties of a physical object are occurrent, mind-independent properties of that object.[3]

What I am suggesting is that Berkeley, to avoid the paradox delineated above, sometimes rejects the view that bodily movements brought about by me constitute an essential element of most, if not all, of my actions. Thus he has Philonous ask Hylas whether the latter, motion being allowed to be no action, can conceive any action beside volition. Hylas replies in effect that he cannot (D 220). And it is clear from the context that what is to be excluded is the stirring of my finger, taken now to be representative of bodily movement. The passivity of such a stirring, explicitly mentioned here, guarantees that at least as far as Berkeley is concerned, the employment of the active mood of the verb is at least misleading; I do not stir my finger, rather it is stirred. Given, moreover, what we know about Berkeley's metaphysics, we may say that according to him my finger is stirred by God. If we are looking for an active stirring, on the other hand, we shall find it on this account, if at all, only in the will.

How does the distinction between stirring my finger and my finger being stirred, drawn in the way that it is, provide a way out of the impasse that we have already mentioned? The answer, it seems to me, is relatively straightforward. My stirring my finger, since it exclusively involves my will, does not, as it were, poach on God's terrain. He continues to be the cause of all my sensations, with regard to which I remain entirely passive. He is not, however, responsible for my sins, which are now to be identified with a proper subset of my volitions. Berkeley, in other words, as I would interpret him, with the appropriate adjustments — the conative aspects of lust would very much have to be emphasized—takes perfectly seriously Christ's admonition that a man who looks at a woman with a lustful eye has already committed adultery with her in his heart, where adultery in the heart, or in the will, is to be identified with adultery *tout court*.

Such an identification, while it eliminates in one fell swoop one obstacle to my being responsible for my actions and one motive for theological skepticism, exacts at the same time a high dialectical price. For it requires us to reject the entailment between my stirring my finger, to return to the original example, and my finger's being stirred. And it might very well be countered not only that the price is too high but that it constitutes a

3. John Locke, *An Essay Concerning Human Understanding*, 2 vols., ed. John W. Yolton (London: J. M. Dent & Sons, 1961). See vol. 1, pp. 105–11, for a discussion of the so-called secondary properties. See also PR 14 and D 151–58.

reductio ad absurdum of the whole procedure, because the entailment in question obviously holds.

That is a powerful objection, and I am not sure that Berkeley or I can satisfactorily answer it. One modest gesture in that direction might be to point out that we are not dealing here in any case with a formal entailment. It is not as though Berkeley denies, for example, an instance of existential generalization in standard logic. Rather, he rejects a large batch of our intuitions concerning what analytically entails what; the alleged entailment between stirring my finger and my finger being stirred, needless to say, is only a paradigm. These intuitions in what is sometimes Berkeley's view must give way to an analysis of action that makes actions purely mental. That the analysis has these counterintuitive consequences hardly counts in its favor. At the same time, however, unless we are prepared audaciously to assert that nothing could induce us to discount these intuitions, we should be willing to admit the possibility that a maximally adequate, Berkeleian analysis of action—its counterintuitive consequences would militate against its being deemed totally adequate— might turn out ultimately to be acceptable. And we should in that event accept it even though it fails to reflect completely what we now mean by action. For there is no guarantee that what we now mean by action is even maximally adequate.

What we encounter here in Berkeley's analysis of action has an instructive parallel in Robert Nozick's recent attempt to list a set of conditions that are individually necessary and jointly sufficient for knowledge.[4] The end result is that knowledge is true belief that "tracks" what is believed. Tracking for Nozick is roughly governed—and for our purposes we need no more than an approximation—by the stipulation that if the proposition believed were false, it would not be believed, and that if it were true, which it is, it would be believed. This definition is ultimately supposed to imply that Descartes, for example, could know that he was sitting by the fireplace writing down his meditations on first philosophy even though he did not know that he was not being systematically duped by an evil genius. This somewhat paradoxical result is supposed to come about because the French philosopher can track the fact that he is sitting by the fireplace writing down his meditations on first philosophy even though he cannot track the fact, if indeed it is one, that there is no evil genius. For even if

4. See Robert Nozick, *Philosophical Explanations* (Cambridge: Harvard University Press, 1981), chap. 3, for this and what follows.

there were an evil genius, he would still presumably believe that there was not one.

Faced with Nozick's challenge to reject the entailment between "Descartes knows that he is sitting by the fireplace writing down his meditations on first philosophy" and "Descartes knows that he is not being systematically duped by an evil genius"—the entailment would be an instance of closure of knowledge where the entailment in question is known—one might react in the same negative manner as some do to the analogous challenge that Berkeley issues. For it seems no more and no less preanalytically perturbing to be told that Descartes can know the one thing without knowing the other than to be told that he committed adultery with a servant—with whom he consequently had a daughter— whether or not she was penetrated by him.

It is important, nonetheless, to be aware of what in both cases the undesirable implications of a negative reaction to the two challenges are supposed to be. Refusal to admit that Descartes could commit adultery with his servant without her being penetrated by him and such like is, as we have already had occasion to note, supposed ultimately to compel us—if we are at all consistent—to resolve a destructive dilemma. Either I abdicate all or most of my responsibility by making God responsible for all or most of my actions, or we provide a not so very thin edge of the wedge to the skeptic by allowing that I, not God, am the cause of at least some sensations. Similarly, a refusal to admit that Descartes can know that he is sitting by the fireplace writing down his meditations on first philosophy, even though he does not know that he is not being systematically duped by an evil genius and such like, would by Nozick's lights, presumably, logically compel us to reject an otherwise attractive account of human knowledge as a kind of tracking of the truth or to embrace the kind of Pyrrhonian skepticism with which Descartes's first *Meditation* *inter alia* has made us familiar. And again Nozick's account of knowledge, like Berkeley's account of action, may fail to reflect completely and, indeed, may constitute a shift in present meanings. For they both seem in their own way to do violence to some of our intuitions concerning the concepts involved. But that in itself, even if true, may not be a sufficient reason for rejecting them, especially if the current concepts assuage our intuitions but only by leaving unresolved the dialectical difficulties that Berkeley and Nozick have to deal with.

II

There is, however, an even more fundamental objection to Berkeley's account of action than that it does violence to our intuitions about what analytically entails what. It is that those volitions with which Berkeley identifies actions are, if not intrinsically mysterious, explanatorily otiose. Thus there is no reason to postulate them and a fortiori no reason to identify actions with them. Such an identification is merely an ad hoc device to which Berkeley has recourse in a vain effort to extricate himself from the dialectical difficulties already mentioned and probably of his own making.

It seems to me, nonetheless, Berkeley's dialectical difficulties aside, that there are persuasive, if not compelling, reasons to postulate volitions or something analogous to them. Furthermore, to brush these reasons aside or ignore them altogether is in effect uncritically to commit oneself to a philosophical position some of whose shortcomings recourse to volitions was meant to redress. Thus C.C.W. Taylor in an otherwise insightful article entitled "Action and Inaction in Berkeley" informs us in an approving gloss of some well-known remarks made by G.E.M. Anscombe in this regard that in "order to get my hand to move all that I have to do is to move it, and if I can't move it, all the willing in the world won't get it to move."[5] The first part of this quotation is, needless to say, trivially true and could offend no one, not even Berkeley in his interactionist moments. Obviously, if I cannot move my hand, then neither a willing, which is presumably the same thing as a volition, nor anything else will get it to move. But we still want to know whether a volition will do the trick, when I can move my hand. As for the second part of the quotation, if it is not to be equally trivial, it must be interpreted as a way of rejecting the following question: in or by doing what do I move my hand? Taylor, in other words, proposes, as if it were somehow self-evident, an analogue in the philosophy of action to direct realism in the philosophy of perception, where the proscribed entities that might have posed an obstacle to such realism are now volitions instead of sensations.

A possible difficulty for such a proposal is, needless to say, provided by the example William James reports of a patient who, having lost sensation in one arm, is asked to put the hand of that arm on top of her head while her eyes are closed and is at the same time prevented from doing so. Such

5. See *Essays on Berkeley: A Tercentennial Celebration*, ed. John Foster and Howard Robinson (Oxford: Clarendon Press, 1985), p. 219.

a patient ordinarily, according to James, will be surprised on opening her eyes to discover that the movement in question has not occurred.[6] It is in order to explain this surprise—why would or should the patient be surprised if she had done nothing?—that has led philosophers, James included, to have recourse to volitions. And then by a series of moves with which we are familiar from the argument from illusion in the philosophy of perception we are pressed to concede that even when the patient does move her arm—subjectively there is supposed to be no difference from the earlier case—there is a volition in the offing.

James, of course, was writing more than two hundred years after Berkeley, but it is hard to believe that the latter's commitment to volitions, as well as that of a host of philosophers before and after him—volitions constituted an element of philosophical orthodoxy that spanned the different philosophical schools—was not inspired at least in part by the considerations that moved James. For any philosopher who was prepared to employ variants of the argument from illusion based on the relativity of perception and who had an appropriate concern for consistency—conditions that Berkeley *inter alia* satisfies admirably—could not but be impressed by the kind of example that James adduces.[7]

But if volitions are not theoretically otiose, are they not, nonetheless, intrinsically mysterious? Taylor suggests as much when he speaks, with Berkeley in mind, of the "obscurity surrounding the notion of an act of will."[8] If there is a problem here, it is not to be resolved by identifying volitions with, for example, desires and then, in an attempt to discredit the former, making much of the fact that desires alone are not sufficient to cause my body to move.[9] It may, however, be true that in order to avoid that kind of identification we shall have to identify volitions with the actions themselves. As Wittgenstein has one of his imaginary interlocutors say in *Philosophical Investigations*, "Willing, if it is not to be a sort of

6. *Principles of Psychology* (New York: Henry Holt, 1905), vol. 2, p. 105. For a good discussion of James's experiment, see G.N.A. Vesey, "Volition," *Philosophy* 36 (1961), pp. 352–65.

7. PR 14, D 178 ff., where Berkeley discusses perceptual relativity. On the usual reading of the *Dialogues* the fact of perceptual relativity is supposed to force us ultimately to regard sweetness, for example, as existing only in the mind, in much the same way that experiments like that of James are supposed to force us to talk of volitions—again existing only in the mind and ultimately, or so Berkeley would sometimes have it, to be identified with actions.

8. Taylor, "Action and Inaction in Berkeley," in *Essays on Berkeley: A Tercentennial Celebration*, p. 218.

9. Jonathan Bennett, *Locke, Berkeley, Hume: Central Themes* (Oxford: Clarendon Press, 1971), pp. 207–8.

wishing, must be the action itself. It cannot be allowed to stop anywhere short of the action." And then, without enclosing it in quotation marks, he immediately adds, "[I]f it is the action, then it is so in the ordinary sense of the word; so it is speaking, writing, walking, lifting a thing, imagining something."[10] If this line of thought is on the right track, then Berkeley, given volitions, would have a reason independent of his dialectical difficulties, to which I alluded at the beginning of this essay, for making the kind of identification of volition and action that Wittgenstein has in mind.

III

I turn now to a different criticism of volitions that is designed to show that if they are not explanatorily otiose, for the reasons given, or intrinsically mysterious, they are, nonetheless, logically impossible because they would commit us to a vicious infinite regress. This criticism originates with Ryle and has been directed by Jonathan Bennett specifically against Berkeley. The criticism in essence is that if volitions are to explain intentional action and indeed to render them possible, they must themselves be actions. But then we should have to introduce a second batch of volitions to explain the first batch and render them possible and so on *ad infinitum*. As a result, no one would in principle be able to do anything or will anything.[11]

One may, Berkeley aside for a moment, be led to wonder why Bennett is so sure that a volition would itself have to be an action if it is to explain and, indeed, render possible intentional action. Why could action—the notion of intentional action turns out to be pleonastic, as Bennett employs it—not be something that takes place when two nonactions, a volition and a set of bodily movements, come together? Or, since Bennett links the notion of an action to that of a performance, why could a performance not consist of elements that are not themselves performances?

But even if Bennett could supply us with a positive answer to this question, it should not bother Berkeley. If actions are performances, then Berkeley's volitions are indeed performances. Does that commit him to a vicious infinite regress? Not at all; since volitions and intentional action are on his view coterminous, there can be no question of importing a

10. Ludwig Wittgenstein, *Philosophical Investigations*, 2d ed. (Oxford: Basil Blackwell, 1963), p. 615.
11. Bennett, *Locke, Berkeley, Hume*, p. 207.

second batch of volitions in order to explain how the first batch got that way. And Berkeley's actions, far from being logically impossible, proliferate: James's patient, for example, *does* put her hand on top of her head, even though the corresponding bodily movements are not in the offing. That does not mean or, at least, need not mean that on Berkeley's theory I can generally do whatever I want. Some desires have contents that are so indeterminate that they fail to provide a useful blueprint for a volition. Or the blueprint may be so complex, at least from my point of view, that I do not know how to translate it into a volition. It should be remembered in this regard that if volitions are indeed to be actions in all their concreteness, then they must be made to sacrifice the indeterminacy that we commonly associate with mental contents. They must by the same token be made to conform to more exigent standards of performance than those that we normally impose, say, upon decisions. For while it may require skill to make the right decision, it is not generally very hard to make some kind of decision.

IV

The upshot of all this would seem to be, then, that Berkeley's volitions are usually supposed to be actions without the external physical husk that is ordinarily taken to constitute an essential part of them. My inability to do what I want has, as a result, nothing to do with that husk or how it came into being, in case it does come into being. Nor does Berkeley's God *pace* Taylor, in what he takes to be a key criticism, make himself responsible for the wicked deeds I want to do but am unable to do.[12] It is in terms of Berkeley's sometime identification of volition and action—an identification that Taylor himself emphasizes[13]—not I but, if anyone, God who desires the husk. I desire the fruit of action within the husk, and by hypothesis the action does not take place.

Our metaphor of the husk and the fruit assumes, needless to say, that one may remove the husk while the fruit remains essentially the same. The assumption is undoubtedly legitimate because the *principium individuationis* for the fruit is not the husk. It is not so clear, however that the *principium individuationis* of an action may not have something to do

12. Taylor, "Action and Inaction in Berkeley," p. 224.
13. Ibid., p. 223.

with sets of bodily movements. That this possibility does not seem to have occurred to Berkeley is probably related to his conviction that mental contents are in themselves completely determinate and self-individuating. This conviction, as is well known, plays a key role in his polemic against Locke on the existence of abstract general ideas (IN 12). It is, furthermore, as I have already had occasion to note, a requirement at least in the case of volitions if we are to follow Berkeley when he identifies them with actions. For it is one thing to effect a kind of mentalistic reduction of action—if we have been right, the standard criticisms of such a procedure are inconclusive and often present difficulties of their own—it is quite another thing to countenance the possibility that what we vulgarly take to be two actions because there are two different sets of bodily movements involved should turn out to be only one because in both cases the same imperfectly specified volition is in the offing.

We should, incidentally, have the same feeling—going to the roots of it would be another matter—that something has gone badly awry, as we have when we are informed that an analogous mentalistic reduction of physical objects is supposed to yield at best twins where we should have expected one and the same object. Or at least that is supposed to be the yield when we concentrate on the fact that two minds are involved (D 247). Here we have two objects where we expected there to be one. In the case that interests us, we have one action where we expected there to be two.

For those of us who have doubts about the determinacy of mental contents, it might be a good idea to reconsider the variation on the argument from illusion that James offers us based on the experience of his patient who has lost sensation in her arm. It is this argument, I have tried to suggest, that convinced the tradition, if it had had any doubts on that score, of the existence of volitions in the first place. It was then open to Berkeley to identify them without remainder with actions. It may be, however, that what the argument compels us to accept, if it compels us at all, are volitions now seen as dynamic blueprints for action instead of as actions themselves. In this respect they would resemble desires, which, as I have already indicated, may be seen as blueprints for volitions. But the former lack the dynamism of the latter. And it is this characteristic of volitions that explains the surprise of James's patient when in the circumstances she discovers that her arm has not gone up.

Another way of viewing what I am trying to get across would be to see a volition as a kind of rehearsal for action. Like a literal rehearsal it can take place without that for which it is a rehearsal taking place—James's patient's arm does not rise, and the play might be canceled at the last minute—but unlike a literal rehearsal it may be a rehearsal for two actions that differ in intrinsic detail and not just two different performances of what is intrinsically the same play. And just as the performance of a play is to be distinguished from its rehearsal, so the performance of an action, whichever action it turns out precisely to be, is to be distinguished from the volition that prepared it and made it possible. At the same time, a rehearsal of an action is sufficiently like an action itself to account for the surprise of James's patient, just as one may be surprised to learn that one was only rehearsing a play when all along one was convinced that one was engaged in an actual performance. Indeed, what essentially distinguishes a rehearsal of an action, a volition, from an action itself is not an element of agency present in the former though not the latter—it is present in both—but the determinateness of that agency which a volition cut off from the body lacks. And if I am right, it is because of that lack of determinacy that a volition *pace* Berkeley loses the name action.[14]

14. This line of thought clearly seems to commit us—if indeed mental contents are indeterminate—to the view that there are no purely mental actions. But I take this to be more an argument in favor than a criticism of the position in question.

10

On Imlay's
"Berkeley and Action"

Catherine Wilson

Professor Imlay's interesting and wide-ranging essay is intended to show that despite the problems with Berkeley's theory of voluntary action, there is something to be learned from the attempts of this immaterialist to give action a place in his system. This attempt, Imlay thinks, requires Berkeley to appeal to the much-maligned notion of a volition. Though Imlay does not think Berkeley really has a coherent theory of action, he thinks that volitions in some dress or other may play a role in the analysis of an action. His suggestion at the end is that a volition might be something like a rehearsal for an action, and he explains this with the help of a case borrowed from William James.

I agree with Imlay on two of the main points he makes in his essay: first, that Berkeley does not have a coherent theory of action; second, that the notion of a volition might be deserving of and capable of rehabilitation. But I disagree with him on two other points. First, I can make no philosophical connection between Berkeleian idealism and the moral doctrine that sin is in the will, and I do not think that Imlay's discussion of volitions establishes such a connection. Second, if volitions are to be rehabilitated, it seems to me that one of the lessons taught by the failure of Berkeley's theory of action is that they should not be conceived as parts of actions or as causes of actions, as Imlay is still inclined to do. Although a "rational reconstruction" is often objectionable when it requires us to write off much of what a philosopher says about a subject, in order to get a more coherent theory—the theory he should have held—I proceed with such a reconstruction anyway, hoping that the noncausal account of volitions I give is one Berkeley might eventually have agreed to as more consistent with his idealism.[1]

Let me first retrace the apparent problems with what little Berkeley does have to say on the subject of action. Berkeley thinks that the human soul is active, that it wills, and that through its willing, actions occur for which reward and punishment are deserved. He thinks, for example, that I can willingly turn my head and so bring about a different visual experience in myself. But he also thinks that I can willingly move my hand to kill someone in a war, write out a death warrant, or just murder someone. His belief in effective human agency, he thought, distinguished his position from that of Malebranche, who thought that our volitions were inefficacious without the help of God. But to be consistent with the rest of Berkeley's philosophy, this effectiveness must not depend on my mind being able to produce any changes in "material substance," since that substance does not exist.

The charge brought against Berkeley by C.C.W. Taylor, in a recent paper cited by Imlay, is that his assertion that there are human actions and that it is we who bear the responsibility for them is impossible to articulate if real things are only constellations of ideas. For we can produce new constellations of ideas, hence new configurations of objects, only to the extent that we engage in fantasy. To produce changes in real things we would have to be able to produce new constellations of ideas in such a way that the change was not merely an imaginary change. To be sure, we can define nonimaginary changes as those in which God cooperates to bring about corresponding configurations and experiences in other

---

1. Such an account inevitably undermines Berkeley's argument for God's existence— depending as it does on the premise that only volitions have causal efficacy—and so cannot accommodate his defense of commonsense realism. Thus, implicitly, it is an account of "Berkeley without God." For an account explicitly on this theme but quite independent of Berkeley's theory of action, see Margaret Atherton, "Berkeley Without God," and Charles McCracken's rejoinder, Essays 13 and 14 in this volume.

minds. But we then lose the notion of agency that Berkeley was trying to defend. For then it seems that if the activity of God is a necessary condition of my having made a change in real objects, we fall back into Malebranche's occasionalism with regard to the will and into the conventional objection that God is then the author of sin. Taylor thinks that Berkeley's fallback position is that it is enough for moral responsibility that I will something to come about, even if I cannot actually effect a change in a real object. Agency consists, in this case, in the having of "volitions," where a volition is defined as what you have when you subtract from an action the effecting of a change in real objects. But in that case it is just good luck if God cooperates to make my volitions effective, and this cannot have been what Berkeley intended. Taylor concludes that Berkeley is forced to say, like Wittgenstein in the *Tractatus*, that "even if all that we wish for were to happen, still this would be only a favor granted by fate."[2]

Despite Taylor's suggestion that Berkeley actually held such a view, which developed into a psychological theory of passivity, helplessness, and dependence that is hard to endorse, I do not see that his metaphysics really precludes a theory of agency and moral responsibility. To show that he really does not need to end up in this state of passivity, I propose to separate the question of causal insularity in Berkeley from the question of the existence and nature of volitions. I agree that causal insularity does not negate the distinction between actions that are my responsibility and actions that are not. Then I argue that volitions need not be conceived as efficacious or inefficacious causes, so that admitting volitions does not commit the idealist to a thesis of inefficaciousness.

1. Does Action Require Causal Interaction?

First let us imagine something along the lines of a Leibnizian monad: a being alone in a sea of nonbeing with God. We leave it open for the moment

2. C.C.W. Taylor quotes PC 107, an early passage from Berkeley's notebooks: "Strange impotence of men. Man without God. Wretcheder than a stone or tree, he having only the power to be miserable by his unperformed wills, these having no power at all." But there are similar gestures of futility made in a religious context by Malebranche, and it is probable that Berkeley is quoting them as examples of doctrine with which he disagrees. See Taylor, "Action and Inaction in Berkeley," in *Essays on Berkeley: A Tercentennial Celebration*, ed. John Foster and Howard Robinson, (Oxford: Clarendon Press, 1985), p. 225.

whether this monad is a pure spirit, an ensemble of mind and body, or a piece of "thinking matter." For all I know, I am such a monad, according to the Cartesian premise that whatever I experience, I could experience this same thing even if I were such a monad. The question now is, would it be possible to say that this being acts and bears responsibility for its actions?

At first one is tempted to say that I cannot act unless I am causally related to an external world with independent reality, and that I cannot do right and wrong if I cannot harm anyone, if there are no other spirits in the world. Just as Grice tried to show that there is necessarily a causal component to perception by showing that if there is no causal connection between a clock and my "sense-datum" of a clock, I cannot be seeing it, so a causal theorist of action of this type will argue that if there is no causal connection between me, another person's body, and a stick outside my mind, I cannot hit anyone with a stick.

But in claiming that action implies causal contact with external objects, we are imagining a person shut up, as it were, in a room and unable to get into contact with things, so that he is neither dangerous nor useful. Grice's argument that "we would say" that a person in the presence of a clock but not causally affected by it could not be seeing it, regardless of the quality of his sense-data, is convincing only insofar as we conceive this person as unable to get into contact with that clock. If we think of our monad as in any way shut up in its own mind—and as shut off from its body—it might indeed seem that it cannot do anything for good or ill.

But of course the Berkeleian soul is not shut up in its own mind or shut off from contact with external material objects, because according to the hypothesis, *there are no such things.* Being a monad is not like being shut up in a room or being unable to exercise any control over your face or limbs. There is nothing you are prevented from doing, so there is after all no limitation imposed on your action. *Qua* monad, you can even conduct an empirical study of perception based on light waves, the retina, and so forth. And we have another reason to question whether the proposed entailment holds when failure to make contact is not in question. I can be sure that I act and sure that I do bear responsibility even though I am not sure that I am not such a monad. (This is more or less the situation Imlay is, I think, referring to in his discussion of Nozick's claim about "tracking.") So the claim that there are right and wrong actions, just and unjust punishments, does not after all imply that other minds exist or that I am causally related to them or to any external object. It is enough that it should be to me as though there are other minds that can be made happy or miserable, and that I should seem to be able to influence them through my own body and other instruments, so long as it is stipulated that this seeming is not an illusion on my part, the result of my hallucinating the situation. If I am, just now, a monad alone in a sea of nonbeing with God and jab my colleague with a pencil, then *no matter what ontology is in effect*, it seems that I have hurt that other person and should bear the consequences.

Now you might hold that if I am a such a monad, then this seeming to have hurt someone is after all the result of an illusion on my part, for I am deceived in believing that I am not such a monad. But I do not see that this follows. Perhaps I do believe that I am such a monad; even if I do not, this seeming to have hurt someone is not the *result* of believing falsely that I am not a monad, but the result of what I see, hear, and otherwise experience.

But note that once I establish that, metaphysically speaking, there are other minds or external things, then the causal contact rule holds, for then it would be a defect in me if I were unable to influence them. And remember that for Berkeley we can know, somehow or other, that there are other spirits. So there is after all a defect in me: I cannot act on them myself. But this defect is compensated for by God's help. People think they can attack Berkeley for making God the author of sin, but his reply seems appropriate. If we were to accept material substance and mind-body interaction, the existence of God would still be a contributing cause of any result, insofar as everything is one of God's creatures and moved by his laws.[3] The fact that God's action is necessary to ensure that other spirits experience sufferings corresponding to my actions could only take away from my responsibility—given that we have established that monads are responsible if other spirits do not exist—if we construed this as a means by which our access to others was blocked rather than made possible.

2. Do "Volitions" Exist?

Though Berkeley should have left well enough alone here, he took, according to Taylor and Imlay, a step that, in my view, was unnecessary, the step of locating the sinfulness of an "action" in the will. As he says to Johnson, "Difficulties about the principle of moral actions will cease if we

3. Or so one might think is implied by the fourth paragraph of Berkeley's second letter (November 25, 1729) to Johnson (*Works* II, 281).

consider that all guilt is in the will, and that our ideas, from whatever cause they are produced, are alike inert."[4] Note that we are no longer specially concerned with metaphysical idealism at this point. A materialist too can believe in volitions and believe that guilt is in the will.

I here agree with Imlay that there are volitions, and I will go farther by arguing that Berkeley is correct to suggest that it is they that are morally evaluated. But if guilt does lie in the will, it cannot lie in the having of volitions in the sense Berkeley sometimes seems to have in mind—the occurrence of a pure mental act undifferentiated by its content. For Berkeley's claim that volitions are wholly distinct from ideas—that they only result in ideas—means that volitions are not individuated for Berkeley according to what they are volitions of. And this means that the idea of a sinful volition is nonsense. If we want to allow for sinful volitions, we need to build mental content back into them. And this means violating Berkeley's distinction between volitions and ideas.[5] Volitions, in order to be at all useful in philosophical analysis, need, I think, to be seen as certain kinds of experiences.

First, let us look at the various things the historical Berkeley says about volitions, in order to see what is salvageable and what is not. His remarks occur mainly in his notebooks, where he says for example: "The act of the Will or volition is not uneasiness for that uneasiness may be without volition" (PC 611). "The Will not distinct from particular Volitions" (PC 615). "To say ye Will is a power. Volition is an act. This is idem per idem" (PC 621). Thus we know that the will is not a faculty that produces volitions; rather, our having volitions is what we call having a will. And we know that it is not informative to say that volitions are acts. And we know, finally, that volitions should not be confused with desires, wants, wishes, and feelings of need or uneasiness. All of these terms refer to attitudes I may have toward an object or state of affairs. These attitudes may or may not lead me to perform some voluntary action but are not any more tightly connected with my doing something voluntarily. Berkeley tries to establish this nonidentification by saying that we will not desire things or feel uneasy in the lack of them in heaven, though we will still perform voluntary actions (PC 610). This seems to me a little spurious. Perhaps it is a condition of our doing anything that we need to be desirous, uneasy, and so forth. Nevertheless, Berkeley is surely right to say that this does

---

4. Taylor quoting Berkeley, "Action and Inaction in Berkeley," p. 225.
5. For an exploration of Berkeley's difficulties here, see Robert Muehlmann, "Berkeley's Problem of Sighted Agency," Essay 8 in this volume.

not mean that there is an identity of reference here. And this is, I think, unique among Berkeley's theoretical statements about the will; and it is one we ought to keep.

Why not suppose then that having a volition is simply a special experience on its own? In this way we can be faithful to the spirit of Berkeley's idealism and even to his (logically independent) doctrine that guilt lies in the will, even while trampling down his claim that volitions are entirely different from ideas. The difficulty here is that antipsychologistic philosophers influenced by Wittgenstein, Ryle, and Austin have repeatedly failed to find a special experience that occurs when we do something voluntarily. Ryleans caricature volitions as little gestures made by actors in my inner mental theater, which my body copies or fails to copy. Wittgensteinians note that introspection fails to deliver them up, that there is nothing subjective that all my voluntary actions have in common. Austinians point out that the various distinctions we make in ordinary language between voluntary and involuntary, intentional and unintentional, purposeful and inadvertent, and like actions do not depend on the presence or absence of volitions. In general, philosophers treat them as part of the verbiage (along with sense-data) left over from the Jamesian days when philosophy and psychology were not distinct, and psychology has no use for them either at this point, treating them as refugees from philosophy.

The critics having had their fun, volitions, Imlay suggests, need a sympathetic look. Are we certain that voluntary action is not in some way subjectively marked out? If so, he argues, Berkeley was not entirely wrong. Imlay now discusses a case first brought forward by Godfrey Vesey from James's *Principles of Psychology*. A certain lady believes, on the basis of her proprioceptive sensations, though with her eyes closed, that she has performed a voluntary action. She is then surprised when she opens them to find that she has not. We can even imagine that we have this experience of being surprised, say, 50 percent of the time. I think I am reaching out my hand for a cup of coffee; it looks to me and feels to me as though I have. Yet a split second later, there is my hand still lying in my lap, the cup is on the table, and I am feeling amazed! Perhaps the next time it succeeds, and I manage to perform the action of getting the coffee. There seems to be no logical reason this could not happen often, at least until the feeling of surprise was eventually extinguished by repetition.

James's clinical case indicates that when we do something voluntarily, we have ways of knowing that we do it voluntarily. (More surprisingly, perhaps, another person might have access to information about whether I am going to do something, for studies are said to show activation in certain brain regions a few milliseconds before a person is aware of making a voluntary movement.)

Note that the claim that there may be first- or third-person access to "voluntariness" does not solve any philosophical problems about responsibility. We cannot suppose that it is in virtue of some brain state that a person is responsible for a deed, just because that brain state is a necessary and sufficient condition of any deed. For we have to ask, how did that volitional state arise? Not by being willed, for then we would have an infinite regress. If I had to be in a volitional state to get myself into a volitional state, we would be in trouble. So the volitional state must be something I find myself in. But then, if volitional states determine responsibility, then a state I merely find myself in can make me blameworthy, which is absurd. The kinds of volitions that James's experiment turned up or that brain research may turn up do not help very much with the problems of moral accountability. There are various things I have done: become a teacher of philosophy, sat for an exam, lifted a finger. All of these things are in some sense my fault or to my credit, or whatever. But I did not have a volition associated with the first or the second; my having done those things and their being ascribable to me has to do with the whole pattern of life; they are not the summation of some set of volitions.

Suppose, however, we press on with trying to identify volitions with what this lady has when it seems to her that she put her hand on top of her head. Imlay suggests that volitions might in this case be construed as being like rehearsals. What was thought to be a play can turn out to have been only a rehearsal (if no one comes, for example, and it is decided to schedule the performance for later). And what was thought to be an action can turn out to have been only a volition. But a rehearsal can never be a play, for the right context and sequelae are missing, and a volition can never be an action.

How might this help in our discussion of responsibility? If we were to extend Imlay's account, it would, I think, go something like this: We normally criticize the play rather than the rehearsal because the play is what we see: rehearsals are normally closed to the public. But the content and the performance of the play are all there in the rehearsal, and it would be just as appropriate to criticize the rehearsal as the play. Similarly, we normally criticize actions because we perceive them. But if we could look into people's hearts (or brains) and read their volitions in advance of their performing any action, these volitions would be appropriate objects of moral praise and blame.

I agree with Imlay that if we knew what people's volitions were, we would react to them with moral judgment. Nevertheless, we cannot be completely happy with the action-performance analogy. The difference between a performance and a rehearsal consists in what the actors tell themselves, the absence of ticket sales, an audience, perhaps in a sloppier performance, one that stops and starts. But there is no difference in how it seems to me at the time between a volition, on Imlay's account, and an action. This suggests to me that volitions are just *the subjective experience of doing something voluntarily*. Like the subjective experience of seeing a pair of antlers on a coatrack, which may or may not correspond to reality, volitions may or may not correspond to actions. Just as you may either hallucinate or perceive, so you may have a volition-illusion or perform an action.[6]

The mistake made by traditional defenders of volitions was like that made by sense-data theorists. They wanted to make a volition a component of every voluntary action and of every experience that seemed to the subject to be one of voluntary action, just as the sense-data theorists wanted to make sense-data the common element in hallucinating and perceiving. But we do not find them in our actions any more than we find sense-data in our ordinary perceptions, and that is why we cannot, as Vesey noticed, "subtract" the fact that my arm goes up from the fact that I raise my arm.[7] And just as sense-data are not effects, volitions are not causes.

If volitions are not causes but certain experiences, then the problem of whether volitions cause bodily movements, changes in objects, and new experiences in other people, or only prod God to cause them, is otiose, and there is no problem for a Berkeleian. However, Berkeley himself makes things difficult for his defender by saying explicitly that the will is "active" (PC 706) and not to be identified with sensations of uneasiness or "ideas" (PC 613), which are of course passive. But where sometimes he thinks of "the will" as *something*—"purus actus or rather pure Spirit not imaginable, not sensible, not intelligible, in no wise the object of ye Understanding, no wise perceivable" (PC 828), which issues in various effects (PC 788)—sometimes he indicates that it is not a particular faculty (PC 643)

---

6. See J. M. Hinton, *Experiences* (Oxford: Clarendon Press, 1973), pp. 37 ff., on "perception-illusion disjunctions" as a means of avoiding the common element, sense-data and skepticism.

7. G.N.A. Vesey, "Volition," *Philosophy* 36 (1961), p. 352.

and seems rather to identify it with the sum total of volitions. As is sometimes observed, when it comes to the will, Berkeley seems to be abandoning his campaign against abstract ideas and metaphysical notions of force. But this is in some ways a crude objection: Berkeley is torn between the position that our wills are not metaphysical entities but given to us in immediate experience and the position that they correspond to no idea. His real problem is to explain how we can experience ourselves as active, even if we lack any idea of a volition.

Now, it seems to me that Berkeley and any other student of the voluntary should simply press ahead here and maintain that our status as metaphysically active agents is revealed to us in our conscious experiences—our volitions—without our having a specific idea of the will. It might be said that no mere experience of voluntary action can guarantee that we are metaphysically free—that is, have free will. And indeed, perhaps we cannot know this and can only know that we conceive ourselves as free: in that case the having of volitions would have to be included in the account of why we do conceive ourselves this way.

Imlay, as we have seen, approves the doctrine that guilt is in the will, but argues that Berkeley cannot solve the problem of causation: he treats volitions as causes, but when pressed must admit either that they are inefficacious or that they might obviate the need for a God. Imlay presses his point, in effect, asking Berkeley whether he thinks that bodily movements brought about by me constitute an essential element of (most of) my actions. What can Berkeley say here? His first impulse will be graciously to concede that they do constitute such an element, provided we understand "bodily movements" as congeries of *ideas* rather than as motions of material substance. But this will get him into trouble. If I am the cause of some ideas, as Imlay asks, how can I be sure that I am not the cause of all of them and that God does not exist?

But it is only to the extent that Berkeley is prepared to take volitions themselves as causes rather than as evidence of our status as metaphysically active agents that he creates trouble for himself. He should simply have stuck to his immaterialist account, without bringing them in. For if he does not admit that they are causes, he does not have to explain what they cause—for example, "bodily movements"—or how they cause it (thanks to God).

Let me summarize how not making volitions causes solves the problem he is faced with. Taylor posed the problem as follows: We know that

(1)   changes in real things are changes in what we perceive.

So,

(2)   changes in real things are changes in our ideas.

But then, since

(3)   our ideas of real things are independent of the will,

it follows that

(4)   my will cannot produce changes in real things.

And either

    (4a) I cannot produce changes in real things, I cannot act—at best I
         can produce volitions which signal God to act—

or else

    (4b) I can produce my own ideas, in which case there is no need to
         posit a God.

Let us try to work through an example in Berkeley's terms to see whether
we must wind up at (4a) or (4b). Suppose that a person voluntarily picks up
a stick and hits a child. This means a real object, a stick, is brought into
contact with a real object, a hand, and that this real hand moves this real
stick forcefully against a real child, which suffers real pain. The result is
that, for the childbeater, the stick is perceived and felt as being in the
hand, that contact is felt with the child through the stick. For the usual
Cartesian reasons, nothing in what we have said commits us to the
existence of material substance. The only difficulty is this: if all of our
ideas of real things are independent of the will, I cannot make the idea of
the stick be in my idea of my hand, so that I cannot effect a change in a real
thing.

    But did Berkeley argue that in picking up a stick I am making the idea
of the stick be in the idea of my hand? Does "A picked up a stick" entail "A
made the idea of the stick be in his idea of his hand?" No! For Berkeley it
just means, ideationally speaking, the stick first was not, but now is
(through a series of intermediate states), in A's hand. A did something
such that, ideationally speaking, the stick is now in A's hand. Then the
question is, what did A do?

    Berkeley's answer is easy: A picked up the stick, just as Anscombe and
the other post-Wittgensteinians would like. This does not mean that
ideationally A did something independent of the existence of a real stick.
Especially it does not mean that A had a pick-up-the-stick volition where
this is conceived mereologically as a part of the action of picking up a stick,
or as part of the action of hallucinating that A has picked up a stick, or as
A's being given by God the idea that A has picked up a stick. Rather,

having a pick-up-the-stick volition just is either the experience of picking up a material stick, hallucinating it, or being given the idea of picking it up by God.

3. Idealism and the Good and Evil Will

There is a danger, then, in trying to get more out of idealism than any coherent metaphysical theory can deliver. Do we get out of Wittgenstein's fatalism-pessimism? No. Nor, I think, do we get out of it Christian ethics. Imlay suggests that Berkeley would agree with Jesus that to look on someone forbidden with lust in your heart is as immoral as committing adultery with that person. Probably Berkeley would agree with that, but for reasons that are not intrinsically related to idealism. For remember that Berkeley does want to distinguish unease, desire, velleity, wanting, and wishing from having a volition. Between the fleeting thought and the volitional leap there lie various stages of entertaining, planning, deciding, and even restrained or curtailed movements. Condemning or approving certain thoughts, wishes, and so forth, as opposed to certain world-altering actions, as evil or good is thus a matter different from condemning or approving volitions as opposed to alterations in objects. Contrast the case in which James's paralyzed patient has an idle but unchristian wish to commit adultery with the experimenter, quickly rejected as absurd, and the case in which she actually experiences an adulterous volition, one that is not induced experimentally but that arises from the depths of her being. A strict moralist will, like one of the old Puritans, reproach herself even for fleeting, frivolous thoughts, as these are inconsistent with moral seriousness. A lax moralist will not even reproach herself with having experienced a full-scale volition, taking refuge in the observation that nothing actually happened, no harm was experienced by anybody—after all she was paralyzed! A moralist of medium strictness might reproach herself, not for fleeting thoughts, but for thoughts that are repeatedly dwelled on or turned over, that enter into her plans, or that she in some ways identifies with herself. But the degree of strictness one adopts with oneself or others seems unrelated to the choice of ontology. I may, unlike Berkeley, believe in the existence of material objects that causally interact with my mind and be a Puritan when it comes to morals; or I may believe that objects are only congeries of ideas, yet hold myself blameless in case none of these other objects is perceived to undergo any change in consequence of my volitions. We have all, I suppose, experienced inner dialogues running approximately as follows: "You wanted to do that!" "Admitted, but I didn't do it, did I?" "But if circumstances had not intervened . . . ?" "What does anyone know about that!" These dialogues prove that we may be genuinely in doubt, in the particular case, about the relative contribution to moral good or ill made by inner intentions versus outward results. And they suggest to me that there is no general answer to the question, Which is more important, intentions or results? One can only try to correct unbalanced evaluations where they stand out. Some hard cases present themselves under this heading. For example, we might think that some experiences—whether they are sensory experiences or fantasies—are in and of themselves bad to have whether or not they affect people's behavior. The attempt to control spectatorship of sadistic sports or consumption of sadistic films is based not simply on beliefs about what people are likely to do as a consequence of their exposure, but on beliefs about what sort of images it is good to have in your mind: we know that it was in some way not right for people to experience public executions in the nineteenth century in a mood of pleasure. On the other side, we recognize that one should not be too hard on people, too intrusive of their private worlds, and that antisocial fantasies may not only have a stabilizing effect in the wider society but may be prized as manifestations of spontaneity, freedom, or love.

To conclude, then, I disagree with Imlay's specific conception of a volition: I do not think that volitions are rehearsals for actions; such rehearsals may occur without the will being engaged at all and are pure presentations or ideas, contrary to what Berkeley himself insists. Nor do I think that volitions can be parts of actions. Here I follow the lead of J. M. Hinton, who, in his arguments against sense-data, employed the notion of a "perception-illusion disjunction." Having a volition is either having the experience of doing something voluntarily or having the illusion that you are doing so. Second, I disagree with Imlay's suggestion that Berkeley's theory that only souls and their ideas are real commits us to evaluating volitions rather than actions, though I agree with him that it is sometimes experiences and volitions, rather than the effects that contingently and sometimes unexpectedly follow from them, that we need to and do evaluate.

And perhaps this idea would have been impossible to formulate in the absence of the idealist episode of the eighteenth century. In any case, it seems to me that Imlay has brought out an interesting connection between the Berkeleian doctrine that "sin is in the will" because my agency does not, rigorously speaking, extend beyond myself, and its Kantian counterpart: the doctrine that the only thing that can be called absolutely good is the good will because of the inevitable slippage between intentions and results in the empirical world. The creative misunderstanding of another person's doctrines is a well-known vehicle of philosophical progress. Here we are faced with the possibility that Berkeley might have misunderstood his own doctrines in supposing that his discovery that experience did not entail the existence of—and in fact actually excluded—a multiplicity of material objects external to the experiencer could also validate Protestant inwardness, which traditionally has been contrasted with the Catholic emphasis on "works." It is worth reflecting on similar motivations in the case of the pietistic Kant.

The emergence of subjectivity is, as Imlay's essay shows us, a broad phenomenon reaching into theory of morals as well as theory of knowledge. And his essay is a reminder that where a theory seems sketchy, incoherent, or mostly absent, as Berkeley's theory of the will does, it is precisely there that we ought to devote some effort, for the evasion is likely to be hiding something of importance.

11

Berkeley's Case Against Realism About Dynamics

Lisa Downing

W hile *De Motu*, Berkeley's treatise on the philosophical foundations of mechanics, has frequently been cited for the surprisingly modern ring of certain of its passages, it has not often
been taken as seriously as Berkeley hoped it would be. Even A. A. Luce,
in his editor's introduction, describes *De Motu* as a modest work, of limited
scope:

> The *De Motu* is written in good, correct Latin, but in construction
> and balance the workmanship falls below Berkeley's usual stan-
> dards. The title is ambitious for so brief a tract, and may lead the
> reader to expect a more sustained argument than he will find. A
> more modest title, say *Motion without Matter*, would fitly describe

This essay was the winner of the third annual Colin and Ailsa Turbayne International
Berkeley Essay Prize Competition (1992).
    Thanks to Margaret Wilson and Abraham Roth for helpful comments on an earlier version
of this paper.

its scope and content. Regarded as a treatise on motion in general, it is a slight and disappointing work; but viewed from a narrower angle, it is of absorbing interest and high importance. It is the application of immaterialism to contemporary problems of motion, and should be read as such. . . . [A]part from the *Principles* the *De Motu* would be nonsense. (*Works* IV, 3–4)

There are good general reasons to think, however, that Berkeley's aims in writing the book were as ambitious as the title he chose. As Luce notes, Berkeley wrote the essay in hopes that it would win a prize offered by the Paris Academy of Sciences. He could hardly have expected a tract on the scientific consequences of immaterialism to receive serious consideration. It is also clear from *De Motu* itself that Berkeley saw himself as offering solutions to major conceptual problems confronting contemporary mechanics, problems that, he takes it, should be evident to any philosophically informed reader.

Moreover, although *De Motu* is certainly consistent with Berkeley's early works and the views he puts forward are undoubtedly motivated in part by his metaphysics, he goes out of his way not to mention or overtly invoke any immaterialist or idealist tenets. The most general metaphysical claims that Berkeley appeals to in *De Motu* sound blandly Cartesian: "There are two supreme classes of things, body and soul" (DM 21). "Besides corporeal things there is the other class, *viz.* thinking things" (DM 25). Of course, Berkeley himself would ultimately maintain that these bodies, or corporeal things, are not substances but bundles of ideas that are dependent upon thinking things; however, he is careful never to take this step explicitly in *De Motu*.[1] It seem, then, that Berkeley himself did not suppose that his conclusions in *De Motu* depended upon the truth of immaterialism.

One of Berkeley's central contentions in *De Motu* is that dynamics is problematic because positing physical forces is nonsensical. The most important and most general problem with positing forces, Berkeley maintains, is that they are supposed to be corporeal, that is, physical

---

1. In fact, one might well describe Berkeley as attempting in *De Motu* to pass himself off as an odd kind of Cartesian. For another example, see DM 53, where Berkeley speaks uncharacteristically of a faculty of pure intellect (which, as it turns out, has spirit and the actions of spirit as its sole objects). There seems nothing dishonest in any of this: Berkeley does not say anything that contradicts his own metaphysical views. It is clear, however, that this presentation is strategic—to avoid alienating the scientific audience he hopes to convince. Such rhetorical tactics are quite characteristic of Berkeley.

qualities, yet they are also supposed to be active, that is, they are supposed to be efficient causes of motion.[2] He proffers an instrumentalist interpretation of Newtonian dynamics that avoids the difficulties he claims are involved in a realistic interpretation.

A careful examination of Berkeley's attack on dynamical realism in *De Motu* reveals specific grounds for disputing Luce's evaluation of the work. The main task of this essay is to reconstruct Berkeley's central argument for his contention that dynamics cannot be understood realistically. The argument is original and interesting and is certainly the sort of sustained argument that Luce claims is lacking in *De Motu*. It does not, moreover, rely on immaterialism or idealism; in fact, it is not based on any distinctively *metaphysical* views at all. Rather, the argument is rooted in Berkeley's rigidly empiricist epistemological views and a certain thesis about the requirements of reference.

The Argument

Berkeley's target in *De Motu* is, as has been noted, *a certain kind* of realism about dynamics. It supposes, first, that forces are corporeal. This was certainly one obvious way of interpreting Newton's dynamics (and one followed by many later Newtonians), although it was by no means the only way or a way obviously advocated by Newton. Berkeley specifically declines to treat "spiritual force," which, he says, is not properly a subject for physics: "Those who derive the principle of motion from spirits mean by *spirit* either a corporeal thing or an incorporeal; if a corporeal thing, however tenuous, yet the difficulty recurs; if an incorporeal thing, however true it may be, yet it does not properly belong to physics" (DM 42). (Berkeley would, no doubt, maintain that the only sensible way of understanding the claim that there are spiritual forces is as merely stating that spirits cause the motions of bodies, but he does not argue this point in *De Motu*.) He assumes that no third kind of status (other than corporeal or spiritual) is available, an assumption shared by adherents of the mechanical philosophy.

The dynamical realism Berkeley attacks also supposes that forces are *causes* of motion. Certainly Newton and his followers accorded this status to at least some forces, although they may have thought that certain

---

2. See DM 5, 28, 29, 31, 67, 70.

forces (e.g., attraction) could be reduced to more basic ones (e.g., impulse or repulsion).

The first premise of Berkeley's argument is taken from this sort of dynamical realism:

(1) Physical forces are supposed to be active (i.e., causally efficacious) qualities of body.

The argument's second premise is not a broad metaphysical claim about the total passivity of body, but is importantly restricted:

(2) But all the *known qualities* of body are passive.

Berkeley maintains and supports (2) in two central passages:

> All that which we know to which we have given the name *body* contains nothing in itself which could be the principle of motion or its efficient cause; for impenetrability, extension, and figure neither include nor connote any power of producing motion; nay, on the contrary, if we review singly those qualities of body, and whatever other qualities there may be, we shall see that they are all in fact passive and that there is nothing active in them which can in any way be understood as the source and principle of motion. (DM 22)

> Take away from the idea of body extension, solidity, and figure, and nothing will remain. But those qualities are indifferent to motion, nor do they contain anything which could be called the principle of motion. *This is clear from our very ideas.* (DM 29; emphasis added)

Berkeley's qualification in DM 22, "and whatever other qualities there may be," is, of course, crucial, since he is committed to the existence of more qualities of body than the corpuscularian "primary" qualities he cagily lists. In Berkeley's view, color is a physical quality inseparable and unabstractable from (visible) extension. Likewise, temperature, taste, and smell are legitimate qualities of body. The known qualities of body are the sensible qualities.[3] (DM 29, by contrast, seems somewhat disingenu-

---

3. One might wonder whether impenetrability is sensible. It seems, however, that Berkeley means it to be equivalent to solidity, that is, hardness, which is perfectly tangible.

ous insofar as it suggests that the corpuscularian concept of body exhausts the real qualities of body.)

But how is it established that the sensible qualities are uniformly passive? How can Berkeley rule out the possibility, for example, that solidity is an active quality that endows a body with the power to repel other solid bodies? DM 29 provides the beginnings of an answer—the passivity of the qualities of body is supposed to be clear from our ideas of those qualities. Now, for Berkeley, our ideas of sensible qualities are all ideas of sense or ideas of imagination (which do not differ in kind from ideas of sense).[4] Thus, when Berkeley recommends that we "review . . . those qualities of body," he is directing us to recollect our sensory experiences, not to consult intellectual or abstract concepts. Even so, it is unclear how our sensory experience of the qualities of bodies could rule out those qualities being active, unless by "sensible quality" Berkeley *just means* "quality-as-sensed." If Berkeley were using "quality" in this special sense, it would follow from the plausible premise that we never directly perceive causal power, that none of the sensible qualities are active; extension (i.e., extension-as-sensed) is thus passive, and likewise for solidity and the rest. To put it another way, once it is granted that we do not sense any activity in sensing solidity, Berkeley is free to stipulate that "the sensible quality of solidity" is solidity stripped of any unsensed active aspect, which, if it existed, could be regarded as a separate quality.

That this is in fact Berkeley's line of reasoning here is confirmed by his clear use of it in a related section of *De Motu* where he argues that motion is passive: "Hence it is that many suspect that motion is not mere passivity in bodies. But if we understand by it *that which in the movement of a body is an object to the senses,* no one can doubt that it is entirely passive" (DM 49; emphasis added). Thus (2) amounts to the relatively uncontroversial claim that we do not directly sense any causal powers in body; the qualities-as-sensed of bodies are passive.

Clearly, then, (2) is much weaker than the claim that body *is* passive. It is *so* weak, however, that it seems that little of significance could follow from it: in particular its truth could not be taken to rule out the possibility that bodies might *have* active qualities, causal powers. Interestingly, however, Berkeley does not attempt to conclude that a body cannot *have*

4. DM 21 and 53 confirm that Berkeley does not abandon or revise this opinion in *De Motu.*

active qualities; rather, he argues that it is nonsensical to *posit* any such qualities:

> And so about body we can boldly state as established fact that it is not the principle of motion. But if anyone maintains that the term *body* covers in its meaning occult quality, virtue, form, and essence, besides solid extension and its modes, we must just leave him to his useless disputation with no ideas behind it, and to his abuse of names which express nothing distinctly. But the sounder philosophical method, it would seem, abstains as far as possible from abstract and general notions (if *notions* is the right term for things which cannot be understood). (DM 23)

> The contents of the idea of body we know; but what we know in body is agreed not to be the principle of motion. But those who as well maintain something unknown in body of which they have no idea and which they call the principle of motion, are in fact simply stating that the principle of motion is unknown, and one would be ashamed to linger long on subtleties of this sort. (DM 24)

> If therefore by the term *body* be meant that which we conceive, obviously the principle of motion cannot be sought therein, that is, no part or attribute thereof is the true, efficient cause of the production of motion. But to employ a term, and conceive nothing by it is quite unworthy of a philosopher. (DM 29)

> From what has been said it is clear that those who affirm that active force, action, and the principle of motion are really in bodies are adopting an opinion not based on experience, are supporting it with obscure and general terms, and do not well understand their own meaning. (DM 31)

A preliminary unpacking of the argument of these passages might look like this: From (1) and (2), Berkeley deduces

(3) force is an unknown quality of bodies.

From (3), he concludes that

(4) the term 'force' is empty.[5]

And (4), he supposes, rules out dynamical realism by dictating that force terms do not name anything.

How compelling is this argument? The first thing to note is, given the interpretation of (2) deduced above from Berkeley's attempts to support it, (3) amounts merely to the claim that we have no direct sensory experience of force.[6] But then, does (4) follow from (3)? A significantly qualified version of (4) follows readily enough:

(4a) The term 'force' is empty of sensory significance.

But (4a) does not seem nearly damning enough to rule out dynamical realism.

The Significance of Force Terms

In the passages cited, Berkeley emphasizes the vacuity of dynamical terms. One obvious way of interpreting his remarks is as claiming that the term 'force' is *utterly without significance*, that is, meaningless. This claim would seem to be strong enough to rule out dynamical realism. Two distinguished commentators, Karl Popper and Gerd Buchdahl, have represented Berkeley as arguing in this way. The resulting account of Berkeley's argument, however, is seriously oversimplified because it is based on a misrepresentation of Berkeley's semantic views. A brief excursion into Berkeley's views on the significance of force terms is therefore required in order to arrive at a more precise understanding of (4).

Popper sees Berkeley as basing a claim that dynamical terms are meaningless on the thesis that "to have meaning, a word must stand for an idea."[7] Buchdahl, while taking note of the exception made for general

---

5. And, of course, so too are other terms for forces, for example, 'gravity'.

6. One might object that, strictly speaking, (3) only follows from (1) and (2) if it is supposed that force is *nothing but* activity. (The idea is that we might have some sensory access to forces without having access to their activity.) This is not a serious objection, however, since 'force' could simply be replaced by 'the activity of force' in (3) and (4). It would follow, then, that we cannot intelligibly posit *forces* in the sense of (1), forces that are active.

7. Karl Popper, "Berkeley as a Precursor of Mach and Einstein," in *Berkeley's Principles of Human Knowledge: Critical Studies*, ed. G. W. Engle and G. Taylor (Belmont, Calif.:

terms, attributes very nearly the same semantic view to Berkeley and seems to see this view as a primary source of his antirealism about dynamics.[8]

For convenience, I refer to the semantic thesis that every meaningful word must stand for an idea as "strict Lockeanism," although it represents something of an oversimplification of Locke's own semantic views.[9] The important point, for my purposes, is that Berkeley emphatically rejected strict Lockeanism (which he did indeed associate with Locke)[10] as early as 1708, when he wrote the "Draft Introduction to the Principles." In the published introduction, Berkeley attacks strict Lockeanism as the source of the doctrine of abstract ideas and argues that language may be significant despite not suggesting ideas, for example, by provoking certain emotions.[11] Most significantly, in the seventh dialogue of *Alciphron*, he argues for a broader exception to strict Lockeanism: "A discourse, therefore, that directs how to act or excites to the doing or forbearance of an action may, it seems, be useful and significant, although the words whereof it is composed should not bring each a distinct idea into our minds" (A VII, 5, 292). Berkeley's primary *example* of a discourse that has significance in virtue of its use is Newtonian dynamics (A VII, 7). Force terms, he holds, acquire a sort of significance through their role in guiding action (A VII, 8, 296–97).

Of course, one might interpret Berkeley as simply having changed his mind about the significance of force terms sometime between publishing *De Motu* and publishing *Alciphron* (i.e., between 1721 and 1732). There are good reasons, however, for supposing that the two works are consistent on this issue. One important consideration is the previously noted

---

Wadsworth, 1968), p. 96.

8. Gerd Buchdahl, *Metaphysics and the Philosophy of Science* (Cambridge: MIT Press, 1969), p. 289.

9. Given Locke's discussion of language in book 3 of the *Essay*, it is certainly prima facie plausible to attribute to Locke the view that significant words, excepting particles, stand for ideas. The question whether *Berkeley* was right to attribute this view to Locke is complicated by further questions about the extent to which Locke and Berkeley have a common understanding of what ideas are. John Locke, *An Essay Concerning Human Understanding*, ed. Peter H. Nidditch, (Oxford: Clarendon Press, 1975). (References to Locke's *Essay* in what follows are by book, chapter, and section number.)

10. This is evident from the fact that Berkeley held that the doctrine of abstract ideas was motivated by the thesis that every significant word must stand for a determinate idea, and from the fact that Locke, of course, was the explicit target of Berkeley's antiabstractionism. PC 667 also contains a telling allusion to Locke's semantic views.

11. See IN 20.

fact that Berkeley consistently maintained (from 1708 or so, when he wrote the "Draft Introduction to the Principles," throughout his philosophical career) that words *could* be significant despite not suggesting ideas. And this fact alone requires interpreting Berkeley as occasionally overstating his point in *De Motu* for rhetorical effect. Such passages (e.g., DM 29) are readily understood as making the point that employing a term *as a name* and conceiving nothing by it (i.e., having no associated idea or notion) is "unworthy of a philosopher." Moreover, the fact that Berkeley footnoted *De Motu* approvingly in *Siris* (section 250), published in 1744, and republished *De Motu* in 1752 indicates that Berkeley saw the essay as consistent with his later views.

A comprehensive look at Berkeley's semantic views, then, makes clear that he would not have argued that dynamical terms lack *all* significance. Rather, the cited passages from *De Motu* should be understood as asserting that dynamical terms lack a particular sort of significance, the sort of significance that would allow them to *refer*. This thesis is strong enough to rule out dynamical realism:

(4b) The term 'force' is empty of any significance adequate to secure reference.[12]

If force terms do not name anything, then it is nonsensical to posit forces.

The Role of Berkeley's Empiricism in Supporting the Argument

The crucial move in Berkeley's argument, then, is the leap from (4a), the claim that force terms lack sensory significance, to (4b). How is this leap to be justified? Evidently, a bridge is needed: Berkeley needs to argue that the only significance appropriate for securing the reference of force terms is sensory significance. In effect, Berkeley defends a more general claim, from which (4b), given (1) and (4a), follows. His bridge is this:

12. Here and throughout, by 'secure reference' I mean "secure reference, all else permitting." Of course, no matter how clear our force concepts are, force terms will not refer if forces do not exist.

(Br) The only significance appropriate for securing the reference of terms
      for physical items is sensory significance.[13]

Berkeley attempts to support (Br) in several passages, most notably DM
21:

> To throw light on nature it is idle to adduce things which are
> neither evident to the senses, nor intelligible to reason. Let us see
> then what sense and experience tell us, and reason that rests upon
> them. There are two supreme classes of things, body and soul.
> By the help of sense we know the extended thing, solid, mobile,
> figured, and endowed with other qualities which meet the senses,
> but the sentient, percipient, thinking thing we know by a certain
> internal consciousness. Further we see that those things are plainly
> different from one another, and quite heterogeneous. I speak of things
> known; for of the unknown it is profitless to speak.

In DM 21, Berkeley outlines an epistemology that justifies (Br). From
other passages in *De Motu*, we can fill out the account as follows: The
sources of knowledge are threefold—sense, imagination, and reflection on
mental processes ("internal consciousness" or "intellect"). Imagination,
however, is parasitic on sensation; nothing can be imagined that is not of
a sensible kind, possessed of sensible qualities: "For nothing enters the
imagination which from the nature of the thing cannot be perceived by
sense, since indeed the imagination is nothing else than the faculty which
represents sensible things either actually existing or at least possible"
(DM 53). Reflection can supply us with knowledge only of spirits and their
activities: "Pure intellect . . . is concerned only with spiritual and inex-
tended things, such as our minds, their states, passions, virtues, and such
like" (DM 53). This is certainly a rigidly empiricist epistemology, and one
that might well have been resisted by Berkeley's more Cartesian readers.
Certainly the limited scope allotted to "intellect" would have seemed quite
mistaken to Descartes. Leibniz, moreover, held that the intellect is the
source of a *metaphysical* notion of force that provides a necessary

---

13. This bridge has an air of anachronism about it that is easily dispelled by seeing it as
a consequence of two more general and more obviously Berkeleian principles: "You cannot
name anything of which you cannot conceive" and "Conceiving of something physical
requires having an idea of it." In what follows, I focus on (Br) itself because it is precisely
what is required for Berkeley's case against dynamical realism and because a discussion of
the nature of "conceiving" would take me too far afield.

foundation for physics.[14] Berkeley's empiricism, which he does not defend against alternative epistemologies, rules out any such picture of how we attain a concept of force.

What makes this account still more restrictive, and what enables it to justify (Br), is that Berkeley builds into it such a great divide between sense/imagination and reflection that it is illegitimate to use reflection on mental processes to give content to terms for physical things (and, likewise, illegitimate to use imagination to give content to terms for spiritual things). Locke's empiricism, by contrast, includes no such restriction. Locke maintains that we acquire our most clear and distinct idea of active power from reflection on the operations of our minds. He holds, further, that this very idea of active power, so derived, is applicable to bodies, although an idea of active power can only be *derived* from bodies in an obscure form.[15]

Berkeley supports the restriction by eloquent appeals to the heterogeneity of body and spirit:

> A thinking, active thing is given which we experience as the principle of motion in ourselves. This we call *soul, mind,* and *spirit.* Extended thing also is given, inert, impenetrable, moveable, totally different from the former and constituting a new genus. Anaxagoras, wisest of men, was the first to grasp the great difference between thinking things and extended things, and he asserted that the mind has nothing in common with bodies, as is established from the first book of Aristotle's *De Anima.* Of the moderns Descartes has put the same point most forcibly. What was left clear by him others have rendered involved and difficult by their obscure terms. (DM 30)

This restriction is crucial for Berkeley, since he admits, even insists, that we have some notion of spiritual activity or force: "Besides corporeal

---

14. See "A Specimen of Dynamics," p. 119, "New System of Nature," p. 139, and "On Nature Itself," p. 159, in *Philosophical Essays,* ed. Roger Ariew and Daniel Garber, (Indianapolis: Hackett Publishing Co., 1989). Interestingly, in the *Nouveaux Essais,* Leibniz seems to endorse Locke's account (briefly described below) of the origins of the idea of active power. One suspects, however, that the agreement is somewhat superficial; Leibniz seems to be using Locke to make the point that forces are soul-like. Leibniz, *New Essays on Human Understanding,* ed. Peter Remnant and Jonathan Bennett (Cambridge: Cambridge University Press, 1981), pp. 169–72 (II, xxi, 1–4).

15. Locke explicitly mentions the possibility that matter might in fact not possess any truly active powers, but he clearly holds that it makes sense to suppose that matter has such powers. *Essay,* II, xxi, 2–4.

things there is the other class, *viz.* thinking things, and that there is in them the power of moving bodies we have learned by personal experience" (DM 25). "[W]e feel it [mind] as a faculty of altering both our own state and that of other things, and that is properly called vital, and puts a wide distinction between soul and bodies" (DM 33). This restriction might appear to be easily the weakest step in Berkeley's argument against dynamical realism. Given that a notion of activity is readily available, it is not at all clear why that notion should not be applicable to the physical realm, so that it could give the dynamicists' use of the term 'force' enough significance to permit reference and save realism.

Antiabstractionism as Support for the Argument

One suspects that Berkeley would respond to such a suggestion (and to Locke, as I interpret him) by denouncing abstraction. And indeed, it seems that Berkeley has an antiabstractionist argument available to block such a move. Although he does not make such an argument in *De Motu* (unsurprisingly, since he does not explicitly consider the objection made above), he does allude to its main ingredient: "Too much abstraction, on the one hand, or the division of things truly inseparable, and on the other hand composition or rather confusion of very different things have perplexed the nature of motion" (DM 47). The argument, modeled on one he offers in several other works, would run like this:[16] What is impossible is inconceivable. Therefore, what cannot exist separately (as two things) cannot be conceived of as existing separately. Now, it is not possible for a spirit's activity to exist apart from the spirit. Therefore, it is not possible to conceive of a spirit's activity existing apart from the spirit. Therefore, we cannot attain any notion of spiritual activity, separate from spirit, that we could then *transfer* to the corporeal domain.[17]

The argument thus constructed on Berkeley's behalf is significantly different from those he actually makes in attacking abstract ideas, in that what is under attack is something more general than abstract *ideas*, that

16. See *First Draft of the Introduction to the Principles* (*Works* II, 125); *Defense of Free-Thinking in Mathematics* (*Works* IV, 134); and A VII, 6, 333–34.

17. This argument might at first glance appear to beg the question, but it does not. It does not require assuming that activity could not exist in body without spirit, but only that a particular spirit's activity could not exist without that spirit. The argument then (purportedly) blocks an attempt to extract a separate notion of activity from a particular active spirit.

is, separate or abstract *conceptions*. This shift is necessary, of course, since Berkeley maintains that we cannot have ideas of spirits or their actions. I take it that this generalization of the argument is legitimate for two reasons. First, Berkeley does hold that we somehow conceive of spirits and their actions (i.e., we have notions of them), although we do not do so "by way of idea." Second, Berkeley holds that what is impossible cannot be conceived of *at all:* it is not just that we cannot form *ideas* of impossibilities. It is clear from PR 143 that Berkeley does object to this sort of abstraction and does consider it to *be* a sort of abstraction. "It will not be amiss to add, that the doctrine of *abstract ideas* hath had no small share in rendering those sciences intricate and obscure, which are particularly conversant about spiritual things. Men have imagined they could frame abstract notions of the powers and acts of the mind, and consider them prescinded, as well from the mind or spirit itself, as from their respective objects and effects." There are three obvious ways to resist the argument. First, one might simply deny the first premise. However, although this premise might seem questionable, it was a commonplace of seventeenth- and eighteenth-century philosophy.[18] (Whatever is conceivable is noncontradictory and thus, it was thought, possible, since God *could* make it so.) Second, one might (in a Humean mood, perhaps) assert that it *is* possible for a particular instance of spiritual activity to exist without spirit. Although Berkeley himself went through a Humean phase with respect to his view of spirit (wherein he identified spirits with bundles of volitions), his considered view rules out this response by dictating that particular volitions and ideas require the support of spiritual substance, the essence of which is to will and to perceive/understand.[19] This conception of spirit, or mind, certainly would have seemed familiar and uncontroversial to Berkeley's Cartesian readers. And although it doubtless seems more controversial to present-day readers, it could scarcely be called unintuitive. Third, one might try to turn Berkeley's own alternative to abstraction against him. Although Berkeley argues that we cannot form an abstract idea of triangularity, he does

---

18. It was accepted, in particular, by defenders of abstraction. See Julius Weinberg, *Abstraction, Relation, and Induction* (Madison: University of Wisconsin Press, 1965), pp. 17–18; Douglas Jesseph, *Berkeley's Philosophy of Mathematics* (Ph.D. diss., Princeton University, 1987), p. 21; and Kenneth P. Winkler, *Berkeley: An Interpretation* (Oxford: Clarendon Press, 1989), pp. 37–38.

19. For evidence of Berkeley's Humean phase, see PC 615, 478a, 712. For an account of the changes and tensions in Berkeley's view of spirit, see Charles McCracken, "Berkeley's Notion of Spirit," *History of European Ideas* 7 (1986), pp. 597–602.

acknowledge that "a man may consider a figure merely as triangular, without attending to the particular qualities of the angles, or relations of the sides" (IN 16). Presumably, then, he would also allow that we can selectively attend to activity, that is, consider a spirit's activity without attending to other aspects of its spiritual nature. Is this selective attention not enough, one might ask, to ensure that when I talk of physical forces, that talk is not so empty as to be obviously nonreferring? Berkeley, it seems, would simply have to insist that something somehow more distinct and concrete—a directly applicable idea or notion—is required to make sense of force terms as potentially referring. This undefended (while not obviously implausible) position on the requisites of reference, then, is in effect the foundation for his claim, in *De Motu*, that positing forces is nonsensical. The position itself seems quite Lockean, which is unsurprising, since Berkeley's semantic views are derived from Locke's (although, as I have shown, Berkeley rejects what he sees as strict Lockeanism about meaning/significance).[20] When this requirement for reference is combined with Berkeley's anti-Lockean views on abstraction, however, the results, as we have seen, are quite un-Lockean.

Underdetermination as Grounds for Antirealism?

W. H. Newton-Smith attributes a very different argument against dynamical realism to Berkeley.[21] Newton-Smith sees Berkeley as foreshadowing Duhem and Quine by premising his argument against scientific realism on the "thesis of the underdetermination of theory by data." He bases this interpretation on one intriguing section of *De Motu*:

> It is clear, moreover, that force is not a thing certain and determinate, from the fact that great men advance very different opinions, even contrary opinions, about it, and yet in their results attain the

20. "For the signification and use of Words, depending on that connexion, which the Mind makes between its *Ideas*, and the Sounds it uses as Signs of them, it is necessary, in the Application of Names to things, that the Mind should have distinct *Ideas* of the Things, and retain also the particular Name that belongs to every one, with its peculiar appropriation to that *Idea*" (*Essay*, III, iii, 2).

21. W. H. Newton-Smith, "Berkeley's Philosophy of Science," in *Essays on Berkeley: A Tercentennial Celebration*, ed. John Foster and Howard Robinson (Oxford: Clarendon Press, 1985), pp. 149–61; hereafter, N-S, followed by page number.

truth. For Newton says that impressed force consists in action alone, and is the action exerted on the body to change its state, and does not remain after the action. Torricelli contends that a certain heap or aggregate of forces impressed by percussion is received into the mobile body, and there remains and constitutes impetus. Borelli and others say much the same. But although Newton and Torricelli seem to be disagreeing with one another, they each advance consistent views, and the thing is sufficiently well explained by both. For all forces attributed to bodies are mathematical hypotheses just as are attractive forces in planets and sun. But mathematical entities have no stable essence in the nature of things; and they depend on the notion of the definer. Whence the same thing can be explained in different ways. (DM 67)

The first thing to note about Newton-Smith's interpretation is that it attributes a gross non sequitur to Berkeley. Newton-Smith paraphrases Berkeley's argument in this passage as follows: "Forces are not determinate since Newton and Torricelli tell different stories about them" (N-S, p. 157). But, of course, a mere example of two contradictory theories that have so far both agreed with observation has no implications for realism. Antirealist consequences for dynamics might be held to follow from the limited underdetermination thesis that both theories "make exactly the same predictions" and "fare equally well on any principle of theory choice which is of epistemic value" (N-S, p. 156), but nowhere in this passage does Berkeley support any such claim, nor is it clear that he *makes* one. Certainly, there is absolutely no textual evidence that Berkeley ever entertained the thesis that Newton-Smith sees him as assuming without argument, the thesis (labeled UTD by Newton-Smith) that "for any subject matter there will be a pair of evidentially equivalent theories which are logically incompatible" (N-S, p. 156), that "for any Newton there is a Torricelli" (N-S, p. 158–59).

Interestingly, Newton-Smith seems to acknowledge that his interpretation leaves Berkeley's position looking rather embarrassing; the main virtue of the interpretation, as he sees it, is that it gives Berkeley's views "contemporary significance": "Berkeley's semantical instrumentalism rests then on an entirely speculative conjecture of UTD. While there is no good reason to think the conjecture is true, his philosophy of science would be appropriate should it be true. And while the science of his day did not render the conjecture plausible, the arguments of Duhem and Quine have generated sufficient interest in UTD to give Berkeley's philosophy of science contemporary significance" (N-S, p. 159). Newton-Smith, however, misunderstands Berkeley's point in the passage. A closer examination of the latter half of the passage shows that Berkeley's argument is very nearly the reverse of the argument Newton-Smith attributes to him. Berkeley argues that *because* dynamical terms refer to nothing in the nature of things, so that forces are mere fictions, seemingly contradictory theories may be equally satisfactory, for they may work equally well and provide equally good scientific explanations (in Berkeley's sense of "scientific explanation"). Berkeley notes that the theories are not really inconsistent, for they do not make literal claims, and their significance derives from their results. Thus the plurality of equally adequate dynamic theories is for Berkeley a *consequence* of the fact that force terms do not refer to any underlying entities.[22] Berkeley's point in the first sentence of the quoted passage is just that in the proliferation of dynamical theories, we should see the effects of employing nonreferential terms in mechanics.

Berkeley's "semantical instrumentalism," as Newton-Smith labels it, is thus grounded (as far as his explicit arguments in *De Motu* are concerned) in his *semantics* and epistemology, not in a Quinean thesis about underdetermination.[23]

The Argument's Rhetorical Role and Implications

To recapitulate, Berkeley's argument against dynamical realism can be broken down as follows:

(1)   Physical forces are supposed to be active qualities of body.
(2)   But all the *known* qualities of body are passive.
(3)   Force is an unknown quality of bodies [from (1) and (2)].
(4a) The term 'force' is empty of sensory significance [from (3)].
(Br) The only significance appropriate for securing the reference of terms for physical items is sensory significance.
(4b) The term 'force' is empty of any significance adequate to secure reference [from (Br), (1), and (4a)].

22. Here I am in agreement with Popper, who, unlike Newton-Smith, in my view correctly understands the direction of Berkeley's argument in this passage. See Popper, "Berkeley as a Precursor of Mach and Einstein," 94–95.

23. I do agree with Newton-Smith's basic characterization of Berkeley's instrumentalism; see N-S, p. 150.

Premise 4b rules out dynamical realism, for if force terms do not name anything, then dynamical realism is fundamentally confused. The bridge (Br) is supported by appeal to a strictly empiricist epistemology and might be further shored up by antiabstractionism and a thesis about the conceptual requirements for reference.

Given the intricacy of this argument, one might well wonder what advantage Berkeley saw in offering it instead of arguing that dynamical realism is impossible because body *is* passive, that is, bodies are never efficient causes. After all, Berkeley did hold that only spirits are causally efficacious. The obvious way of arguing for this metaphysical thesis, however, would have exposed Berkeley's more controversial metaphysical views, which he evidently sought to keep under wraps in *De Motu*.[24] Berkeley does allude in *De Motu* to various grounds (none of them immaterialist or idealist) for thinking that body *is* passive; for example, he appeals to a Cartesian conception of God's relation to the world.[25] However, Berkeley's central argument against dynamical realism does not employ the metaphysical thesis but rather (2), a much weaker claim. Berkeley might rightly have expected (2) to be much more appealing than the metaphysical thesis to anyone with a skeptical bent, who might be inclined to deny that we can be sure of our grasp of the nature of body (or of God's relation to the world). Since Berkeley was quite sensitive to the possibility of skepticism and was always concerned to combat it, one might plausibly speculate that this sensitivity shaped his choice of argument here. Moreover, Berkeley might reasonably have expected many readers, especially the skeptically inclined, to jump immediately from (3) to a rejection of dynamical realism simply out of a horror of occult qualities.[26] (Berkeley seems deliberately to obscure the fact that he has only really argued that forces are *unsensed* in order to encourage this leap; still, even a reader who noted that fact might be inclined to make the leap out of vaguely empiricist sentiments.)

Of course, the most fundamental reason why Berkeley gave *this* argument is the simple fact that he held the semantic and epistemological views that make it a compelling argument against realism about dynamics.

One very interesting implication of this analysis of Berkeley's argument should be noted: The argument, when generalized, does not rule out

24. The argument of PR 25 is easily extended into an argument against dynamical realism. I agree with Phillip Cummins's claim that the argument of this passage presupposes idealism. See Essay 6 in this volume.

25. See DM 34.

26. A horror Berkeley is careful to cultivate in *De Motu*. See DM 4.

realism about all theoretical (i.e., unobserved) entities, or even all *unob-servable* entities. Rather, it applies only against entities that are supposed not to possess qualities *of a sensible kind* (i.e, extension [visible or tangible], color, taste, smell, sound). Thus, Berkeley maintains in *De Motu* that it's nonsensical to posit *unimaginable* entities.[27] Theoretical particles that are supposed to possess figure and motion count as imaginable by Berkeley's criteria: "And here it may not be amiss to observe that figures and motions which cannot be actually felt by us, but only imagined, may nevertheless be esteemed tangible ideas, forasmuch as they are of the same kind with the objects of touch, and as the imagination drew them from that sense" (TVV 51). Thus, Berkeley's case against realism in *De Motu* does not rule out positing such particles, but does proscribe any (realistically understood) attribution of forces to particles. In this respect, Berkeley's instrumentalism about dynamics is in harmony with his apparently realistic corpuscularian speculations in *Siris*.[28]

27. Likewise, it is nonsensical to posit unimaginable qualities of otherwise imaginable things.

28. Berkeley does retain his dynamical antirealism in *Siris:* "Sir Isaac Newton asks, Have not the minute particles of bodies certain forces or powers by which they act on one another, as well as on the particles of light, for producing most of the phenomena in nature? But, in reality, those minute particles are only agitated according to certain laws of nature, by some other agent, wherein the force exists and not it them, which have only the motion" (S 250; cf. S 155, 234, 246).

PART III

Vision and Perceptual Objects

12

Seeing Distance from a Berkeleian Perspective

Robert Schwartz

A lthough Berkeley's *An Essay Towards a New Theory of Vision* contains a probing examination of a range of topics in vision theory, the aspect of this work most discussed and criticized has been his account of distance perception. Now, while many of these criticisms have some point, I believe that readings of Berkeley often misconceive the significance of crucial aspects of his psychology of perception and fail to appreciate the full force of his problems and proposals. Perhaps the extent to which Berkeley's ideas have been differently understood and received can be highlighted by comparing a few quota-

This essay is excerpted from a much longer one on Berkeley's views on distance perception, which, in turn, constitutes the first chapter of my book *Vision: Variations on Some Berkeleian Themes* (Oxford: Basil Blackwell, 1994). Phillip Cummins commented on this essay at the University of Western Ontario's conference on Berkeley's Metaphysics. I hope I have answered some of his questions in my book.

tions from representative philosophical and psychological works. Consider first the contrasting remarks of Alan Donagan,

> Although Berkeley's theory of vision was generally received as true for over a century, so much of it depends on the false proposition that distance cannot be immediately seen that it has long been discredited,[1]

and Julian Hochberg,

> The most influential theory of space perception in Western thought has been that distance is not a direct visual sensation at all. Instead . . . memories of the grasping or walking motions that have been made in the past . . . provide the idea of distance.[2]

Donagan, along with numerous other commentators, is convinced that the idea that distance perception is not immediate "has been long discredited." Yet if one turns to a standard psychological text, such as Hochberg's one finds a much different assessment of this claim.

The following selections from George Pitcher and Herman von Helmholtz are likewise in sharp contrast. Pitcher writes that

> [W]hatever a person immediately (or directly) sees he has incorrigible knowledge of. . . . Berkeley is firm in his espousal of [this]. . . . Many philosophers through the ages have certainly accepted something like it as axiomatic.[3]

And here is Helmholtz:

> We are not in the habit of observing our sensations accurately. . . . Thus in most cases some special assistance and training are needed in order to observe these subjective sensations.[4]

Pitcher is right when he says that many philosophers have taken it as axiomatic that we have incorrigible knowledge of our sensory states. But

1. "Berkeley's Theory of the Immediate Objects of Vision," in *Studies in Perception*, ed. Peter Machamer and Robert Turnbull (Columbus: Ohio State University Press, 1978), p. 332.
2. *Perception* (Englewood Cliffs, N.J.: Prentice-Hall, 1965), p. 43.
3. *Berkeley* (London: Routledge & Kegan Paul, 1977), p. 97.
4. *Treatise on Physiological Optics*, vol. 3, ed. James Southall, (New York: Dover, 1950), p. 6.

Helmholtz's account of our ability to report on our sense experience better reflects the position of most visual theorists working in the Berkeleian tradition, including, I would argue, Berkeley himself. The next quotations provide another striking case of conflicting viewpoints. Bertrand Russell insists that

> Berkeley's theory of vision, according to which everything looks flat, is disproved by the stereoscope.[5]

But James Sully demurs:

> Some years ago it was commonly thought that, thanks to the argument of the Berkeleyans aided by experiments of Wheatstone and others the derivative nature of visual space was amply demonstrated.[6]

Russell has been joined by other critics in citing Wheatstone's invention of the stereoscope as damaging to Berkeley's line of thought. As Sully points out, however, developments in vision theory support no such conclusion. Indeed, many of the early stereoscope experiments were taken to strengthen Berkeley's position.

The passage in the *New Theory* that has been the subject of severest criticism appears right at the beginning. In section 2 Berkeley says, "It is, I think, agreed by all that distance, of itself and immediately, can not be seen." In section 11 he goes on, "[I]t is plain that distance is in its own nature imperceptible." In considering these passages I think it important to separate several issues that can be easily run together: (i) Berkeley's account of our ideas of distance, (ii) the claim that ideas of distance gained by sight are not immediate, and (iii) the claim that, in and of itself, distance is imperceptible by sight. While critical discussions tend to focus on (ii), Berkeley himself is mainly concerned with (i) and (iii). As Berkeley says, (ii) was generally accepted by all.

For Berkeley and for other vision theorists, the claim that some idea is not immediate is an empirical claim about the process that leads to our having that idea. Ideas are "not immediate" when they are the result of operations that involve the processing of mental items. In contrast, immediate ideas are ideas brought to mind by purely nonmental goings on.

5. *Human Knowledge: Its Scope and Limits* (New York: Simon & Schuster, 1964), p. 51.
6. "The Question of Visual Perception in Germany, I," *Mind* 9 (1878), p. 1.

The processes that underlie immediate ideas are, on this score, like those that underlie the output of our kidney or liver; they are entirely organic or physiological in nature. In much of the literature on vision, what Berkeley calls 'immediate ideas' are also referred to as 'sensations'.

Berkeley's own version of what makes a process mental is closely tied to the then long prevalent identification of mental states with conscious states. Mental processes were understood to involve manipulating ideas, which were themselves assumed to be states of consciousness. In particular, then, the claim that we do not see distance immediately amounts to the claim that the ideas of distance, derived from sight, depend on mental operations; that is, they are brought to mind via intermediate ideas.

As Berkeley notes, the claim that distance evaluation depends in this way on the registering of pictorial and other cues was widely accepted. It was thought to be a trivial consequence of the one-point argument. "For distance being a line directed endwise to the eye, it projects only one point in the fund of the eye, which point remains invariably the same, whether the distance is larger or smaller" (NTV 2). But if distance perception is not immediate, which aspects of vision might fall under the label 'immediate'? Here matters have been hotly contested throughout the modern history of visual studies. It might seem, for example, that color or neutral color (the black-to-white scale) are obvious candidates. What color or neutral color we perceive is simply determined by the interplay between the properties of light and the physiological natural of our visual receptors. No mental work is needed. Yet this sort of explanation has its problems.

A piece of coal in sunlight looks black, while a lump of sugar indoors looks white. The sunlit coal, however, reflects more white light than the sugar. Treating such phenomena as sensations may thus seem problematic, since there is no direct correlation between the stimulus intensity and the experienced quality. Roughly, two types of theories have been offered to explain the phenomena. On the psychic, or cognitive, theory, it is claimed that we immediately experience a sensation that corresponds to the absolute value of the light. The coal immediately appears white. But then our visual system takes into account the high level of illumination. This combination of information triggers a memory trace of a black quale, which we then experience. The alternative approach claims that no such mental operations are necessary. According to this view, the stimulus is not the absolute intensity of the light but the *ratio* of the light intensities coming from the object and those in its environment. The constant black color of the coal under different illumination is determined by the constant intensity of the *ratios* of the stimuli. It is immediate, a matter of sense.

Similar conflicting approaches turn up in discussions of size and other spatial properties. Consider the moon illusion. Although the size of the retinal image of the moon is the same at its zenith and on the horizon, the moon seems bigger on the horizon. For Berkeley the number of minimum *visibilia* are the same, but we read through our immediate ideas and see the moon differently in the two situations. In recent years, critics of this psychic approach, most prominently Gestaltists and Gibsonians, have argued that the visual appreciation of size is simply triggered by higher-order properties of the stimulus and is not dependent on intermediate sensations of the sort Berkeley and others propose. Examples of these contrasting approaches, psychic versus organic, could be multiplied, but this is no place to consider the merits of each.[7]

If Berkeley's use of the distinction between immediate and nonimmediate ideas is continuous with that characteristic of work on vision both before and after the *New Theory*, it might best be understood to incorporate the following features:

(1) Immediacy depends on the type of processing involved, not on the kind of idea. Even to sight, certain cases of color perception, for example, need not be immediate.

(2) The "immediate" notion does not match up with our ordinary-language 'looks', 'appears', and 'seems' locutions. The sunlit coal *looks* black and the moon *appears* bigger on the horizon, but neither is immediate according to psychic theories.

(3) What is immediately seen does not correspond to judgments that are *noncommittal* regarding how things actually are in the world. We can protect against factual error by claiming that the cat *seems to be* three feet away and not asserting that it *is* three feet away, just as we can avoid commitment to the real color of the fire engine by saying only that it *looks* red. Nevertheless, the red look for Berkeley is immediate, but the three-feet-awayness is not. And on the classic accounts of neutral color and size we are not reporting what we immediately see when we speak guardedly and only say that the sunlit coal *seems to me* to be black or the moon *seems to me* bigger on the horizon.

(4) Immediate ideas of sense did not typically have the epistemological status they took on in twentieth-century philosophical discussions of

---

7. For an account of many of these, see Julian Hochberg, "Perception, I and II," in *Woodworth and Schlossberg's Experimental Psychology*, ed. J. Kling and L. Riggs (New York: Holt, Rinehart & Winston, 1971), pp. 395–550.

the foundations of knowledge and the mind/body problem. For Berkeley, as well as later theorists, although our immediate experiences are mental states, we are not necessarily able to report accurately on them, and they are not incorrigible.

As for the status of distance perception, the one-point argument convinced Berkeley, along with most everyone else, that seeing distance was a two-stage process. In vision, ideas of distance come to us by way of the prior registering of distance cues. In this assumption, Berkeley was in accord with the optics writers of his day as well as with most vision theorists who followed. Berkeley's disagreement with the optic writers was over the nature of our ideas of spatial distance and over the particular kind of mental processing involved in vision. It was not over whether nonorganic or psychic operations were required for distance perception. As the psychologist James J. Gibson critically remarked not long ago, the one-point argument "states the problem of perception of the third dimension, or depth perception, as it has been studied . . . for over 250 years."[8] Although Berkeley may be most remembered for saying that distance is not immediate, his more original and controversial ideas in the study of vision are found elsewhere. Recall, Berkeley also claimed that, in and of itself, distance is imperceptible to sight. Our visual experience lacks any inherent qualities of spatiality from which we could *derive* our ideas of space. This latter claim, although related, is different from the claim that spatial perception is nonimmediate. To see this, consider again our perception of the black coal in sunlight. According to the psychic theory this is a two-stage process, the black color is not immediately perceived. Yet this black color idea is an idea of sight, and under more standard lighting conditions a black color could be an immediate sensation.

Berkeley maintains that the situation is different in the case of distance. Our idea of distance is not a visual idea at all, nor is it a construct of visual ideas, nor is it in any way derivable from visual experience by reason, similarity, or analogy. Our concept of distance in general is derived from movement experience, not sight, and the content of any specific distance idea is entirely tangible. For Berkeley, distance is not a property of our visual experience, just as color and distance are not properties of our

8. "Three Kinds of Distance That Can Be Seen or How Bishop Berkeley Went Wrong," in *Studies in Perception: Festschrift for Fabio Mettelli*, ed. G. Flores D'Arcais (Milan: Martello-Guinti, 1976), p. 83. It was Gibson's own work that did much to challenge the paradigm and assumptions underlying the traditional claim that distance perception is not immediate.

olfactory field. We may be able to tell by the lemony smell that the object is yellow, but yellow is not a quality of the odor. Similarly, as the lemony smell gets stronger, we may be able to tell that the object is approaching, but distance is not a property of smell. We could not, moreover, acquire our ideas of color or distance if all we had to go on was smell.

Intuitively, however, vision seems different from smell; there appears to be something inherently spatial to our visual sensations. But according to Berkeley, this everyday, "vulgar" intuition is incorrect. A major reason for Berkeley's claim that distance, in particular, is not an attribute of our visual field comes from his understanding of the implications of the one-point argument, and in this he was again joined by most theorists. What was more controversial and more original was his further claim that vision lacks the wherewithal to provide us with *any* of our ordinary (physical) spatial ideas, and this includes ideas of size, shape, orientation, and direction. Berkeley does not, however, subscribe to the doctrine some others were to adopt, that our visual field has no intrinsic order. For Berkeley, it does not follow from an allowance that our visual field has inherent structure that it makes sense to treat that field as a *spatial* realm to which our ordinary geometric ideas can be meaningfully applied or from which they can be derived.

The dilemma of the inverted image is an important case in point. We say that the man looks erect, but then are puzzled by the fact that the retinal image is inverted. The puzzle dissolves when we realize that it makes no sense to describe our *phenomenal field* as itself erect or upside down, as if it were located in the same space as the retinal image and could be compared to it with respect to some common idea of spatial orientation. We can, of course, come to use visual information to determine whether an object is up or down, but this depends on correlations with the tangible. We could not develop our ideas of spatial orientation from visual experience alone. Such experience lacks any intrinsic qualities of spatial upness or downess to serve as a basis for acquiring these ideas. The same holds for our ideas of right and left. Our use of spatial terms to describe our phenomenal field is not to be taken literally. It is derived from our habits of interpreting the tangible significance of our visual experience.

Berkeley's approach to the supposed distance properties of vision is of a piece. Berkeley does not claim that our visual experiences are flat (spatially two-dimensional) rather than voluminous (spatially three-dimensional), a claim that many did take to be a consequence of the one-point argument. Instead, he says the claim that the immediate objects of perception are planes and not solids makes no sense. His reasons for holding this position, I think, are not quite D. M. Armstrong's: "[F]latness presupposes the existence of three dimensions, for it is only *surfaces* which can be said to be flat or not flat, and surfaces must be surfaces of *volumes*, and volumes are three dimensional. Now Berkeley denies that objects are immediately seen as three dimensional, and so he must deny they are seen flat."[9] Nor, I believe, would Berkeley distinguish the case of location from that of distance in the way Armstrong suggests: "I can see immediately that the man is to the left of the tree, and that the leaves of the tree are above its trunk (more strictly, all I immediately see are certain man-like, leaf-like, and trunk-like colored shapes arranged in this way), but I can not immediately see that the tree-like shape is more, or less, distant than the man-like shape."[10] Berkeley claims, instead, that our visual field, like our olfactory field, lacks anything comparable to our ideas of both spatial distance and spatial direction. With regard to distance, however, "all agreed." A point anywhere along a line of sight projects the same point on our retina whether near or far. There is no presentation of the third dimension per se in the stimulus and, in turn, in our visual field. There is nothing in our visual field, for example, that increases in size as the distance of the point increases.

This version of the one-point argument does not depend, as has often been claimed, on the assumption that distance cues are necessarily ambiguous. Cues could be unambiguous (e.g., brightness could vary directly with distance) without affecting Berkeley's main point here. No matter how unambiguously such brightness ideas corresponded to distances, they would not themselves be ideas of distance. We cannot, therefore, acquire distance ideas, as we acquire color ideas, on the basis of visual experience alone. A spirit with sight but no tangible sense could not have our ordinary ideas of space (see NTV 153–59). Talk of the voluminousness or distance properties of our visual experience is strictly derivative, reflecting the spatial or tangible significance we have come to assign to visual phenomena.[11]

But then, did not the invention of the stereoscope and experiments on retinal disparity show that Berkeley and those who agreed with him were mistaken? Many critics have assumed that these findings overturn or severely challenge Berkeley's theories. Such claims, however, are particu-

9. *Berkeley's Theory of Vision* (Melbourne: Melbourne University Press, 1960), p. 6.
10. Ibid., p. 5.
11. In other sections of the *New Theory*, Berkeley argues that the same holds for size, shape, direction, and orientation. His claims in these cases, however, do not depend on the one-point argument in the way his distance thesis does.

larly puzzling when one looks at the actual developments in the scientific study of vision. As Sully reminds us, many prominent theorists (including, to an extent, Wheatstone himself) took the stereoscope experiments to support Berkeley's views. Why the discrepancy? In order to answer this question, I think it necessary to separate again Berkeley's different claims about the nature of distance perception [(i), (ii), (iii) above].

Perhaps the easiest misunderstanding to clear up is the idea that Wheatstone's invention proved that distance perception is immediate. For a long while it had been known that, within a limited range, objects at different distances from the viewer project noncongruent images on the retina. Only objects on the plane of focus strike corresponding points on both retinas; the retinal projections from all other objects strike disparate points (see Fig. 1).

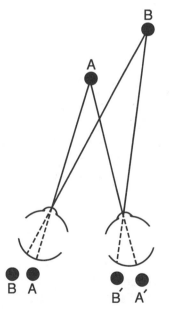

Fig. 1. Retinal disparity: the distance B–A is less than the distance B′–A′.

What the stereoscope showed was that the disparity of the images did indeed effect or play a role in distance perception. It did not undermine the one-point argument; rather, it indicated that there was another cue, retinal disparity, that vision could and did tap in trying to work out distance relations. According to most models of binocular vision, this was taken to mean that the visual system first registers disparity information and then uses it to derive distance. The model was a two-stage operation, and in this way not different from the nonimmediate processing models found in dealing with pictorial and kinesthetic cues to distance.

In fact, experiments with the stereoscope were used to argue in favor of a two-stage solution to another problem that was most prominent in Berkeley's time and thereafter. This is the problem of accounting for the fact that we do not see double even though each eye is capable of producing its own visual experience.[12] According to one account, the organic model, we are wired so that nerve impulses from corresponding retinal points come together and merge into a single impulse that then travels to higher brain centers, triggering but a single experience. The fact that objects not on the focal plane do not project to corresponding retinal points, therefore, poses a challenge to organic models of single vision. Moreover, workers like Helmholtz thought they could demonstrate by means of stereoscope experiments that fusion does not occur at a neural level and that we do have the distinct experiences associated with each eye. "These experiments show . . . the content of each separate field comes to consciousness without being fused with the other field by means of organic mechanisms; and that, therefore, the fusion of the two fields in one common image, when it does occur, is a psychic act."[13]

If the invention of the stereoscope did not demonstrate that distance perception is immediate, did it not at least deal a blow to Berkeley's further claim that distance is not a quality of visual experience? Anyone who has looked through a stereoscope has experienced the difference between the voluminous quality of these pictures in contrast to the flatness, or two-dimensional quality, of ordinary pictures. So how, in light of this, could Berkeley maintain that distance is not an attribute of our visual experience?

Berkeley, I think, would not have denied that the stereoscope scenes look different or are experienced differently from single pictures. He was obviously aware that in ordinary vision we see distance better, and our experience seems more voluminous, when we use two eyes. The reason is that in binocular vision we have powerful, additional cues, for example, conversion, to aid in assessing distance. The stereoscope showed that there is one more cue, binocular disparity, that could help. We have noted, too, that Berkeley did not claim that our visual field was or looked planar.

12. Berkeley himself does not deal with this problem in NTV.
13. *Physiological Optics*, vol. 3, p. 499. Again, it was not assumed that the average person was aware of or could report on the intermediate sensations.

He says, in fact, that we will derivatively describe as solid, not planar, those visual experiences that we interpret three-dimensionally. Thus, since disparity enhances our appreciation of distance, it is not surprising that visual experiences that include disparity among their cues are described, derivatively, as being more voluminous.

Still, though the stereoscope experiments did not refute Berkeley's position, why were they taken by many to support his ideas, in particular, his claim that vision lacks spatial properties? Here issues are more complex, and I can only begin to sketch out the considerations that were operative. By the time Wheatstone invented the stereoscope, perhaps the major schism in vision research was over the issue of innateness. On one side there were those who, like Berkeley, claimed that our spatial ideas were derived from sense experience. On the other side were those who saw themselves as heirs to the "Kantian" tradition and were convinced that we could not acquire our ideas of space by means of sense. Our ideas of space were an innate imposition of mind. Not only vision, as Berkeley claimed, but our senses in general were thought to be inadequate to supply us with our spatial framework. "[T]here is a *quality produced* out of the inward resources of the mind, to envelop sensations which, as given originally, are not spatial. . . . This last is the Kantian view."[14] In turn, distance perception was not, as Berkeley and others proposed, learned.

On just about every aspect of space perception debates raged over whether the phenomenon was innate or acquired. The stereoscope experiments, however, were taken by many prominent researchers to support the "empiricist" approach on several counts. Two are reasonably nontechnical and worth mentioning here. First, various experiments were thought to demonstrate the importance of learning in distance perception, hence challenging innateness claims. Second, locating in retinal disparity an external physical base for the fullness, or three-dimensionality, of our visual phenomena meant that it was that much more reasonable to explain depth perception as dependent on *sensory* apprehension. It was that much less plausible to assume that spatiality was a nonsensory imposition of

14. William James, *The Principles of Psychology*, vol. 2 (New York: Dover, 1950), p. 252. Whether James and other perceptual psychologists who cite or appeal to Kant correctly understood the implications of Kant's position for empirical theories of vision is a real question. See Gary Hatfield, *The Natural and the Normative* (Cambridge: MIT Press, 1990), esp. chap. 3, for the claim that many theorists misunderstood the empirical implications of Kant's ideas. Hatfield further argues that Kant's empirical claims about vision and touch are much like Berkeley's: "[Kant] makes vision depend upon touch for its ability to perceive objects in depth, thereby implying the standard Berkeleian account" (p. 105).

mind. The discovery of the stereoscope "made the dogma of an innate intuition of space—of space as an inner condition of all experience—less likely than ever before."[15]

This is not to say that everyone in the "non-Kantian" camp agreed with Berkeley that visual experience itself provided no basis for our spatial framework. For example, Ewald Hering, Carl Stumpf, and William James agreed with Berkeley that our idea of space is not an a priori imposition of mind, but they rejected the claim that visual experience could play no role in the construction of our spatial ideas. Most radically, James argued that all of our sensations, including odor, taste, and sound, have a voluminous quality that can serve as a basis for building our conception of space. Still, for James, as well as most other theorists, distance is not a simple or immediate quality of visual sensations. James's claim is only that we can use this sensed voluminousness, in conjunction with the variations in experience of objects as we move about, to construct a visual idea of metric space. Moreover, for many researchers the stereoscope experiments were seen to support Berkeley's thesis about the relevance of movement to our idea of space. For the experiments counted against the view that binocular vision was special or peculiarly different from monocular vision, where the importance of motion and touch were widely taken for granted. "There can be no doubt that the fusion of the two visual images is the result of an act of mental association . . . [and that as is the case with monocular vision] . . . in the binocular idea of depth it is sensations of movement which furnish our primary measure of spatial distance."[16] Or as Herman von Helmholtz saw matters, "The invention of the stereoscope . . . made the difficulty of the Innate Theory more obvious than before and led to another solution which approached much nearer to the older view. . . . This assumes that none of our sensations give us anything more than 'signs' for the external objects and movements, and that we can only learn how to interpret these signs by means of experience and practice."[17] If historically the invention of the stereoscope is not taken to refute Berkeley's claims about the nonimmediacy and imperceptibility of distance by vision, consideration of a related issue can enhance our appreciation of Berkeley's views concerning the importance

15. James J. Gibson, *The Perception of the Visual World* (Boston: Houghton Mifflin, 1950), p. 21.

16. Wilhelm Wundt, *Lectures on Human and Animal Psychology*, trans. J. E. Creighton and E. B. Thorndike (New York: Macmillan, 1896), p. 189.

17. "The Recent Progress of the Theory of Vision," in *Helmholtz on Perception*, ed. R. Warren and R. Warren (New York: Wiley, 1968), p. 110.

of our ideas of movement. The point here is that retinal disparity, by itself, cannot provide information about the absolute distance of an object from a viewer, nor can it, independent of such information, provide a measure of the absolute depth between two objects. The reason is that the amount of disparity is a function of *both* the depth relations and the absolute distance. Two objects close to each other in depth but near the viewer may project the same disparity as two objects widely separated but further away. Disparity measures may serve to recover absolute spatial depth only when conjoined with a means of measuring absolute distance to scale the significance of the disparity.

The geometrical features of the projection of light that prevent disparity from providing independent information of absolute distance is not unique to this cue. It has long been recognized that the pictorial cues cannot indicate absolute spatial measures. This result is just the other side of the geometrical considerations that underwrite the one-point argument. Of the traditional cues only the nonvisual motor cues of convergence and accommodation might seem to vary directly and unambiguously with distance. Given the goal of accounting for how we locate objects in space, it is not surprising that Berkeley attached special prominence to these cues.

Still, in order to evaluate absolute distance it is not enough to have a cue K that varies directly and unambiguously with distance. In addition, we need a scheme for assigning absolute-distance meaning to the values of K. We must know how much distance goes with so much K. I think that an appreciation of this problem plays an important role in Berkeley's insistence on the need for a scheme of visual-motor correlation. And although the issue has not received all that much attention, the problem is a genuine one. As T.G.R. Bower, albeit a recent critic of Berkeley, remarks, in real-life situations "to know how far away an object is *from us* . . . the expression of *how far* must serve to control behavior. . . . The term *absolute distance* serves as shorthand for 'spatial variables translated into a form appropriate for the control of spatial motor movements'."[18]

Just how vision might come to provide such information, Bower argues, is a difficult problem. Convergence, for example, varies with distance, but since the distance between our eyes changes as we grow, the same convergence angle will reflect different distances as we get older. In what way, then, might convergence be calibrated so as to provide accurate distance information? One theory of calibration that has gained some

18. *Development in Infancy* (San Francisco: W. H. Freeman, 1974), pp. 75–76.

currency proposes that such scaling results from correlating visual cues with movement.

> Suppose that you are at some distance D from an object and then take a step toward it so that the distance is reduced by the length Δ of one step. . . . If the visual angle [a measure of the size of the retinal image] prior to the step is α_1, [and] after the step . . . α_2 . . . [i]t can be shown that $\alpha_2/\alpha_1 = D/(D - \Delta)$. Now, suppose that you register your own locomotion in terms of an internal unit corresponding to the size of your pace [and] Δ represents one unit of locomotion. . . . It follows that $D = 1/(1 - \alpha_1/\alpha_2)$ [paces]. [By applying this calibration scheme,] distance to the object, expressed in terms of units of locomotion, can be derived from the ratios of angular sizes of an object seen at two different distances. . . . merely by taking a step toward an unfamiliar object, it is possible to compute the approximate number of paces that you would need to take in order to reach the object.[19]

Now, although Berkeley might have qualms taking Kaufman's equations to describe actual mental computations, the importance of this sort of motor scaling seems to me to lie at the heart of Berkeley's stress on the tangible nature of our distance perceptions. It is not just that behavior provides the ultimate test of distance perception, as the Behaviorists might claim. For Berkeley, and on Kaufman's model, visual experience gains its distance significance via a scheme of motor calibration. And as Kaufman says, echoing Berkeley, "[I]f perceptual space . . . is scaled in terms of locomotion . . . [t]his has profound implications for any theory of perception . . . [especially] how the senses work together."[20] Berkeley's views about the interrelations between the senses, however, are a story for another occasion.

19. Lloyd Kaufman, *Perception: The World Transformed* (Oxford: Oxford University Press, 1979), p. 224 ff.
20. Ibid., p. 226.

13

Berkeley Without God

Margaret Atherton

I n much of his work, Berkeley set himself the twin goals of combating atheism and skepticism. Nowadays, it is the second enterprise that interests philosophers more than the first, especially since Berkeley's proofs for the existence of God are not thought to be any more successful than anyone else's. There has been, then, some interest in the question, What does Berkeley's theory amount to if he is not allowed his proofs for the existence of God? Can there be a viable position that is Berkeleianism without God? To many, the answer to this question must be no. God plays far too important a role in Berkeley's thinking to be eliminable. For Berkeley maintains that for ideas to be perceivable, they must actually be perceived. Thus, things not currently perceived by any finite mind can only be perceivable if God is actually perceiving them. Berkeley's theory, it is said, is unavoidably theocentric. Without God, it collapses into the unlikely view that things exist only when they are actually being perceived.

There is, however, one consideration that suggests a different way of looking at Berkeleianism without God. Berkeley's first book, *An Essay Towards a New Theory of Vision*, in its first and second editions, made absolutely no reference to God whatsoever. (In the third edition, in two places, the phrase "language of nature" is changed to "language of the Author of Nature" [NTV 147 and 152].) The *New Theory* criticizes a theory of perception based on realist or materialist assumptions and, in its place, puts forward a theory of sensory representation, in which ideas represent only other ideas. This theory of sensory representation might be said, in effect, to constitute a Berkeleianism without God. This suggestion is plausible, however, only if the Berkeleianism of the *New Theory* is compatible with the Berkeleianism of the later works. If the proofs for the existence of God Berkeley subsequently introduces require adjustments to his theory that render it incompatible with the God-free *New Theory*, then perhaps those who say that Berkeleianism is unavoidably theocentric are in the right. If this is the case, then it will also mean that in suppressing all mention of God from the *New Theory*, Berkeley was doing something with more far-reaching consequences than his notorious suppression of the facts about *tangibilia*. He was putting the *New Theory* at odds with his final doctrine.[1]

I

When we consider the relation between the *New Theory* and Berkeley's proofs for the existence of God, it is highly significant that when Berkeley published *Alciphron*, he chose to reissue the *New Theory* along with it. *Alciphron*'s most important goal is theological. It is a defense of traditional religion against freethinkers, and it contains very elaborate proofs for the existence of God. In the *Theory of Vision Vindicated*, Berkeley tells us that he published the *New Theory* along with *Alciphron* because he was "persuaded that the *Theory of Vision*, annexed to the *Minute Philosopher*, affords to thinking men a new and unanswerable proof for the existence and immediate operation of God, and the constant conde-

1. The issues are not unconnected, of course. It is maintained Berkeley does not need God in the *New Theory* as he does in the later works, because in the *New Theory* tangible objects are mind-independent. This claim is not entirely compatible with the way in which I prefer to read the *New Theory*. See Margaret Atherton, *Berkeley's Revolution in Vision* (Ithaca: Cornell University Press, 1990).

scending care of his providence" (TVV 1). Thus, in 1732, when Berkeley published *Alciphron*, he indubitably considered the *New Theory* not only to be compatible with but also to provide significant support for the proofs for the existence of God to be found there. What remains at issue, however, is the extent to which the position Berkeley lays forth in *Alciphron* is compatible with what is found in *Principles* and *Three Dialogues*, with the position that is generally identified as Berkeleianism.

Berkeley's ultimate proof for the existence of God in *Alciphron* depends heavily on the results he had achieved in the *New Theory*. He builds to this proof by way of a subproof, which is not found satisfactory by Alciphron, one of Berkeley's representative freethinkers. This subproof sets the stage for the final proof and helps establish its nature. In this first proof, Alciphron concedes that while we can be sure of the existence of whatever we sense, we may also infer the existence of imperceptible things from their sensible effects. What is involved in these sorts of causal inferences is further refined: we can make inferences about the nature of the cause from the nature of the effects, and so, in particular, from rational acts we infer a rational cause. The proof therefore is going to be a matter of showing that there are a number of events that would be otherwise inexplicable unless we assume the existence of a particular rational cause. Euphranor, Berkeley's spokesman, cites a number of examples of such rational events, or motions, as he calls them: "A man with his hand can make no machine so admirable as the hand itself; nor can any of these motions by which we trace out human reason approach the skill and contrivance of those wonderful motions of the heart, and brain, and other vital parts, which do not depend on the will of man" (A IV, 5, 146). These are, then, examples of motions that are rational but in need of an explanation because they are independent of any human reason. Therefore, we can infer the existence of some rational or, indeed, suprarational cause.

Berkeley does not, however, take this proof as it stands to be sufficient to establish the existence of a single God. He therefore adduces some further evidence: these rational motions exhibit a unity in that they are governed by single set of immutable laws. It is concluded that they must be the product of a single agent or mind, which can be identified with God. This first proof is, as I read it, causal. It attempts to establish the existence of God as the best explanation for certain natural events.[2] It

2. The proof is sometimes taken as an analogical argument. The claim we infer rational causes from rational effects is taken to be licensed by a comparison with explanations for

depends upon our willingness to admit as evidence that there are events or motions in nature that are both rational and independent of a human will and that are law-governed. For the proofs to go through, we have to be in a position to accept these as facts.

Alciphron recognizes that the proof for the existence of God just given, depending as it does on the premise that from rational effects we can infer a rational cause, is a version of an argument to the existence of other minds. It requires that we have just as good evidence for the existence of God as we do for other rational human beings. This Alciphron refuses to admit. He is then casting doubt on the strength of the evidence Euphranor has cited, claiming it is not as powerful as the evidence Euphranor has that Alciphron exists, whom he sees and talks to. Euphranor responds by asserting he has better evidence for the existence of God than for the existence of Alciphron (A IV, 5, 147).[3] What is at stake here is the nature of the evidence Euphranor claims to have. Alciphron is maintaining that truly to be evidence of a rational cause, it would have to be of the same sort as the evidence that convinces him of the existence of a human mind, and that is the presence of language. Alciphron is introducing a condition on what it is for natural events or motions to be rational: they must be languagelike.

Berkeley's demonstration that the rational natural motions are languagelike amounts to a lightning tour through the *New Theory of Vision*. What he is seeking to establish is that vision is a language, that our ability to see the world around us, to see people, trees, and houses, is a matter of having learned to understand visual signs. Berkeley's demonstration consists, first, in a discussion of what he regards as a clear case of his account of how we learn to see, that of distance perception. We are undeniably able to see how far away objects are from us, even though this is not information available to us in the visual stimulus. Our success at seeing distance is the result of connecting visual cues, such as faintness,

human actions. Even those, however, who take the initial proof to be analogical suppose that the final "successful" proof is a best-explanation argument. See Michael Hooker, "Berkeley's Argument from Design," in *Berkeley: Critical and Interpretive Essays*, ed. Colin M. Turbayne (Minneapolis: University of Minnesota Press, 1982), pp. 261–70, and A. David Kline, "Berkeley's Divine Language Argument," in *Essays on the Philosophy of George Berkeley*, ed. Ernest Sosa (Boston: Reidel, 1987), pp. 129–42; hereafter, Sosa.

3. This passage is sometimes considered a second subproof, analogical in nature, which is not usually regarded as satisfactory. Since, in the passage in question, Euphranor does not in fact give any of the evidence he alleges he has, I think it better to regard this not as a proof at all but rather as an introduction to the proof Euphranor eventually gives.

which in its own nature has nothing to do with distance, with distance information. Faintness can come to stand for distance because it is reliably correlated with distance in our experience. Seeing distance is therefore something we learned how to do; we learned to read visual distance cues such as faintness as signifying distance information. Berkeley generalizes from the distance case very rapidly. Just as we have to learn to see distance because distance information is not immediately present in visual stimulation, so most of what we see, trees, people, and houses, must be suggested by the lights and colors we are built to register visually. Thus, Berkeley claims that upon the whole, "it seems the proper objects of sight are light and colours, with their several shades and degrees; all which, being infinitely diversified and combined, form a language wonderfully adapted to suggest and exhibit to us the distances, figures, situations, dimensions, and various qualities or tangible objects: not by similitude, nor yet by inference of necessary connexion, but by the arbitrary imposition of Providence, just as words suggest the things signified by them" (A IV, 10, 154). This is the conclusion, of course, that Berkeley took most of the *New Theory* to demonstrate, that the natural motions of Alciphron are rational because they can be fit into the rational structure of a language. On the basis of what we see, we can learn what to expect, so as to govern our conduct rationally.

Berkeley's proof for the existence of God follows quite straightforwardly from the claim that vision is the language of nature. If there is a language of nature, there must be a speaker of the language, there must be a divine mind to which we owe the language of nature. The only plausible explanation for the highly rational phenomenon that is the language of nature is that it is due to God. The last proof in *Alciphron* is intended by Berkeley to be understood as a convincing version of the first, and exemplifies the same causal principle, that from rational effects we can infer rational causes. For this proof to go through, we have to accept Berkeley's account of the evidence, his characterization of rational causes. We have to accept the demonstration of the *New Theory*, that sensory ideas constitute a language in which visual ideas represent other ideas. For the proofs in *Alciphron* to hold, we have to, at least, accept that what Berkeley says in the *New Theory* is true. Berkeley must first establish his theory of sensory representation as the correct way to understand our knowledge of the natural world; then he can use it as evidence for the existence of God. So Berkeley's theory, as developed in the *New Theory*, must be independent of the theological use to which he puts it, and cannot require the existence or the cooperation of God in order to be true. The

New Theory, then, from the perspective of *Alciphron*, constitutes Berkeleianism without God.

There is, however, a problem with drawing conclusions about the nature of Berkeleianism based on *Alciphron*. This is because *Alciphron* makes no mention of the issue of the mind-dependent status of the natural world. Indeed, the effects that in *Alciphron* are explained by appealing to God are referred to as "motions." There is no indication of the fact that, for Berkeley, these motions have the status of ideas. There is a sense, then, in which Berkeley's attitude in *Alciphron* is a throwback to the one he expressed in the *New Theory*, where he failed to point out that the tangible objects that visual ideas signify are themselves mind-dependent. Since the need to make use of God, which Berkeley's theory faces in its canonical form, is generally supposed to arise from the absence of a mind-independent material world to provide stability, it might be supposed that it is not appropriate, based on *Alciphron* to make generalizations about the nature of Berkeleianism. It might be the case that there are two versions of Berkeleianism. In the one laid out in the *New Theory* and *Alciphron*, Berkeley's account of the natural world is not theocentric and can be used as evidence in a proof for the existence of God. In the other, found in *Principles* and *Three Dialogues*, Berkeley's account of nature is unavoidably theocentric, and God's existence is proved by other means. It is not, on the face of it, likely that in the course of his life Berkeley leapt back and forth between two incompatible positions, but since the way in which *Principles* and *Three Dialogues* are often read has this result, it is necessary to show that the complete statement of his position that Berkeley gives in *Principles* and *Three Dialogues* is nonetheless compatible with the somewhat more cautiously expressed claims of the *New Theory* and *Alciphron*.

II

Berkeley proves the existence of God twice in *The Principles of Human Knowledge*, once in sections 25–33, at the end of the introductory section summarizing his doctrine, and once in sections 145–55, at the very end of the book. The placement of these proofs not only indicates the importance of this issue within Berkeley's overall plan, but also supports the view that Berkeley took his proof for the existence of God to be the culmination of his theory, for which the rest provided support. While the occurrences of the proof differ in detail, they do not differ significantly from each other, in the sense that each relies on roughly the same body of evidence. The second occasion on which Berkeley proves God's existence, a proof that makes reference to other minds, ought appropriately to be regarded as an enrichment of the first. While in both cases the primary evidence Berkeley relies on are ideas rather than, as in *Alciphron*, "rational motions," the arguments do not otherwise differ significantly from that of *Alciphron*.

Berkeley begins his proof in PR 26 by claiming ideas need causes, and proceeds to establish by a process of elimination that they must be caused by spiritual substance or mind. (Ideas, being inert, cannot cause other ideas, and so must be caused by a substance. Since there is no such thing as corporeal substance, they must be caused by spiritual substance.) Although I experience some of my ideas as having been caused by myself ("It is no more than willing, and straightway this or that idea arises in my fancy" PR 28), many other ideas, in particular, sensory ideas, are not like this but are experienced as involuntary. These ideas, the ones that are independent of my will, are caused by some other will or spirit (PR 29). Thus, this proof, like the *Alciphron* proof, is causal. Since the "rational motions" of *Alciphron* have been identified in the *Principles* as ideas, Berkeley is able to argue more straightforwardly that their cause must be something mental, or rational, and argues that God is the best explanation for our ideas.

As in *Alciphron*, the nature of the evidence must be further refined before Berkeley can plausibly argue that the cause of our ideas is God.[4] Berkeley gives a description of the ways in which the ideas he is going to ascribe to God differ from human productions.

> The ideas of sense are more strong, lively, and distinct than those of the imagination; they have likewise a steadiness, order and coherence, and are not excited at random, as those which are the effects

---

4. Jonathan Bennett, as A. C. Grayling points out, has unaccountably ignored this part of Berkeley's proof in his influential discussion of Berkeley's proofs for the existence of God, although he does nevertheless criticize Berkeley for having given a proof that falls far short of theism. It is certainly true that at the place where Bennett halts his discussion of Berkeley's proof, Berkeley has done no more than show that my involuntary ideas are caused by some mind or other besides my own. See Jonathan Bennett, *Locke, Berkeley, Hume: Central Themes* (Oxford: Oxford University Press, 1971); idem, "Berkeley and God," reprinted in *Locke and Berkeley: A Collection of Critical Essays*, ed. C. B. Martin and D. M. Armstrong (Notre Dame, Ind.: University of Notre Dame Press, 1968), pp. 380–99; and A. C. Grayling, *Berkeley: The Central Arguments* (LaSalle, Ill.: Open Court, 1986).

of human wills often are, but in a regular train or series, the admirable connexion whereof sufficiently testifies the wisdom and benevolence of its Author. Now the set rules or established methods, wherein the mind we depend on excites in us the ideas of sense, are called the *Laws of Nature:* and these we learn by experience, which teaches us that such and such ideas are attended with such and such other ideas, in the ordinary course of things. (PR 30)

This passage, in a highly condensed form, refers to the same sorts of reasons that led Berkeley in *Alciphron* to describe our ideas as language-like: they have the order and coherence that allows us to learn what to expect, that is, to learn to understand them. As in *Alciphron*, Berkeley argues the specific character of our ideas of nature indicates they must be the effects of a suprarational mind, or God. While the reference to language is lacking, otherwise this proof parallels the proof in *Alciphron*. Like that one, this depends upon the claim that our ideas are law-governed and independent of our will.[5]

The proof for the existence of God Berkeley gives at the end of the *Principles*, like the proof in *Alciphron*, is enriched by a comparison with the way in which we know other persons, or other minds. Berkeley's point is that the inference that leads us to God is as good as and in fact better than the inference we make to the existence of other minds. Just as we do not see a person directly, but rather infer the person's existence from "such a certain collection of ideas, as directs us to think there is a distinct principle of thought and motion like to our selves" (PR 148), so we infer the existence of God. Presumably (this is not spelled out with respect to other finite minds) it is not just any ideas that lead us to suppose we are in the presence of another person, but only those to be explained as deriving from a rational agent. Similarly, in the proof for the existence of God, the emphasis is on the complexity of the evidence that leads us to attribute some of what we experience to God.

5. For those who like to see proofs laid out in a series of numbered steps, the one just discussed might go something like this:

(1) Ideas can only be caused by a mind.
(2) I am not the cause of ideas of sense.
(3) Therefore they are caused by some other mind.
(4) Ideas of sense are more coherent and orderly than any caused by a finite mind.
(5) Therefore they are caused by God.

But, though there be some things which convince us human agents are concerned in producing them; yet it is evident to every one that those things which are called the words of Nature, that is, the far greater part of the ideas or sensations perceived by us, are not produced by, or dependent on the wills of men. There is therefore some other spirit that causes them; since it is repugnant that they should subsist by themselves. See *Sect.* 29. But if we attentively consider the constant regularity, order, and concatenation of natural things, the surprising magnificence, beauty, and perfection of the larger, and the exquisite contrivance of the smaller parts of the creation, together with the never enough admired laws of pain and pleasure, and the instincts or natural inclinations, appetites, and passions of animals; I say if we consider all these things, and at the same time attend to the meaning and import of the attributes, one, eternal, infinitely wise, good, and perfect, we shall clearly perceive that they belong to the aforesaid spirit, *who works all in all*, and *by whom all things consist.* (PR 146)

Berkeley's proof here, as in *Alciphron*, requires us to see the effects that we attribute to God not just as independent of our will but as exhibiting a certain kind of rational structure.

While the language analogy, the explicit comparison between our ideas of the natural world and a language, is absent from Berkeley's proof for the existence of God in the *Principles*, it is not entirely missing from the *Principles* itself. Berkeley refers to the language analogy explicitly in PR 44, in which he goes over the results of the *New Theory*,[6] and makes use of it in PR 65, in his answer to the eleventh objection. This objection asks why there appears to be a clockwork of nature, if all the various inner parts have no causal efficacy. Berkeley's answer, in part, is that the connections observed are not causal but those of sign to thing signified. Further, he writes:

[T]he reason why ideas are formed into machines, that is, artificial and regular combinations, is the same with that for combining

---

6. "It is, I say, evident from what has been said in the foregoing parts of this treatise, and in *Sect.* 147, and elsewhere of the essay concerning vision, that visible ideas are the language whereby the governing spirit, on whom we depend, informs us what tangible ideas he is about to imprint upon us, in case we excite this or that motion in our own bodies." It is clear from this passage Berkeley regards the language analogy as established by the argument of the *Principles*.

letters into words. That a few original ideas may be made to signify a great number of effects and actions, it is necessary they be variously combined together: and to the end their use be permanent and universal, these combinations must be made by *rule*, and with *wise contrivance*. By this means abundance of information is conveyed unto us, concerning what we are to expect from such and such actions, and what methods are proper to be taken, for the exciting such and such ideas: which in effect is all that I conceive to be distinctly meant, when it is said that by discerning the figure, texture, and mechanism of the inward parts of bodies, whether natural or artificial, we may attain to know the several uses and properties depending thereon, or the nature of the thing.

Finally, in PR 108, he compares natural scientists to grammarians, who are able to go beyond the ability of ordinary people in understanding the signs of nature and to write the grammar or rules for their use.[7] It seems reasonable to suppose that the rational structure that, in the *Principles*, Berkeley argues must be the effect of God is the same as the language of nature, whose existence he demonstrated in the *New Theory* and referred to in *Alciphron*. Berkeley's proof for the existence of God in the *Principles* does not require the traditional argument from design, as Grayling has it, but rather the enriched version of this argument, as found in *Alciphron*, which presupposes the results of the *New Theory*. As in *Alciphron*, the proofs for the existence of God in the *Principles* assume the truth of the theory of sensory representation developed in the *New Theory*.

III

But even if the proof of the *Principles* is entirely compatible with the proof given in *Alciphron*, it might be supposed that the same cannot be said of the way in which Berkeley sets about proving the existence of God in *Three Dialogues Between Hylas and Philonous*. For it is generally

---

7. Curiously, in the first edition, Berkeley made much more explicit use of the language analogy in PR 108, writing, for example, "It appears from *Sect*. LXVI, etc. that the steady, consistent methods of Nature, may not unfitly be stiled the *language* of its *Author*, whereby he discovers His *attributes* to our view, and directs us how to act for the convenience and felicity of life." I have no theory to account for Berkeley's deletion of this and other sentences from PR 108.

supposed that in *Three Dialogues* Berkeley introduces a new proof for the existence of God, a proof Jonathan Bennett has called the continuity argument.[8] And it is, after all, the continuity argument that has led people to claim Berkeley's theory is intrinsically theocentric, because it purports to show God must exist to perceive the tree when there is no one about in the quad. The crucial passage runs as follows:

> When I deny sensible things an existence out of the mind, I do not mean my mind in particular, but all minds. Now it is plain they have an existence exterior to my mind, since I find them by experience to be independent of it. There is therefore some other mind wherein they exist, during the intervals between the times of my perceiving them: as likewise they did before my birth, and would do after my supposed annihilation. And as the same is true, with regard to all other finite created spirits; it necessarily follows, there is an *omnipresent eternal Mind*, which knows, and comprehends all things, and exhibits them to our view in such a manner, and according to such rules as he himself hath ordained, and are by us termed the *Laws of Nature*. (D 230)

This argument is supposed to differ from the one given in the *Principles* because it argues God must exist, not to be the cause of the ideas we do have, but to perceive the ideas we do not have. The *Principles* God functions as a cause—He is to be seen primarily as an agent, a will— whereas the *Three Dialogues* God preserves the continuing existence of things and is primarily (or, rather, additionally) a perceiver, an understanding. Such an assessment, however, not only requires a particular way of reading *Three Dialogues*, which can be questioned, but also requires taking the *Principles* to be about God only as a cause. According to this assessment, the *Principles* argument is what has been called a "pure passivity" argument. The account I have given so far of the *Principles*

---

8. Although Jonathan Bennett has focused attention on the problem of the two proofs for the existence of God and given them the names by which they are now commonly known, the idea that *Dialogues* contain a new proof is not new with him. See the editor's introduction, *Works* II, 152: "In the *Principles* (Sect. 29) God was adduced as the *cause* of our percepts, and of our perceptual experiences, and only incidentally (Sects. 48 and 91) is He brought in as the *upholder* of sensory things when they are not being perceived by us. The emphasis is now transposed: the argument is that the existence of God must be granted in order to account for the continuous existence of the natural order; the notion of God as cause is slipped in in a quite casual way."

suggests this is not the case. When the *Principles* argument is properly understood, it is clear that the arguments of the *Principles* and *Three Dialogues* are very similar.[9]

Since the proof in the *Principles* does not stop with the conclusion that some other spirit causes our involuntary ideas, it does not simply establish the existence of God as a will or agent. The ideas whose existence depend upon God do not occur randomly or incoherently, but instead display the sort of order that leads Berkeley to describe them as languagelike. God is not a random cause or blind agent, but causes our ideas according to a plan, the laws of nature, by virtue of which our ideas are meaningful. It cannot be correct, therefore, to see Berkeley as offering at any stage an argument that just trades on God's volitions, an argument to be otherwise supplemented by another about his role as an understanding. The argument that establishes that the cause of our ideas is *God* rests on the claim that these ideas are rational in structure, requiring a rational cause.[10]

In arguing that our involuntary ideas are also orderly or meaningful, Berkeley is presenting a picture of our ideas as having an existence that is distinct from any particular (finite) perceiver. Consider the case of distance perception, discussed extensively in the *New Theory of Vision*. When I stand on my front steps and look to the corner, I may be said to see how far away the corner is from me. But, of course, all that I register visually, all that I immediately perceive, is light and colors. These lights and colors, therefore, suggest to me distance, which, according to Berke-

9. This position is also shared by Grayling and Winkler and is compatible with Winkler's claim that Berkeley's Divine Agent is both will and understanding. Michael Ayers has shown the continuity argument of D 230 is an enrichment of and not otherwise distinct from the central proof for the existence of God in D 212–15, but he wants to distinguish what he renames the "distinctness argument" from the "pure passivity argument" he finds in the *Principles*. It is not like Ayers to be taken in by Bennett, but I think he is wrong in agreeing with Bennett that the *Principles* contains a "pure passivity" argument. See Grayling, *Berkeley: The Central Arguments*; Kenneth P. Winkler, *Berkeley: An Interpretation* (Oxford: Oxford University Press, 1989); and M. R. Ayers, "Divine Ideas and Berkeley's Proofs of God's Existence," in Sosa, pp. 115–28.

10. The best evidence, according to Ayers, Berkeley thought he had two arguments for the existence of God comes at D 240, where Berkeley says: "From the effects I see produced, I conclude there are actions; and because actions, volitions; and because there are volitions, there must be a will. Again, the things I perceive must have an existence, they or their archtypes, out of my mind: but being ideas, neither they nor their archtypes can exist otherwise than in an understanding: there is therefore an understanding. But will and understanding constitute in the strictest sense a mind or spirit. The powerful cause of my ideas, is in strict propriety of speech a *spirit*." The conclusion of this passage suggests, however, that a single causal argument requires the operation of a being who has both will and understanding.

ley, I experience tangibly or kinesthetically. There is a way or ways it feels to go from where I am standing to the corner. Because visual experiences are reliably correlated with tangible experiences, I come to learn what distance looks like, or I come to read my visual experiences as having a distance meaning. Just as the immediate visual experiences are independent of my will, so the distance meanings with which my visual experiences are invested are also involuntary. They are a habit I fall into when my visual and tangible experiences are regularly correlated. The existence of the distance meaning is dependent on these regular correlations and is therefore distinct from my own existence. The standards I learn and employ, while cashed out in terms of my tangible and kinesthetic experiences, are nevertheless independent of my mind.

Exactly the same can be said about any of my experiences of sensible things. If I am seeing a cherry, then my immediate visual experiences stand for a range of perceptual experiences with which these immediate visual experiences are reliably correlated and which they have come to mean. The cherry, although mind-dependent, has an existence that is distinct from and independent of *my* mind. Berkeley's claim that our sensory ideas are governed by law amounts to the claim that the sensible things for which our ideas stand have a distinct existence, independent of any particular finite perceiver. From the fact that we do, and therefore can, make sense of our experience because of its regular and orderly (language-like) nature, we can conclude the items of our experience have a distinct existence. This claim is established entirely through the God-free resources of the *New Theory of Vision*.

It is useful, in getting a handle on the way in which sensible things have an existence that is distinct from any particular (finite) perceiver, to keep Berkeley's distinction between immediate and mediate perception in mind. According to Berkeley, I may be said to immediately perceive whatever my sense organs are equipped to register, whereas I mediately perceive those meanings I have learned to attach to what I immediately perceive, which constitutes the greatest part of what I may be said to perceive. I immediately perceive lights and colors, but mediately perceive distance or cherries. Things that are sensible, like cherries or coaches or trees, are all mediately perceived.[11] While it seems reasonable to say what

11. NTV 9, D 174–75. The account I am giving here is the one I defend in *Berkeley's Revolution in Vision*. It is not entirely in accordance with others that have appeared in the recent literature. See Winkler's *Berkeley*, pp. 149–61, and George Pappas, "Berkeley and Immediate Perception," in Sosa, pp. 195–213.

I immediately perceive exists in my mind for only so long as I am perceiving it, the same is not true for the sensible things I mediately perceive. Two people do not feel the same twinge of pain or sense the same flash of light, but they do see the same distance or the same cherry. Just as the immediate ideas I hear and see are different but of the same coach (so long as they form part of the same congeries of ideas I have come to expect to mean coach), so the immediate ideas you and I have are of the same coach. On the basis of what I immediately see, I expect to be able to touch the coach, and I expect you to be able to touch it too. We can be confident we attach the same meanings to what we perceive, because our perceptions are governed by the same laws of nature.

The distinction between immediate and mediate perception is also useful in understanding how Berkeley thinks he can argue it is God who causes our ideas. Berkeley himself says God causes ideas in us in the same way in which I cause ideas in myself, but it is, I believe, more helpful to think about the more strictly analogous situation where I cause ideas in someone else by speaking to them, by making noises they hear as meaningful. Berkeley thinks, after all, it is a strength of his position that his argument that God is the cause of our ideas relies on the same evidence as that by which we convince ourselves that other minds exist. But it is not apprehension of immediately perceived sounds that convinces us that we are in the presence of another mind, but rather the mediate perception of meaningful language. Similarly, what convinces us of the existence of God is the meaningful units we mediately perceive. Looking at things in this way not only makes plain why Berkeley is so clear that the cause of our sensible ideas must be a mind, but also shows that Berkeley's proof for the existence of God depends upon his theory of sensory representation.

Not perhaps surprisingly, what I am saying is that, according to Berkeley, the natural world is mind-dependent, but independent of any particular mind, such as my own, in exactly the same way language is a mind-dependent phenomenon, but independent of any particular mind. If all minds were annihilated, clearly language would also be annihilated; but the existence of language is distinct from that of any one mind, in the same way that the law-governed world we learn about via our senses is independent of any one (finite) mind. The annihilation of a single English speaker does not cause English to go out of existence, and similarly, the items of the natural world are not dependent on the ideas of some one perceiver.

This point is consonant with various remarks Berkeley makes in the *Principles* that have been cited as reflecting his interest in the continued existence of objects. Consider his reply, in PR 48, to the objection that so long as the existence of things depends on their being perceived, then everything goes out of existence whenever it is not being perceived:

> For though we hold indeed the objects of sense to be nothing else but ideas which cannot exist unperceived; yet we may not hence conclude they have no existence except only while they are perceived by us, since there may be some other spirit that perceives them, though we do not. Wherever bodies are said to have no existence without the mind, I would not be understood to mean this or that particular mind, but all minds whatsoever. It does not therefore follow from the foregoing principles, that bodies are annihilated and created every moment, or exist not at all during the intervals between our perception of them.

To be a sensible body is reliably to present a certain range of experiences to perceivers. Sensible bodies will continue to exist so long as the conditions exist that enable perceivers to make sense of their experiences, to experience them as bodies.[12] Berkeley, of course, further supposes that God is the cause of those conditions that enable perceivers to understand what they are perceiving. Ultimately, through the laws that preserve the regularities that allow us to make sense of what we perceive, God preserves the continued existence of sensible things. The issue of the distinct and continuous existence of sensible things is not absent from the *Principles*. In the *Principles*, the proof for the existence of God, from the premise that our experiences are orderly and according to the laws of nature, establishes the existence of a God who is responsible through these laws of nature for the distinct and continued existence of sensible things.

It is finally interesting to note there are two entries in the *Philosophical Commentaries* that are relevant to our understanding of Berkeley's proof for the existence of God. PC 838 reads: "Every sensation of mine which happens in consequence of the general, known Laws of nature and is from without i.e. independent of my Will demonstrates the Being of a God. i.e. of an unextended incorporeal Spirit wch is omniscient, omni-

---

12. This thought seems to be what is captured by the more phenomenalist passages of the *Principles*, such as PR 3: "The table I write on, I say, exists, that is, I see it and feel it; and if I were out of my study I should say it existed, meaning thereby that if I was in my study I might perceive it, or that some other spirit actually does perceive it."

potent etc." This entry indicates Berkeley considered the proof for the existence of God to follow not only from the fact that ideas are independent of my will but also from the fact that my sensations are in accordance with the laws of nature. A further entry also shows Berkeley's conception of the independence of my ideas is not limited to their independence of my will: "I will grant you that extension, Colour etc may be said to be without the Mind in a double respect i.e. as independent of our Will & as distinct from the Mind" (PC 882). These entries make clear Berkeley was thinking about the issues surrounding the distinct existence of ideas before he published the *Principles*, and further suggest it is unlikely they would form part of a new proof, introduced only in *Three Dialogues*.

Once it becomes clear the position in the *Principles* is that God is the cause of ideas that are both independent of my will and distinct from my understanding, then it is hard to find any new element introduced in *Three Dialogues*. Berkeley's proof for the existence of God spreads over several pages of the second dialogue, or more accurately, it is discussed twice, once at D 212–13 and again, after a digression where Berkeley distinguishes his position from that of Malebranche, at D 214–15. The second occurrence is a fairly straightforward causal argument, not different in any way from that of the *Principles*:

> It is evident that the things I perceive are my own ideas, and that no idea can exist unless it be in a mind. Nor is it less plain that these ideas or things by me perceived, either themselves or their archtypes exist independently of my mind, since I know myself not to be their author, it being out of my power to determine at pleasure, what particular ideas I shall be affected with upon opening my eyes or ears. They must therefore exist in some other mind, whose will it is they should be exhibited to me.

Michael Ayers says of this argument that Berkeley has built into it "certain elements of the Passivity Argument,"[13] and if by this he means that it relies, as does the *Principles'* proof, on the claim that sensible ideas are independent of my will, then this is certainly the case. Ayers is also of the opinion, however, that the first occurrence of the proof, at D 212–13, lacks any reference to passivity, but this seems to me less clear. Berkeley says, in D 212: "To me it is evident, for the reasons you allow of, that sensible things cannot exist otherwise than in a mind or spirit. Whence I

---

13. Ayers, "Divine Ideas," p. 121.

conclude, not that they have no real existence, but that seeing they depend not on my thought, and have an existence distinct from being perceived by me, *there must be some other mind wherein they exist.* As sure therefore as the sensible world really exists, so sure is there an infinite omnipresent spirit who contains and supports it." The only reason I can see for distinguishing this proof from the one given slightly later in *Three Dialogues*, or from the proof in the *Principles*, is that here Berkeley speaks of his ideas as independent of his *thought* instead of independent of his *will*. But I think this is to place too much weight on an implied sharp distinction between will and understanding. Berkeley is quite prepared to use "thought" as a general term for what goes on in his mind, and he is suspicious of attempts to separate the will from the understanding. I think it is reasonable to see this proof, too, as arguing for the need to provide an explanation for ideas that are both causally independent and ontologically distinct from my mind. There is no serious discrepancy between the proofs of the *Principles* and the proofs of the second dialogue.

Furthermore, once it becomes clear Berkeley was arguing from the start that sensible things, while mind-dependent, are distinct from my mind, then it is also clear, as Ayers and Grayling argue, that the "continuity argument" of D 230 does not present a startling departure from what has gone before. For since what makes it possible for us to perceive the world of sensible things is their dependence on the laws of nature, then it is obvious this world is not only distinct but continuous, preserved by the continuing operations of the laws of nature. Thus the "continuity argument," far from introducing any novelties, is, as Ayers says, an "enrichment," doing no more than spelling out the implications of what has gone before.

IV

It seems reasonable to say, then, that from the beginning, Berkeley intends our sense experience to be of sensible things having a continued and distinct existence. From entries in his philosophical notebooks to *Alciphron*, Berkeley has based his argument for the existence of God on the claim that the natural world is governed by law, and hence is meaningful to us. We can reject Berkeley's proof for the existence of God and still accept his theory of sensory representation. We can accept that we live in a world in which, thanks to the regular and orderly nature of our experience, we perceive distance or cherries or trees in the quad. Without God, we obviously lack a cause or an explanation for the theory of sensory representation, but the theory itself stands.[14]

In arguing for the existence of a viable Berkeleianism without God, I am not trying to downplay the importance of theological considerations in Berkeley's own motivations. On the contrary, I believe them to be central. I am only claiming that Berkeley's theological purposes required him to have a freestanding theory of sensory representation to which he could then appeal in proving the existence of God. If it is concluded that Berkeley's proof for the existence of God is unconvincing, then we have no account of the cause of sensory representation, but the details of the theory are untouched.[15]

14. In what I am saying here, I am agreeing with Grayling, who argues there is a lot of value left to Berkeley's theory even if God is removed. I am going slightly beyond his claims, however, in seeing the residue as consisting not only in the view of the world, as Grayling has it, as mental, together with a negative thesis about materialism, but also in a positive theory of sensory representation. I have written more about this in *Berkeley's Revolution in Vision*.

15. This essay took its inspiration from a paper Charles McCracken read at an International Berkeley Society session at the 1991 Central Division Meetings of the APA, in which he complained that the doctrine of the *New Theory* cannot be used as a guide to understanding the theologically based doctrines of the *Principles* and *Dialogues*. I do not know that what I have written here satisfies him any more than what I said to him there, but this is my considered response. I am also grateful to Robert Schwartz and Robert McKim for their help, as well as to Lorne Falkenstein, who commented on this essay at the University of Western Ontario's conference on Berkeley's Metaphysics.

14

Godless Immaterialism:
On Atherton's Berkeley

Charles J. McCracken

During the last half century Berkeley's philosophy has been construed as a species of commonsense realism by a number of its interpreters, where "commonsense realism" has usually been understood to consist in the claims (1) that bodies really have the properties they appear to us to have and (2) that bodies exist whether or not they are being perceived by any finite perceiver. Now, Berkeley accepts both these claims, so his philosophy (in contrast, say, to the philosophies of Descartes or Locke, which reject the first claim) belongs to the family of commonsense realist philosophies. Such a reading of Berkeley has usually taken his realism to be underpinned by his theology: a world of things exists, whether we perceive it or not, because it is held in existence by an all-perceiving God. Thus A. A. Luce, foremost apostle of the commonsense realist interpretation of Berkeley's metaphysics, declared that Berkeley's "conception of God as an omnipresent spirit all-encompassing and all-penetrating was no pious ornament of the system but its very ground and foundation."[1] And T. E. Jessop, another notable defender of the realist interpretation of Berkeley, called Berkeley's concept of God the "crowning doctrine" of his philosophy, explaining that Berkeley's "obstinately real world is too vast, too lasting (existing before us and after us), too orderly, to be dependent on any finite minds. The mind it depends on must be commensurate with it. We must therefore infer a cosmic mind."[2] Several recent defenders of the realist interpretation of Berkeley's philosophy, however, seem to take the view that his realism is intelligible independent of the doctrine of an all-perceiving God.[3] One defender of this view is Margaret Atherton, and it is her view of the matter I want to examine here.

In *Berkeley's Revolution in Vision*[4] Atherton has given us a splendid commentary, one that contributes substantially to our understanding of Berkeley and deserves a place on the shelf beside the fine studies of Berkeley's theory of vision by David Armstrong[5] and Colin M. Turbayne.[6] At the end of her commentary on the *New Theory* (BRV, part 3), Atherton proposes an interpretation of Berkeley's metaphysical realism—an interpretation in which God is conspicuous by his absence ('God' in fact does not appear in the index of her book), though she does not there expressly address the question whether God plays an indispensable role in a realist reading of Berkeley. But in "Berkeley Without God,"[7] she explicitly defends the thesis that Berkeleian realism does not require God as what Luce called "its very ground and foundation." I want first to discuss her interpretation of Berkeley in BRV and then to say something about the argument she develops in "Berkeley Without God."

According to Atherthon, Berkeley's chief aim in both the *New Theory* and the *Principles* is to present a "theory of sensory representation," a theory, that is, of what it is that sensible qualities represent to the mind that perceives them (and a theory, moreover, that differs radically from that of his predecessors). "The *Principles*, like the *New Theory*, can be

1. *The Dialectic of Immaterialism* (London: Hodder & Stoughten, 1963), p. 189.

2. T. E. Jessop, *George Berkeley* (London: Longmans, Green, 1959), p. 30.

3. See esp. John W. Yolton, *Perceptual Acquaintance from Descartes to Reid* (Oxford: Basil Blackwell, 1984), chaps. 7 and 11, and A. C. Grayling, *Berkeley: The Central Arguments* (La Salle, Ill.: Open Court, 1986), esp. pp. 201–10. God seems to play no indispensable role in Yolton's realist construal of Berkeley; Grayling fully acknowledges the centrality of God in Berkeley's version of immaterialism but holds that a "non-theistic reworking of Berkeley's central arguments" is possible.

4. Ithaca: Cornell University Press (1990); hereafter, BRV.

5. *Berkeley's Theory of Vision* (Melbourne: Melbourne University Press, 1960).

6. *The Myth of Metaphor* (Columbia: University of South Carolina Press, 1971).

7. Essay 13 in this volume.

seen as primarily concerned with the nature of what is represented by sensible qualities" (BRV, p. 22). The chief difference between the *Principles* and the *New Theory* is in the scope of the theory of sensory representation they present. The *New Theory* limits itself to the representative nature of the qualities we perceive by *sight*, qualities that are construed as signs, not of the properties of mind-independent material substances, but of the qualities that we do (or can) perceive by touch. In the *Principles* the thesis is made perfectly general: the qualities perceived by any of our senses represent not the properties of mind-independent material substances but qualities that are (or can be) perceived by our other senses. It is this theory that Atherton takes to constitute the core of Berkeley's immaterialism. Now, the doctrine that ideas constitute a "language" that represents other ideas is certainly one of Berkeley's major tenets, but it is a mistake to suppose that it is the chief tenet the *Principles* aims to establish. The chief aim of the *Principles*, it seems to me, is to prove that there are no substances save spirits and that bodies exist only because they are perceived by spirits.

But a more serious objection is that Atherton's view of the relation between the aims of the *Principles* and the aims of the *New Theory* leads her, I think, to misconstrue Berkeley's philosophy. In interpreting that philosophy, she holds we should distinguish two different theses, the thesis of *idealism* and the thesis of *immaterialism*. It has been the failure to distinguish these theses, she thinks, that has led many interpreters to construe Berkeley's philosophy in a way that makes it less plausible and less compatible with common sense than it really is. The thesis of "idealism" she characterizes as

> [t]he view that sensible objects exist only in the mind, that in sense perception what the perceiver immediately perceives are ideas of sense. . . . [This view] comes down to the relatively uncontroversial claim that sensations are ways of experiencing which happen to beings with minds capable of having experiences and which therefore are dependent upon the various sensory apparatus by means of which such beings have experience. There are clearly no ways of experiencing or perceiving in the absence of perceivers; hence sensations or sensible objects do not exist without the mind. (BRV, pp. 233–34)

Thus construed, the thesis of idealism takes "sensible objects" or "ideas of sense" to be "ways of experiencing" or "ways of perceiving," and the thesis amounts only to the innocuous and commonsensical doctrine that "ways of experiencing" or "ways of perceiving" cannot be mind-independent. Seeing, for example, is one way of experiencing, feeling by touch another; and it would be absurd to suggest that seeing or feeling by touch could happen independently of a perceiver that sees or feels.[8]

Now, it is hardly surprising that Atherton finds Berkeley's idealism, thus construed, "relatively uncontroversial," or that she can hold that it does not conflict with common sense (BRV 235) and does not require any theological underpinning. But is it correct to suppose that what Berkeley means by 'a sensible object' or an 'idea of sense' is a "way of perceiving"? Does he not mean, by 'sensible object' or 'idea', *what* is seen or what is felt, rather than the seeing of it or feeling of it? Atherton's construal of idealism forces on us at once the question of what, on this view of idealism, the status of the object seen or felt is and how that object is related to our "way of perceiving" it, that is, to our seeing it or feeling it.

I can think of only three answers to this question: we must suppose that Berkeley holds either, first, that we cannot distinguish between seeing something and the object seen, feeling something and the object felt, and so forth; or, second, that although we can distinguish our seeing or feeling something from what we see or feel, it is impossible to conceive that the object could exist unless it were seen or felt; or, third, that we can distinguish between our seeing or feeling something and what is seen or felt, but that when it is said that the *esse* of an idea is *percipi*, all that is meant is that the seeing or feeling of something is mind-dependent not that the object seen or felt is.

If we adopt the first answer, then although the thesis that seeing and feeling are mental events (and so are mind-dependent) will be uncontroversial and compatible with common sense, Berkeley's idealism will also involve a highly controversial and uncommonsensical thesis, namely, that the *seeing* of a red patch is itself *red*, that the *feeling* of a spherical shape is *itself* spherical, and so forth, for it will hold that we cannot distinguish seeing and feeling from what is seen or felt. Suppose, however, we adopt the second answer, that ideas are distinguishable from mental events like seeing or feeling but are not separable or abstractable from them and that since the mental event (the seeing or feeling) is mind-dependent so is the

8. It is noteworthy that throughout BRV Atherton equates expressions like "the way in which we see," "the way in which we feel," "ways of perceiving," and "ways of experiencing" with expressions like "the content of our ideas" (p. 208), "the visual qualities" or "tangible qualities" of something (p. 210), "the proper objects of vision" (p. 226), "an idea" (p. 228), "sensible objects," "ideas of sense," and "sensations" (p. 234).

object we see or feel. In my view that really *is* what Berkeley holds. But it is not the innocuous and relatively uncontroversial "idealism" Atherton attributes to him, for it involves the highly controversial claim that it is impossible to separate conceptually the object perceived from the perceiving of it—impossible to conceive, say, that something spherical could exist unperceived.

Finally, the third answer—that we can distinguish the spherical object perceived from the perceiving of it, and that the latter is mind-dependent, while the former is not—would be, I grant, uncontroversial and commonsensical. But it is manifestly not Berkeley's doctrine, for it is explicitly of things like shape (figure) that Berkeley says, "their *esse* is *percipi*, nor is it possible they should have any existence out of minds or thinking things which perceive them" (PR 3).

These three alternatives are the only ways I can understand the thesis that Atherton calls "idealism," and it seems to me that, depending on which of them one adopts, one gets either a doctrine that is very far from being uncontroversial and commonsensical or a doctrine that is indeed uncontroversial and commonsensical but very far from Berkeley's view.

But it may seem that I have not given a fair airing to Atherton's interpretation of Berkeley, for I have found fault with her construal of "idealism" without considering the thesis she takes to be the other leg of Berkeley's metaphysics, the "thesis of immaterialism." For it might be unobjectionable to use "idealism" in the somewhat idiosyncratic way that Atherton uses it—namely, for the admittedly commonsensical view that seeing, feeling, hearing, and so on, are mental events and so mind-dependent—provided her interpretation of immaterialism satisfied my demand that we be given an account of the nature of the *objects* seen, felt, or heard. But here, too, if I understand her view, Atherton does not give an account of what Berkeley thinks the objects are that we perceive.

By "immaterialism" Atherton means a theory of sensory representation, that is, a thesis about what is *represented* by our ideas. The thesis of immaterialism, she notes (BRV, p. 233), can be expressed either negatively or positively. Expressed positively it is the claim that ideas represent only other ideas; expressed negatively it is simply the denial that ideas represent something that is *not* an idea (for example, they do not represent material substances). The *New Theory* was limited to showing that visual ideas do not represent properties of mind-independent entities but instead represent other ideas—tangible ideas of distance, magnitude, and situation. The *Principles* makes the thesis more general: no ideas represent mind-independent things; all ideas represent only other ideas.

Now, for Berkeley, Atherton rightly stresses, no one of our senses, taken by itself, is adequate to the job of perceiving the whole physical object; rather, the qualities perceived by any one of our senses represent to us other qualities of the object that can be perceived by our other senses. Thus a mountain is not the proper object of any one sense—that is, by no one of our senses alone can we perceive all of a mountain's properties. But the qualities perceived by any one sense—for example, the colors we see when we look at a mountain—represent to us other qualities of the mountain that can be perceived by our other senses if we use them to inspect the mountain. While this thesis about the nature of sensory representation may not express one of our commonsense beliefs, it is not incompatible with any of those beliefs. And it is the defense of it, in both its positive and negative forms, that is the work of the *Principles* and the *Three Dialogues*.

What ought to be taken to be Berkeley's unique contribution in the *New Theory* is his account of visual representation. Similarly, then, we can see Berkeley in the *Principles* and *Three Dialogues* as asking a question about the nature of sensory representation and not a question about the nature of sensory objects. The focus of Berkeley's immaterialism and what distinguishes it from materialism is an account of the ways in which sensory ideas represent, rather than a claim that sensory objects exist only 'in the mind' (BRV, p. 2).

Now, I want first to note that the thesis of immaterialism, thus construed, does not solve the problem about the object of perception that I raised when discussing the thesis of idealism, for the immaterialist thesis as construed by Atherton is a doctrine not about "the nature of the sensory object" but about how the qualities perceived by one sense represent other qualities that can be perceived by a different sense. So the problem of the status of the object perceived is unresolved by the immaterialist thesis, as it is now construed. But furthermore, the thesis that ideas do not represent mind-independent things but rather represent other ideas, while certainly an important Berkeleian doctrine, will not— either by itself or when taken together with the innocuous "idealist" thesis that mental events like seeing and feeling are mind-dependent— give us Berkeley's philosophy. The reason for this is that the immaterialist thesis, as Atherton states it, is perfectly consistent with a purely phenomenalistic theory like Mill's. Our ideas represent other ideas—ideas that we will have if we perform certain actions, or would have if we performed them. Nothing in this thesis prevents us from supposing that the ideas that we are not now having but that are represented by the ideas we *are* now having are anything other than permanent possibilities of perception—things, that is, that are perceivable. When I see a certain configuration of light and color, it represents to me certain tactile qualities that would be perceived were I, or somebody else endowed with a sense of touch, to stretch out a hand in a certain direction. Ideas, so construed, represent perceivable qualities. But while that is of course part of Berkeley's immaterialist doctrine, it is not the whole of it, nor is it sufficient to give us what sets his theory apart from a theory like Mill's.

For Berkeley the ideas perceived by one sense do indeed represent ideas perceivable by another sense if someone performs certain acts; but even those ideas now represented to me but not now perceived by me must, on Berkeley's doctrine, now actually be perceived by some perceiver or other. If they were not, he holds, they would not now be perceivable by me. When Philonous persuaded Hylas that it would be contradictory to suppose that a sensible object might exist and yet not be perceivable, Hylas replied, "Yes, Philonous, I grant the existence of a sensible thing consists in being perceivable but not in being actually perceived." To which Philonous responded, "And what is perceivable but an idea? And can an idea exist without being actually perceived? These are points long since agreed between us" (D 234). Now, immaterialism, as construed by Atherton, holds that what the ideas or qualities perceived by one sense represent is an object that consists of qualities perceivable by other senses, and that is perfectly compatible with the view here suggested by Hylas, the view that "the existence of a sensible thing consists in being perceivable"—the very doctrine Mill and other phenomenalists have taught.

But to get Berkeley's immaterialism we must add to the thesis Hylas admits the one Philonous insists on: nothing is perceivable unless it is an idea, and no idea can exist without being actually perceived by somebody. Berkeley thought (and here his view really *was* commonsensical) that if something is now perceivable by me, then it must now exist. Since what is perceivable, according to him, is an idea and since ideas "subsist not by themselves," they can only now exist (and so now be perceivable by me) if they are supported by or exist in some mind or spiritual substance (PR 8). I do not propose to defend this claim or to suggest that it is preferable to Millsian phenomenalism, for I do not think it is; but I do say, what seems to me incontestable, that this is Berkeley's characteristic doctrine; it is why he holds that what is perceivable (ideas) cannot exist "without being actually perceived"; and it is what separates his immaterialism from phenomenalist theories like Mill's. Further, a chief aim of the *Principles* and *Three Dialogues* is to establish this thesis: that no object is now perceived or perceivable unless it now exists in some mind—that is, unless it is now actually perceived by somebody.

Now, the thesis, as just stated, is far removed from common sense, for it means that there are now no houses, mountains, or rivers *unless* somebody is now perceiving them.[9] But everyone knows how Berkeley proposes to reconcile this view with common sense: there *is* somebody who "neither slumbers nor sleeps," who perceives all things always. Without God there is no actual perceiver of ideas not now perceived by any finite perceiver—in which case, according to Berkeley, such ideas are not even now perceivable: For "what is perceivable but an idea? And can an idea exist without being actually perceived?" Without the theological component of his doctrine, I can see no way of even trying to render Berkeley's view compatible with our commonsense beliefs about bodies save by transforming it into a doctrine like Mill's—a doctrine that holds that to assert that an object exists is to say that certain qualities are perceivable under some specifiable set of conditions. And I believe this is in fact what Atherton does in trying to show that Berkeley's position, even when taken independently of its theological framework, is far more compatible with common sense than it is usually thought to be.

For the twin theses that she takes to be the pillars of Berkeleianism— the "idealist" thesis that ways of perceiving are not mind-independent and the "immaterialist" thesis that one sensible quality represents another— are perfectly consonant with a theologically neutral theory like Mill's phenomenalism. But when one adds to those theses the ones that are in my view central to the *Principles* and *Three Dialogues*—that there are no substances save minds and that bodies exist (and so are perceivable) only because they are actually perceived by some mind—then one gets a theory that, stripped of its theological undergirding, is so remote from common sense that, so far as I know, it has had no defenders.[10]

In "Berkeley Without God" (Essay 13 in this volume), Atherton explicitly defends the thesis that was implicit in *Berkeley's Revolution in Vision*, arguing that Berkeley's immaterialism is compatible with common sense even if one gives up Berkeley's theological commitments. She gives

9. This is in contrast to that "opinion strangely prevailing amongst men, that houses, mountains, rivers, and in a word all sensible objects have an existence natural or real distinct from their being perceived by the understanding" (PR 4).

10. In "What *Does* Berkeley's God See in the Quad?" *Archiv für Geschichte der Philosophie* (1979), I have tried to show that even with its theological underpinning Berkeley's immaterialism is not really a species of commonsense realism.

two arguments to support this claim. The first argument is like that defended in BRV: the central aim of both the *New Theory* and the *Principles* is the development and defense of a "theory of sensory representation," the theory that sensible qualities represent, not material substances, but other sensible qualities, a doctrine compatible with our commonsense beliefs; the *New Theory*'s defense of this doctrine relies neither implicitly nor explicitly on theism; and the defense of this doctrine given in the *Principles* is "compatible" with the defense of it given in the *New Theory*. From this Atherton concludes that the central doctrine of the *Principles* itself does not presuppose theism. She grants, of course, that from that central doctrine Berkeley tried (by what she thinks are unconvincing arguments) to prove the existence of God, but she concludes that "we can reject Berkeley's proof for the existence of God and still accept his theory of sensory representation" and so can defend "a viable Berkeleianism without God" (247–48).

To this I think it must be replied that if by "Berkeleianism" or "immaterialism" we mean only the "theory of sensory representation," then perhaps one can defend "Berkeleianism without God." But, as I have tried to show, this theory of sensory representation, taken by itself, is compatible with a variety of theories—compatible in particular not only with Berkeley's theistic immaterialism but with various versions of phenomenalism. And that one can have phenomenalism without God is what Mill, Mach, Russell, Ayer, and others have long since shown us. The theory of sensory representation is, certainly, a necessary component of the doctrine developed in the *Principles* and *Three Dialogues;* but it is not sufficient, by itself, to give us the full-blown immaterialism of those works, for that teaches not just that ideas represent other ideas but, further, that bodies are just collections of ideas and so cannot exist unless actually perceived by some mind. Hence I think it is a mistake to suggest that the theory of sensory representation constitutes the core of Berkeley's immaterialism, and it is thus at least misleading to say that the "theory of sensory representation" might be said, in effect, to constitute a "Berkeleianism without God." Somebody might equally plausibly say, "Descartes is one of the chief architects of the mechanical theory of nature; now, I accept that theory, although I reject dualism, and so I subscribe to Cartesianism without the mind." Surely it would be less misleading simply to say, "I'm a mechanist." So too, one may say, "Berkeley is one of the chief architects of the theory of sensory representation; now, I accept that theory, although I do not accept his theism, and so I subscribe to

Berkeleianism without God." But it would be less misleading simply to say, "I'm a phenomenalist."

The second line of argument developed in "Berkeley Without God," however, seems to go beyond simply identifying Berkeley's immaterialism with his theory of sensory representation. Here Atherton argues that Berkeley provides reasons for believing that a world of real things exists independently of his own mind—reasons that do not presuppose the existence of God. If she is right about this, then there may indeed be reasons to count Berkeley's doctrine as a species of commonsense realism even when it is stripped of its theological commitments. Her argument for this claim, as I understand it, runs as follows: By our senses we immediately perceive such things as light, colors, odors, flavors, textures—in effect the so-called proper objects of the senses. But we only *mediately* perceive physical objects—cherries and trees, for example. For by not one of our senses, or even by all our senses taken collectively, do we immediately perceive *all* the properties we attribute to a cherry; or, put otherwise, by the word "cherry" we mean something having a certain color, shape, texture, flavor, and so forth, and such a thing cannot be immediately perceived by any one of our senses, or even by all of our senses collectively, for at any time there will always be some properties of the cherry that we are not perceiving.

> According to Berkeley, I may be said to immediately perceive whatever my sense organs are equipped to register, whereas I mediately perceive those meanings I have learned to attach to what I immediately perceive, which constitutes the greatest part of what I may be said to perceive. I immediately perceive lights and colors, but mediately perceive distance or cherries. Things that are sensible, like cherries or coaches or trees, are all mediately perceived. While it seems reasonable to say what I immediately perceive exists in my mind for only so long as I am perceiving it, the same is not true for the sensible things I mediately perceive. (243–44)

Now, it is my sense experience itself that teaches me that ideas occur in regular (and thus predictable) ways, so that when I see the color of a cherry, without having yet felt or tasted it, I can anticipate, from the orderliness of my previous sense experience, what texture or flavor will be disclosed to my senses if I do touch it or taste it. Thus by means of the law-governed relations of the ideas that we immediately perceive, like color and texture, we learn to perceive mediately physical objects like a cherry (i.e., a whole congeries of sensible qualities including those we do not now immediately perceive).

> If I am seeing a cherry, then my immediate visual experiences stand for a range of perceptual experiences with which these immediate visual experiences are reliably correlated and which they have come to mean. The cherry, although mind-dependent, has an existence that is distinct from and independent of *my* mind. Berkeley's claim that our sensory ideas are governed by law amounts to the claim that the sensible things for which our ideas stand have a distinct existence, independent of any particular finite perceiver. From the fact that we do, and therefore can, make sense of our experience because of its regular and orderly (languagelike) nature, we can conclude the items of our experience have a distinct existence. This claim is established entirely through the God-free resources of the *New Theory of Vision*. (243)

On Atherton's reading of Berkeley, only after he has thus grounded his belief in the independent existence of a world of physical objects does he undertake to prove the existence of God. Furthermore, she argues, Berkeley's proof of God's existence actually depends on the already-established existence of a world of physical objects, for it argues, in effect, that the hypothesis that God exists offers the best causal explanation of the existence of such a world. Berkeley's justification for our common-sense belief in a world of physical objects must therefore be independent of his theological doctrines, since it is from the existence of such a world that he infers the existence of a God as its cause.

Now, I certainly think Atherton is right that for Berkeley it is not the case that any single sense immediately perceives all the qualities we ascribe to physical objects like a cherry or a tree; nor is it the case that at any given time all our senses collectively perceive all the qualities we take the cherry or the tree to have at that time. On the other hand, it is the case for Berkeley that any qualities of the cherry or tree *I* do not now perceive must be perceived by *some* perceiver or other; were he to give up that claim, he would give up the very core of his doctrine, namely, that things are collections of sensible qualities and that the existence of sensible qualities depends on their being perceived by someone (though not necessarily by me). Atherton, I think, agrees that this *is* Berkeley's doctrine, for she writes: "Not perhaps surprisingly, what I am saying is that, according to Berkeley, the natural world is mind-dependent, but independent of any particular mind, such as my own, in exactly the same way that language is a mind-dependent phenomenon, but independent of any particular mind" (244). But what then are we to say of all those qualities of the cherry that I am not now perceiving? Shall we say that although they must now be *perceivable* either by me or by some perceiver, no one need now in fact be perceiving them? Then we view those qualities not as actually perceived ideas but as permanent possibilities of perception ("perceivable but not actually perceived," as Hylas puts it), and we again transform Berkeleianism into Millsian phenomenalism. Or shall we say that those sensible qualities not now perceived by me are nonetheless now actually perceived by some other perceiver or perceivers? But who then are those other perceivers if we jettison Berkeley's doctrine of an infinite perceiver? I can see only two answers to this question. One is that these other (finite) perceivers are simply one or another of those familiar sentient beings our experience acquaints us with—other human beings or perhaps dogs, cats, goldfish, or mites. But in fact we have no good reason at all to suppose that all the qualities of the cherry not now perceived by me are now actually being perceived by some of those other sentient beings our experience has made familiar to us; and in any case, the view that the bodies that make up the natural world exist only because they are perceived by human beings, dogs, cats, goldfish, mites, and the like, is surely very far removed from our commonsense view of things. A second possible answer is that there are innumerable (possibly infinitely many) finite perceivers *besides* those our experience acquaints us with and that one or another of *these* perceivers is always perceiving the qualities of the cherry or tree that are not being perceived by either me or any of the more familiar sentient beings. But this is a hypothesis at least as exotically metaphysical as Berkeley's theory of the infinite perceiver and one for which there seem no better arguments than those he gave for his theological doctrines. So, by it, no progress is made toward a Berkeleianism free of dubious metaphysical encumbrances.

My conclusion is that "Berkeleianism without God" *either* turns out to be some form of nontheistic phenomenalism—in which case I think it simply misleading to call it Berkeleianism (or even immaterialism)—*or* it results in a doctrine that carries us at least as deeply into esoteric metaphysics and away from commonsense realism as did Berkeley's own theistic immaterialism.[11]

11. I am indebted to Katherine McCracken for improvements in this essay that her critical reading of it led me to make.

Index

action, 171–78, 184–96
act-object distinction, 10–13, 48, 54, 60–62, 74, 167–68, 252
agency. See action; causation (activity, volitions); ideas (guiding)
Allaire, E. B., 2–4, 8, 13–14, 19, 39–44, 54 n. 15, 68, 85, 97 n. 13, 98, 103 n. 23
Anaxagoras, 207
Anscombe, G. E. M., 176, 193
Aquinas, T., 40, 61 n. 25
argument from illusion, 177, 180
Aristotle, 2, 8, 29 n. 4, 33 n. 9, 40, 76, 93–94, 97, 99, 207
Armstrong, D. M., 224, 250
Atherton, M., 18, 102 n. 22, 135 n. 5, 184 n. 1, 232 n. 1, 243 n. 11, 250–60
Austin, J. L., 189
Ayer, A. J., 257
Ayers, M. R., 93 n. 5, 101 n. 18, 242 nn. 9–10, 246–47

Beethoven, L. von, 114 n. 9
Bennett, J., 88 n. 31, 178, 237 n. 4, 241
Bergmann, G., 14, 35–37, 41, 44–45
Bolton, M. B., 135 n. 5
Bower, T. G. R., 229
Bracken, H., 3 n. 4, 37 n. 13, 76 n. 16
Bricke, J., 150 n. 2
Buchdahl, G., 203
Butchvarov, P., 150 n. 1

Cambridge Platonists, 14
causation, 2, 15, 27, 29, 76–77, 109, 153–69, 191–92, 200–201, 213, 244
    activity, 27, 87–88, 96, 107–10, 115 n. 13, 201
    God, 18, 27, 103 n. 24, 130–31, 153, 156–57, 171–75, 179, 184–85, 191–94, 213, 231–60; continuity argument for, 241–47; passivity argument for, 168–69, 184 n. 1, 236–47
    natural laws, 233, 239, 241–47
    physical forces, 197–214
    volitions, 15–17, 84–85, 87–88, 96, 102 n. 21, 104, 149–69, 176–81, 183–95
Chisholm, R., 48 n. 4, 62 n. 28, 64
common sense, 18, 64, 103, 105, 172, 184 n. 1, 249, 252–60
comparison model of knowledge, 27–28, 34–35
congeries analysis of mind, 31–32, 80, 89–91, 100–105, 164
Cook, J. W., 122 n. 22
Cottingham, J., 58 n. 22
Cummins, P., 3 nn. 3–4, 15–18, 37 n. 13, 48 n. 3, 68, 85, 91 n. 2, 95 n. 10, 98 n. 14, 100 n. 17, 107 n. 1, 111 n. 5, 122 n. 21, 167 n. 35, 213 n. 24, 217 n.

Dennett, D. C., 14, 49–51, 57 n. 18, 60–62, 65, 69–75, 78–81, 83, 85
Descartes, R., 3, 17, 19, 28–29, 30 n. 5, 42, 47, 49–52, 56–59, 64, 71, 73–74, 77–78, 97, 128, 155, 159, 174–75, 186, 193, 198, 206–7, 209, 213
Dicker, G., 113 n. 8, 114 n. 10, 115 n. 12
Donagan, A., 218
Downing, L., 17
Duhem, P., 113 n. 8, 210

Flage, D., 37 n. 13, 88 n. 33, 118 n. 18
Foucher, S., 51 n. 5
Fraser, A. C., 151 n. 5
Freud, S., 62
Fumerton, R., 119 n. 19
Furlong, E. J., 86 n. 28

Galilei, G., 29, 30 n. 5
Gallois, A., 16 n. 25, 29, 30 n. 5
Gassendi, P., 3
Gibson, J. J., 221–22, 228 n. 15
Goodman, N., 14, 45
Grayling, A. C., 237 n. 4, 242 n. 9, 247, 248
    n. 14, 250 n. 3
Green, T. H., 83
Grice, H. P., 186
Grossman, R., 88 n. 33

Hatfield, G., 227 n. 14
Hausman, A., 3 n. 3, 14, 37 n. 13, 42 n. 3, 44
    n. 5, 47 n. 1, 57 n. 18, 62 n. 28, 67–69,
    73–76, 81, 98 n. 14
Hausman, D., 14, 37 n. 13, 42 n. 3, 47 n. 1,
    57 n. 18, 67–69, 73–76, 81, 98 n. 14
heat-pain argument, 10–13, 101 n. 18, 122
Helmholtz, H. von, 218–19, 226, 228
Hering, E., 228
Hintikka, J., 128
Hinton, J. M., 191 n. 6, 195
Hobbes, T., 3, 7–8
Hochberg, J., 218, 221 n. 7
homunculi, 49–51, 60–64, 71–75, 80
Hooker, M., 233 n. 2
Hume, D., 14, 32, 50 n. 7, 64–65, 68, 72, 75,
    78–81, 83, 85, 102 n. 20, 122 n. 22, 150,
    209

idealism, 1–16, 29–35, 40–43, 48–49, 67,
    73–74, 109–12, 120, 124–25, 183, 188,
    194–95, 198–99, 251–53
ideas, 16, 25, 27, 29, 31–32, 40, 47, 49,
    52–53, 57, 59–60, 62, 64, 70–71, 73,
    97, 102, 108, 112, 123–24, 128, 134,
    157–69, 184, 188, 192–93, 198, 200–
    202, 205, 220, 231
    abstract, 8–9, 27–28, 54 n. 15, 135–37,
        153, 180–81, 192, 208–10
    adverbial account of, 64, 102 n. 22,
        251–53
    as language, 235, 238–40, 242–43, 251
    collections (bundles) of, 1, 9, 41, 100
    guiding, 17, 159–69
    immediate, 219–22
    innate, 42, 58–59, 226–28
    of distance (space), 218, 220–23, 227
    of emotion, 24–25
    of imagination, 160, 164, 201

of memory, 24
of movement, 229–30, 236
of sense, 160, 201, 206, 237–38, 251
passivity of, 161, 167
sensations, 9–11, 54, 61, 100, 120–22,
    152–69, 176, 191, 220, 223, 228
simple, 27
Imlay, R., 17, 183–84, 186–96
immaterialism, 1–2, 9, 41, 184, 186, 193,
    198, 251–54, 260
individuation, 32, 179
inherence, 25, 30, 40–41, 53, 55, 59, 62–64,
    74, 99
inherence account (interpretation), 7–15,
    30, 40–41, 54, 67–69, 74, 85–88, 99–
    101, 103 n. 23, 124 n. 24
instrumentalism, 199, 211–12, 214
intentionality, 47 n. 1, 52, 57, 64, 116
intermittancy objection, 102 n. 19

James, W., 176, 179–81, 183, 189–90, 194,
    227 n. 14, 228
Jesseph, D., 209 n. 18
Jessop, T. E., 88 n. 32, 110 n. 3, 250
Johnson, S., 187

Kant, I., 27, 172, 196, 227
Kaufman, L., 230
Kline, A. D., 233 n. 2

Leibniz, G., 40, 88, 185, 206–7
Lennon, T., 16 n. 25
Lewis, D., 75 n. 15
likeness principle, 11 n. 20, 28, 42–43, 48,
    50, 56–60, 63, 74, 120
Lloyd, A. C., 89 n. 1
Locke, J., 11, 28, 68, 73–74, 77–78, 84–85,
    93, 117, 135, 152, 159, 172, 180, 204,
    207–10
Luce, A. A., 197, 199, 249

Mach, E., 257
Malcolm, N., 49
Malebranche, N., 60 n. 24, 73–74, 77–78,
    184–85, 246
manifest qualities
    argument (MQA), 109–11
    thesis (MQT), 16, 110–12, 114–25
Marc-Wogau, K., 128

master argument, 4–7, 12–13, 16–18, 132, 135, 137–45
McCracken, C. J., 18, 102 n. 22, 184 n. 1, 209 n. 19, 248 n. 15
McCracken, K., 260 n. 11
McKim, R., 145 n. 10, 248 n. 15
Meinong, A. von, 52 n. 11
Mill, J. S., 18, 83, 156 n. 17, 254–57, 260
Moore, G. E., 41, 48 n. 4, 60 n. 24, 62, 122 n. 22
Muehlmann, R. G., 3 n. 4, 6 n. 11, 37 n. 13, 54 n. 16, 68 n. 3, 98 n. 14, 101 n. 18, 188 n. 5

Newton, I., 84, 199, 204, 211, 214 n. 28
Newton-Smith, W. H., 210–12
nominalism, 7–8, 11, 27, 94 n. 7, 127
nominalist interpretation, 7–12
Normore, C., 58 n. 22
notions, 88, 91, 209
Nozick, R., 174–75, 186

Oaklander, N., 3 n. 4
occasionalism, 185
Ockham, W. of, 7–8, 94
one-point argument, 220, 222–24, 229

Pappas, G., 3 n. 4, 4, 12 n. 21, 14 n. 23, 16, 37 n. 13, 47 n., 48 n. 2, 54 n. 15, 68, 86 n. 29, 116 n. 15, 135 n. 4, 243 n. 11
parity argument, 90–91, 95 n. 10
passivity, 92, 173, 185, 191, 200–201, 246
perception
immediate, 18, 55, 60, 95, 111 n. 5, 112–16, 118–20, 168, 218, 243–44, 258
mediate, 95, 113–14, 118, 243–44, 258
perceptual variation (relativity), 5–6, 10, 12–14, 41, 54, 60, 134, 177
personal identity, 94, 104–5
phenomenalism, 18, 33–34, 41, 45, 134, 254–60
Pike, N., 95 n. 11
Pitcher, G., 48 n. 4, 218
Plato, 3, 7–8, 27
Plotinus, 14, 82
Popkin, R., 33 n. 10, 37 n. 13
Popper, K., 203, 212 n. 22
Price, H. H., 40
primary-secondary qualities distinction, 54, 172–73, 200

principle of acquaintance, 36, 80
problem of false belief, 41, 43
pure de re conception, 136–44

Quine, W. V. O., 210, 212
Quirk, R., 121 n. 20

Radner, D., 168 n. 36
Raynor, D., 145 n. 10
realism, 2, 13, 15, 18, 102 n. 19, 103, 112, 184 n. 1
direct, 30 n. 5, 40–42, 45, 54, 176
indirect, 112 n. 6. *See also* representationalism
Reid, T., 100 n. 17, 122 n. 22, 150 n. 3
Reinhardt, L., 145 n. 10
relations, 25–26, 29–30, 32, 35–36, 40, 88 n. 32
representationalism, 11, 14, 27–31, 41–43, 48, 50–60, 64
retinal disparity, 224–25, 229
Roth, A., 214 n. 29
Russell, B., 33 n. 9, 40, 219, 257
Ryle, G., 49, 61 n. 26, 178, 189

Saidel, E., 16 n. 25
Schwartz, R., 17, 248 n. 15
Schwayder, D., 145 n. 10
Sellars, W., 70 n. 7
sensations. *See* ideas
sense-data, 186, 189, 191, 195
sensibles, 107–25
Sergeant, J., 76, 88
skepticism, 2, 13–14, 27–31, 40–43, 64, 73, 173, 175, 213
Skinner, B. F., 49
Spinoza, B., 29–30, 40
Stillingfleet, E., 77
structural analysis, 3–4, 6–13, 18, 23
Stumpf, C., 228
substance
material. *See* immaterialism
mental. *See* causation (God); inherence; congeries analysis of mind
Sully, J., 219, 225

Taylor, C. C. W., 176–77, 179, 184–85, 192
Tipton, I. C., 5–6, 9, 16 n. 25, 89 n. 1, 142 n. 7
Torricelli, E., 211

Turbayne, C. M., 250
Tweyman, S., 166 n. 32

Urmson, J. O., 5

Van Iten, R. J., 11 n. 19, 37 n. 13
verificationism, 133
Vesey, G. N. A., 177 n. 6, 189, 191
volitions. *See* causation

Wagner, S., 145 n. 10
Watson, J. B., 49
Watson, R. A., 3 n. 3, 51 n. 9, 57 n. 20, 68,
    77 n. 18, 86
Waxman, W., 95 n. 11
Weinberg, J., 77 n. 20, 209 n. 18

Wenz, P. S., 4 n. 7
Wheatstone, C., 225, 227
Wilson, C., 17, 150
Wilson, F., 14–15, 70 n. 7, 75 n. 15, 77 n. 19,
    79 n. 22, 80 n. 23
Wilson, M., 214 n. 29
Winkler, K., 37 n. 13, 48 n. 3, 86 n. 27, 87 n.
    30, 88 n. 31, 91 n. 3, 94 n. 7, 97 n. 13,
    102 n. 22, 138 n. 6, 154 n. 13, 162–63,
    165–66, 169 n. 37, 177–78, 185, 189,
    193, 195, 242 n. 9, 243 n. 11
Wittgenstein, L., 29 n. 4, 33 n. 9, 35,
    177–78
Wundt, W., 228 n. 16

Yolton, J., 250 n. 3